A Feminist Legacy

A FEMINIST LEGACY

The Ethics of Wilma Scott Heide and Company

Eleanor Humes Haney

Foreword by

Elizabeth Duncan Koontz

Margaretdaughters, Inc.

Book and cover design by Charlene Eldridge Wheeler

Printed in the United States of America

Library of Congress Cataloging-in-Publication Data

Haney,   Eleanor   Humes.
A feminist legacy.

"Bibliography of works by Wilma Scott Heide": p.
Includes index.
    1. Heide, Wilma Scott, 1921-1985. 2. Feminists–United States–Biography.
3. Feminism–United States–Moral and ethical aspects. 4. National Organization
for Women.   I. Title.
HQ1413.H44H36   1985   305.4′2′0924 [B]   85-21533
ISBN 0-931911-02-8 (pbk.)

Grateful acknowledgement is made for the following:

Permission to quote:

    Brady, Anne Hazlewood: "Bonded," from *Unwritten Testament*. Camden: The Camden Herald, 1972,
p. 20.
    Heide, Wilma Scott: "Feminism for Healthy Social Work," *Smith College School for Social Work Journal*,
Vol. III, #1 (Winter, 1976), pp. 1-4.
    Lorde, Audre: *Sister Outsider*. Crossing Press, Trumansburg, NY, 1984, p. 41.
    Kepler, Patricia Budd, *Declaration of Interdependence and Imperatives* 1975.
    Selected Heide quotes from *Vital Speeches of the Day*. City News Publishing Co., Southold, New York,
1973, pp. 403-408.

Permission to reprint photographs:

    "Members of NOW interrupt Senate Hearings" from NYT Pictures.
    Barbara Evans Crawford, for photo of Heide speaking at ERA rally in Illinois.
    All other photographs were provided by Wilma Scott Heide from her personal collection for reproduc-
tion in this book.

To the following individuals, who have provided assistance in production:

    Barbara Evans Crawford for making possible the reproduction of the NYT photograph;
    Barbara Evans Crawford, Anne Montes and Cathleen Schurr for assistance in proofreading galleys;
    Doris Santercole for photographic restoration and preparation of the early Heide photographs, and for
reproducing the NYT photograph as it appears in *The Rebirth of Feminism* by Judith Hole and Ellen Levine,
Quandrangle Books, New York, 1971.

Dedication

This book is dedicated to the strong company of women and men who worked and struggled with Wilma. Out of that journeying together have come the vision and ethic described in these pages.

Some of the women and men participating in that journey are named. Many others, the majority, are not. I wish especially to thank here those who have contributed by their lives as well as by their words but who have not been specifically identified in this book:

Without the commitments of all of you, this book could not have been written. More important, a profound feminist legacy would not exist.

Thank you very much.

– Eleanor Humes Haney

TABLE OF CONTENTS

FOREWORD

History books are filled with accounts of events and the people – especially men – who made them happen. It is no secret, nor is it acceptable, that entire classes of persons who also contributed to that history were omitted from it. Neither is it acceptable that the practice of omission be continued.

Contributing to the demise of such practices of exclusion and/or omission are the many civil rights and women's organizations, some of which are open to men as well as women.

The subject of this book is one Wilma Scott Heide, who believed that the elimination of discrimination on the basis of sex is a civil rights issue. She saw great similarity between the struggle for minority rights and women's rights before either became "popular" causes. She made the comparison based on a firsthand view marching at Selma, Alabama for enactment of a civil rights law, and marching for passage of the Equal Rights amendment. She spent many hours in discussion with the Reverend Pauli Murray, first female black Epicopal priest and former civil rights lawyer who wrote a treatise on why the 14th amendment to the Constitution does not suffice, as anti-ERA groups have espoused.[1]

The women's movement has been described in various terms. These terms usually reflect the need of the individual to convey a personal opinion, conviction, philosophy, bias and even a confusion of belief. Whatever the description, one usually associates the movement with persons seen in the media or quoted in print, rather than with the complex issues inherent in the movement.

This book about the late Wilma Scott Heide illuminates in dramatic form the early life, the involvement, the philosophy, the convictions, the assumptions and analyses of one who formulated much of the advanced feminist thinking and interpreted the broad range of bias against the female sex. She brought into focus the entwined destructive conditions that have been allowed to exist and prevail against females *and* males.

xii

The reader must peruse carefully the first chapters of the book in order to fully comprehend how the basic, underlying feelings of this woman developed at an early age and permeated her being throughout life. Wilma found a common thread running through all of the inhumanity to "man." When she found societal institutions inconsistent in their charters and proclamations, as compared to their practices, she felt compelled to set these institutions aside and to oppose them at times. More often she found a way to challenge them and cause change.

Wilma's courage was enviable. The courage to follow one's mind and convictions with actions, to act upon the unshakable belief that one person *can* make a difference, was a trait associated with Wilma. She refused to think negatively or to give up because unpleasant encounters or situations might ensue. To be sure, she was a strategist, an analyst, a diagnostician with skills probably developed as she pursued careers in nursing, psychology, teaching, academics, and civil rights activity. But once she had analyzed the situation or issue, developed a plan and approach, she charged ahead.

It was not by accident that this remarkable feminist in the National Organization for Women was elected to the board and subsequently to office in the earliest years. State Commisssions on the Status of Women, supported by the staff of the Women's Bureau of the U.S. Department of Labor, had addressed special problems faced by working women regarding equal pay, conditions at the workplace, protective labor laws, child care, etc. Betty Friedan's book, *The Feminist Mystique,* had dared to bare the innermost feelings of some women regarding their status in the home. But feminist advocates of equal treatment under the law were met with mixed emotions. It was fairly acceptable if women demanded equal pay for the same work done by the same sex, but there were problems with enforcement of the law. "Closet feminists," women and men, needed much examination of the real world before they could grasp the extent of discrimination.

When that small group of women founded NOW, it was an action growing out of frustration and the realization that the usual approaches were not likely to achieve the results needed to relieve the economic and emotional needs of families today. The shoestring operation was carried on through personal contributions and volunteered time, space and materials. The persons in the vanguard gave a great portion of their time and energy. Commitment to the cause of feminism grew rapidly and Heide's prior involvement in the South made her a "natural" for the confrontational approach NOW had come to advocate.

It became quite clear to Heide that the English language provided much justification for discrimination that women and men encountered. Thus, she coined phrases that gave meaning to ideas that refuted the old attitudes and reasonings. There were many times when her zeal to communicate and her own thorough understanding of principles challenged her listeners, who were often far less familiar and sophisticated in their theories of what needed to be changed. But Wilma was also a listener who seldom missed what was being said on either side of issues. She listened equally to those who supported her position, and to those who opposed her. She stored information in her head almost like a computer, and seemed to have instant recall.

History is recorded to preserve events and the characters who are a part of them for civilization, but "herstories" have been omitted. Only a few women are ever mentioned and girls grow up without much knowledge of how women and minorities have contributed to the world. Wilma advocated the writing of "her story" to tell of the contributions of women and to provide role models for girls and women regardless of their race, color, religion, or national origin.

Records and accounts of this century will surely contain the achievements of women's organizations and their impact upon society, its mores and its laws. But these groups must also insure that the writers of the accounts include such great feminist leaders as Wilma Scott Heide.

Perhaps they will point out that her feet were planted firmly in the earth, her eyes were on the future, her head was above the din of discordant voices, her heart was in tune with the people – the high and the mighty and the downtrodden; the dreamers and the doers; the discouraged and the optimists; the weary and the energized; the elderly and the young; and the rainbow colors of humanity.

We who live in the present and those who will live in the future are the beneficiaries of her commitment, dedication and love of people. This is HERSTORY. May the record confirm her true contribution – and the importance of women to civilization and world peace.

– Elizabeth Duncan Koontz

1. It is sad to note the loss of both Wilma Scott Heide and Pauli Murray in May and in June, respectively, 1985.

1

ONE BRIGHT LEGACY

If particular care and attention is not paid to the ladies, we are determined to foment a rebellion....

– Abigail Adams[1]

My silences had not protected me. Your silences will not protect you. But for every real word spoken, for every attempt I had ever made to speak those truths for which I am still seeking, I had made contact with other women while we examined the words to fit a world in which we all believed, bridging our differences.

– Audre Lorde[2]

The rebirth of feminism means, I believe, that She is Risen (She includes He) to redefine and reassign power for life.

– Wilma Scott Heide

Ethics as Story

One rainy day in 1970, members of the National Organization for Women (NOW), Women's Equity Action League (WEAL) and other feminist organizations were scheduled to meet with Assistant Secretary of Labor Arthur Fletcher, to explore enforcement of Executive Order 11246, as amended by Order 11375, to prohibit discrimination based on sex.[3] As the group walked into the main lobby of the Labor Department, they saw a large poster display in three panels about 12 feet wide and 8 feet high, encouraging employers to "Hire the Handicapped." Captions and explanatory material referred to *man*, *men*, *he*, *his*, and *him*; and the pictures, with few exceptions, portrayed black and white males. The poster conveyed to the women the idea that only men were handicapped and/or needed employment. Although many were angered by the sexism, most were willing to ignore it in the interest of meeting with the

Assistant Secretary. One woman however, Wilma Scott Heide, a white woman in her mid-forties, halted and insisted:

> I think we should demand the removal of that exhibit and its replacement immediately. It's unconscionable for the people we have to rely on for government leadership in fair employment enforcement to countenance that sort of thing.

There was an exchange of opinion about what to do. Several felt that to make an issue of the display would antagonize personnel in the Labor Department and jeopardize the securing of strong enforcement procedures. "Come on, Wilma, let's go; we'll be late," urged some.

"We can't do everything at once," observed one.

"It's not that important. If we get side-tracked, we may lose everything," said still another.

But Heide was adamant. "You can go on; I am going to have that thing removed."

The group continued on to its meeting with Fletcher. There, Heide insisted on the poster's replacement. The Assistant Secretary expressed sympathy with her position, but indicated that it was a time-consuming bureaucratic process to remove the exhibit and replace it with another. Finally Heide said, "Come on, let's you and I just go out and change it. You look strong and healthy."

Fletcher, who had been a professional football player, laughed: "I appreciate your sense of humor."

"Go on and appreciate it," responded Heide. "But I'm serious; that thing has to go. And if you won't do it, I'll get it out of here. It was made with tax dollars, and I don't want my money used to violate the laws you are supposed to enforce!"

She continued, "You don't have to go through anything. You have the Executive Order. You're a Black man; how would you feel if it were all white men and it even said just 'white men'?"

Fletcher still demured, and the group eventually went on with the scheduled meeting. But Heide told them she was not going to ignore the poster. The following morning, after discussing the matter with others, she called the Secretary of Labor's office. She informed her hearer that she was calling a press conference in half an hour and intended to ask the photographers to have a picture of the exhibit published and put on television. She wished, she continued, to present the Department's position accurately: Was it indeed true that the Department would not obey the laws and Executive Orders it was supposed to enforce?

The person on the phone asked her to wait a half hour until he could get back to her. When he called back, he assured her that the exhibit would be changed that morning to reflect both sexes in language and both sexes and various races in pictures. He also promised her pictures of the old exhibit and of the new one. Heide agreed to the decision, said that she would not call a press conference, and indicated that she would visit the exhibit later that day and collect the pictures. She concluded with the observation that it was one more time presumably responsible officials changed in order to avoid public embarrassment rather than to affirm moral principle or the law.

At the time of that little "action," Wilma Scott Heide was chairwoman of the Board of the National Organization for Women. This book is about her, about many other women and men who have contributed to, as well as some who have resisted, the rebirth of feminism in this century, and about an ethic that has emerged from and shaped feminist action. My purpose in writing is to tell a story about the vision and life of one woman in concert with others whose experiences have been the articulation of that ethic. The story is written not primarily for historical, sociological or psychological understanding, but for insight into ethics.

It is then, ethics as story. The book begins not with theory, but with story. Good theory is always rooted in story; creative philosophy and theology are rooted in experience. This particular story focuses primarily on Wilma Scott Heide – as a child in the Depression years in southwestern Pennsylvania; as an attendant in a state mental institution trying to bring about some amelioration of living and working conditions there; as a nurse, a sociologist, a wife, and a mother; as an activist for social and economic justice with and for minorities and women; as a prophet and visionary of a transformed society.

This is also a story that has no beginning and no end. It reaches back to eighteenth and nineteenth century feminists; it reaches back into those intimations of a more just and humane social order grasped by women and men of all ages. It reaches forward into the future, as she – and we – become a part of that legacy we give to our children and their children. And as the past is ambiguous, the legacy is both uncertain and hopeful.

As the book is ethics as story, it is also story shaped by ethics. Although I tell the story in largely chronological fashion, I do not mean to suggest that Heide's inspiration and roots came primarily from the past or that the early years of a person's life are the most formative. As feminists, we can seldom turn to the past to find either well-springs of inspiration or roots that sustain us and give us identity. Heide's authority is not reached by having a tradition, a historic community that affords her space in which to stand and a normative perspective to bear on complex issues. Much, perhaps most, of the past – the religious, ethnic, racial, political communities with which many identify – were often alienating for her.[4] The significant soil that nourishes her roots and her creativity are to be found elsewhere – in a vision, in profound fidelity to that vision, in anger, in a sense of self, and in friendships.

Similarly, in the terms of her own personal history, I doubt seriously that Heide's action and thought can be sufficiently understood by examining her early years. I do think that those years are important, but I also find that her life transcends her formative years and context. Heide, for instance, grew up in a home affected by the Depression, but poverty did not generate her ethic and her life. As Alice Rossi has written of earlier feminists:

> It is the charismatic vision of future promise that plays a powerful
> role as a stimulus for action ... Misery and deprivation do not
> themselves prompt revolt; exposure to alternatives does.[5,p.89]

One grows up in communities, with significant others, and among certain
economic and social conditions. My approach is to describe that context and
then explore how Heide responds to it. A response is an interpretive action,
not one of cause and effect. One responds in light of one's values, hopes, fears,
and visions. We live not only in communities and conditions, but we also live
in an ethos, a pattern of values and assumptions and expectations about who
we are and what we are to do. Ethos refers to the moral air we breathe; we no
more live without values than we live without oxygen. We all live by the
principle of trust, for instance. Without trust, there could be no human
community and we would exhaust our days and nights and ourselves
constantly checking and double-checking one another. The differences in our
lives and bearing arise not so much from whether we trust people or not but
whom we trust and about what we trust them.

We respond in light of those values that we have accepted for ourselves as
well as in light of information and feelings we have about others. Those values,
in turn, come in part from the ethos we have been reared in, but at the same
time they are re-interpreted and put together in ways that make sense to us, in
ways that enable us to live and be with at least some degree of integrity.

The story that is told in the following chapters seeks to blend these strands
of personal and moral development and of being shaped by and shaping one's
world. The first chapters of the book trace Heide's life in response to her early
environment, her struggle for personal wholeness, and her efforts to live
responsibly in ever-widening spheres of action. They tell of her moving from
Connellsville, a depressed town in southwestern Pennsylvania, of her
experience as an assistant in a state mental hospital, her years as a nursing
student and practitioner, her involvement in the struggle for racial justice in
the south in the 1950's, marriage and motherhood, and her growing
participation and leadership in NOW, first at the local level and then at the
national level. The struggles, insights, and choices of those years are both
described and interpreted from an ethical perspective; and together – the
narrative and the interpretation – provide the experiential foundation for the
articulation of her ethical vision that is then described in detail.

The Shape of a Feminist Ethic

The ethic that emerges in Heide's life is a particular understanding of
feminism. It is her feminism that integrates vision and value, action and being.
It is the constantly renewing spring which shapes her response to events and
people around her, which gives life and form to her mind and imagination, and
which enables her to act with great flexibility and pragmatism, on the one
hand, and consistency on the other hand.

Humaneness/In the Human Interest

Feminism as an ethic is articulated by Heide with such terms as "in the human interest" and "humane." The overarching principle, or criterion, is humaneness: that which respects, nurtures, and enhances the welfare of all being. Her understanding of that principle is fed from three sources. One is concrete decision and action. What is humane emerges out of lived and shared experiences and emotions, of severe and painful disagreements about what to do, of alienation and loneliness, of communion and support, of outrage and celebration, and always of actions and of living with the consequence of those actions.

A second source of the principle of humaneness is vision and fidelity to that vision. It is an ethic born of hope and imagination. To borrow a biblical phrase, it is nothing less than the vision of a "new heaven and earth," for both the hope and imagination are centered in the human that is also divine. The "human," in vision, is not the apparently fixed part of our being, but the possibility for goodness, or humaneness. Heide is convinced that the human as humaneness is largely uncharted. Hitherto recorded history gives very little understanding of or reason for commitment to humaneness, although humaneness has always existed. Institutions and policy have had little to do with caring for, enhancing or even discovering the humane. It is a relatively untried concept for society as a whole, but its resource can come to us through imagination, fantasy and hope. Is a world of enduring peace possible? Official history says no. Feminist imagination says yes. Is a world of equality, respect, and care for one another possible? We can dream of that kind of world and work to make it come true. We can be prophets engaged in self-fulfilling prophecy.

Third, and this is the lodestone that steadies and grounds imaginative flight, the ethic is centered in the lived daily experience of people, particularly women, who have been in subordinate, marginal and oppressed positions in a culture. The controlling principles and values are those that have been women's responsibilities. Women have been delegated to carry for the whole of society the values and principles of nurture and reconciliation and affiliation. Historically peripheral to the public realm – the "real" world in the eyes of those primarily straight, affluent white men who have been in charge of it – what is called "women's world" is a genuinely real world in which people can learn something of living in alternative ways. Women's world is a world where narrow honor is not at stake, where self and other are not assumed to be in conflict, where time for friendships exists, where tears and emotions are acknowledged and welcomed, where a kiss can heal and is allowed to heal, and where meeting needs of others is taken for granted. This genuinely real world is also a world where lives can be "measured out in coffee spoons," where "women's work" occurs after a grueling or stultifying eight hours out in the "real" world, where sentimentality replaces sentiment, and where competition for favor obscures shared power. This is the real world of most people of both sexes.

A feminist ethic is rooted, therefore, in what has been considered feminine.

> We live in a society and world where too often it appears that art has yielded to pseudoscience, inner and inter-space to outer space, humanities to technology, the expressive to the instrumental, the affective to the cognitive, cooperation to competition, where plowshares have been forged into phallic atomic swords, the so-called "feminine" has yielded to the so-called "masculine," women have yielded to men and even now, girls are carefully taught to yield to boys. The world belongs to what his masculinity has become and its reward, if you can call it that, is power under which terrors the world is groaning. The reward for femininity for her is whatever power he deigns to give her.[6,p.1]

However, this does not finally mean that what is "feminine" is good or that what is "masculine" is bad. The socialization of men and expectations of men do reflect some authentic and valuable dimensions of being human. Further, women are not intrinsically more or less moral than men. But many dimensions of the socialization of women and expectations of women contain resources for the whole of society which have yet to be appreciated and explored publicly.

What is required is elevating the value of the "feminine" and appropriating strengths in both the "feminine" and "masculine." Heide calls this a gynandrous ethic rather than an androgynous one. It is not simply a combination of what has traditionally been called "feminine" and "masculine" but a re-evaluation of both and a selective combining of features of both into something genuinely new and more fully human than what we have experienced so far. When Heide says, "S/he has risen to redefine and reassign power for life," she is affirming precisely both that *she* is risen (the values associated with women's work and lives and women themselves are to rise) and that s/he is *risen* (a new and more humane being can and will come into existence). Rooted in the interpersonal and private spheres of life, the ethic is more interdependent and humane than the ethics that characteristically shape public life, but its intent is to shape both public and private life – for the first time "in the human interest."

Freedom

A distinctive and central corollary of Heide's commitment to humaneness is a view of human nature as radically free. To affirm that human beings are free is to affirm that the possibility – as well as the structure – exists, and that change is as real as limitations.

This conviction enables Heide to be quite realistic about the depths of sexism in the lives of individuals and in society. She addresses over and over the many subtle and blatant ways in which sexism shapes our lives through the values it reflects, the roles and expectations about behavior it imposes, the violence of injustice and destruction it sanctions, and the brokenness of human planetary life it engenders. In our freedom, people can indeed construct such oppressive structures.

But it is also in our freedom that we can arise and accept responsibility for changing those structures. There is a major focus on an analysis of sexism in Heide's ethic; there is an equally major focus on transformation of structures and persons toward humaneness. Heide has consistently been as inspiring as challenging, and both are rooted in a hope that arises out of a view of human nature as free.

An Ethic of Personal and Political Excellence

The ethic that emerges in Heide's speaking, writing, and acting is one of both personal and political excellence. Theories of personal excellence, or *virtue*, as it has been called, have been largely absent from contemporary ethical reflection, but I find an implicit, feminist one in Heide's ethics. One of her recurring phrases and sometimes admonitions is "we must live our values." That is her way of affirming the imperative of personal excellence.

Personal excellence includes the internalizing of the many values identified and affirmed in a gynandrous ethic – values of courage and nurturing and sisterhood, for instance. It also includes the quality of discerning the good. It is this subtle blending of intuitive, experienced, rational, valuing insight and judgment that is so often reflected in Heide's decisions and directions. It is this quality that enables her approach to be creative and pragmatic without falling into expediency or confusion and directionlessness.

Political excellence is both a goal and the criterion of the ways for reaching that goal. Political excellence includes justice, nurturance, choice, and sisterhood (among other qualities) as ends and means. What is significant in Heide's ethic is both the ways these criteria are emphasized and integrated together and the ways in which they are understood or redefined in feminist terms.

Feminist Ethics as a Process

The ethic and the story I am exploring are also mine. I am the author of the book; I am also a participant in the story in a number of ways. I am a feminist, I am an ethicist, and I have become a friend of the person about whom I am writing. I am not writing from some supposed scholarly distance. Indeed, I find the expectation to do that impossible and undesirable. One is not more objective if s/he is removed either in time or emotion from whom or what one is writing about; one simply has a different perspective to bring and may choose to emphasize aspects of one's subject that are different from those I select. I think there would also be a difference in attention to nuance and texture in the material one is using.

Different perspectives illumine different dimensions and can enrich one another. Writing as a participant has its own integrity and contains its own effort to be faithful to the subject matter at hand. Indeed, because I do care intensely about the validity of feminist vision and action, I must take care to describe and interpret as accurately as I can, to identify weaknesses and inconsistencies, and to explore implications.

As a participant-observer, I also share in developing the ethic. This book itself develops the ethic by filtering and ordering the words of Heide and others through my categories and interests. I will suggest some specific ways in which this ethic *should be* part of the continuing development of feminist ethical theory.

There is, however, a dilemma in writing as a friend and participant – whether to refer to Wilma Scott Heide as "Wilma" or "Heide." A person can be trivialized by the premature use of a first name. I have decided to begin with "Heide" in this introductory chapter. Since the next two chapters trace some of her early development, it is appropriate to switch to "Wilma." After that, I will continue to use "Wilma," since readers will then be more at home with her, and I find it a more accurate reflection of the relationship between subject and writer.[7]

The material for the book comes, first of all, from extended conversations with Wilma Scott Heide, sometimes late into the evening, and until she was tired of repeating the past. As Heide told me, "I much prefer creating the future."

The material comes, second, from files and boxes of newspaper clippings, letters, notes, NOW minutes and memos in Heide's basement and in the Schlesinger Library in Cambridge, Massachusetts. I wish to express thanks to Patricia King, Director of the Schlesinger Library, for giving me access to the library papers.

The material comes, third, from conversations with many other people, colleagues and friends and co-participants in the major contemporary movement for justice and transformed humanity. In some instances, I have been able to talk with people in person; in other instances, we have used the telephone, tapes, and letters.

Finally, the material comes from me, living, teaching and participating as a woman in the last two-thirds of the twentieth century. It comes out of those experiences and reflection on them; it comes out of my professional training in theological ethics, particularly with H. Richard Niebuhr at Yale University, whose own ethical insights were often implicitly feminist.

Naming the universe takes time; to borrow from a biblical account, we are still on the second day of creation. The articulation of a feminist ethic is still in its infancy. This book is a contribution to the story of the first two days. The whole story, and the story of the other five (or four, if we are to rest and delight in what we have done) can perhaps never be told. Our task is to share what we can – and that is what this book is all about.

NOTES

1. Quoted in Alice S. Rossi, ed.: *The Feminist Papers: From Adams to de Beauvoir.* Bantam, New York, 1974, pp.10-11.

2. Lorde, Audre: *Sister Outsider.* Crossing Press, Trumansburg, NY, 1984, p.41.

3. Executive Order 11246 was amended in 1967 by Executive Order 11375 to prohibit sex discrimination by Federal contractors and sub-contractors. The Order itself did not specify how the prohibition was to be enforced. The responsibility was delegated to the United States Labor Department. One of the first actions of NOW was to obtain Executive Order 11375.

4. There is one exception to that statement. The liberal legal tradition, represented today by the American Civil Liberties Union, is one she does identify with, has been active in, and on whose National Advisory Board she serves.

5. Rossi, Alice S: "Feminist History in Perspective: Sociological Contributions to Biographical Analysis." *A Sampler of Women's Studies,* ed. by Dorothy Gies McGuigan. University of Michigan Press, Ann Arbor, 1973.

6. Heide, Wilma Scott: "Feminism for Healthy Social Work," *Smith College School for Social Work Journal.* Vol.III, No. 1, Winter 1976, pp. 1-4.

7. I will also follow this procedure with other names, the use of last or first names will reflect both growing familiarity to the reader and to the author.

Wilma and brother Harold, 1925.

2

A SENSE OF SELF

> I think I felt it as a child – that I wanted my life to make a difference. I read about people making history, they did this, and they did that. I wanted to be one of the *they's*.

> – Wilma Scott Heide

Wilma Scott Heide was born on February 26, 1921. At that time her father, William Robert Scott, was a brakeman for the Baltimore and Ohio Railroad. Her mother, Ada Long Scott, was a homemaker. Wilma was the third of four children – Ethel Virginia born in 1916, Ray Eugene in 1920, Wilma Louise in 1921 and Harold Dwight in 1923. When Wilma was born, the family lived in Ferndale, Pennsylvania, now a suburb of Johnstown. In 1932 they moved to Connellsville, fifty miles southeast of Pittsburgh, where Wilma lived until she graduated from high school.

Ferndale was a small, quiet town. The Scotts lived in a single family frame house with a back yard and garden. On Sundays, when the weather allowed, they walked the three miles each way to the Lutheran Church. On stormy or cold days, they rode the street car.

Connellsville was larger than Ferndale and had a more diverse population composed of many ethnic groups who had come there to work in the mines and on the railroads and farms of the region. Although it was predominantly white, there was a small Black population. By the time Wilma moved there, much of the major activity of the mines and the quick rise to wealth, available to a few, were over. The town Wilma knew as a child was still pluralistic but unpretentious and many of it inhabitants close to poverty.

Wilma's family shared some of the situations and values of its neighbors, but it was also unique. Wilma's father was a quiet, intelligent, and thoughtful man; on the heavy side and clean shaven, he had thinning light brown hair and a rounded face. He loved to read and to learn, and as a teenager had left his parents' farm for whatever education he could acquire. By age sixteen he was qualified to teach school. However, he was considered too young and was unable to find a job in education. He started working with the railroad. There he was destined to spend the rest of his life in positions that did not require the skills he had. On one icy winter day he slipped, fell, and thrust a signal flag into his eye, permanently blinding him in that eye. Since the railroad had a rule that only "whole men" could be in more responsible jobs, William Scott remained a laboring man all his life.

He also enjoyed occasionally "playing the stockmarket" and other kinds of gambling. In the 1920's, when the financial future of the family seemed rather secure, Wilma's parents bought a house in Ferndale. During that same period her father began investing in some stocks. The Depression, however, left them with a fifty percent reduction in salary, a mortgage and worthless stocks. All combined, the loss was severe for a family with few financial resources and Wilma grew up during years of real hardships. Nevertheless, her father continued to pursue his love of learning. He purchased a set of Harvard Classics and read on his own – poetry, drama, philosophy, and political economic theory.

Her father's intellectual interest helped create a bond between him and his younger daughter. Although he was respected by and friendly with his colleagues on the railroad and in the town, there were few he could share his questions and ideas with. He turned to Wilma, particularly as she grew older, and she responded eagerly. From an early age, Wilma had been dubbed "serious" by her family and was seen as the child who "had her daddy's brains." The two explored religious, philosophical and particularly economic issues together.

Wilma's mother, Ada Long Scott, was considered a shy, sweet and thoughtful person who preferred to work at home. Small, soft and trim, she had taught school for three years before she married, and then became a homemaker. With a husband away for long periods and with his occasional gambling ventures, Ada Long Scott provided stability for the family and an example and resource of careful administration of very limited resources. When her husband died in 1943, she was left with only a tiny railroad pension. She went back to school at age 50 to the State Teachers College in California, Pennsylvania, to receive an emergency teaching certificate. But then she decided that she had never enjoyed teaching and preferred to work in a store. Until she retired, she worked as a clerk in a local department store, and retired when she was ready – after the post-Christmas rush during her seventieth year. But Wilma's childhood memories of her mother are of a woman who spent her days canning, cooking and cleaning.

Her parents' interests, responsibilities, and values shaped the immediate moral context of Wilma's childhood. From an early age, she heard of *fairness*.

Her father was active in the railroad union (The Brotherhood of Railroad Trainmen) which worked for higher pay, better working conditions, and better living conditions for the railroad families.

He protested a railroad policy known as "bumping," which allowed a person with seniority whose position had been eliminated to take the job of the person immediately below. That person could then do the same, and so on, until the last person (and the one usually most recently hired) was without a job. Since her father was unable to prevent the practice, he went elsewhere to work rather than "bump" the person beneath him. Even in times of hardship he sought to be fair. When it was time to consider the possibility of college for the children, for instance, both parents reasoned that since all could not go, none should go. Such a policy hurt; it hurt Wilma, who wanted desperately to go to college. It hurt her father, who loved learning. But the principle remained, and although the immediate consequence of some of these decisions was restriction and hardship, Wilma, nonetheless, sensed a measure of freedom and possibility. One did not simply have to accept the status quo. However limited the sphere of choice might be, there were still choices.

Within the family, roles were traditionally gender-related. Her father was the economic provider, her mother a homemaker. Attitudes and characteristics also followed traditional lines. Wilma's father was the more authoritative and the one whose views generally prevailed. "Ask your daddy," was a familiar refrain to the children. He was also the disciplinarian and at the same time the one who allowed the children more freedom and risk-taking than did their mother. Wilma's mother, in contrast, tended to defer to her husband and to be more protective of the children. But Wilma's mother had qualities of strength and reliability and administration, keeping the home steady. She knew what she wanted and when and as she could, she took a stand for whatever that was.

The family ethos also emphasized the values of generosity, frugality, and taking responsibility for one's own life within certain restraints. Even in time of real hardship, the Scotts were responsive to the needs of others more desperate than they, primarily railroad people. At the same time, the Scott household was a frugal one. All the children had to earn money to spend on themselves and to contribute to the family's income. It was necessary, and their parents also thought it was intrinsically a good idea. The children cut lawns, shined shoes, collected bottles and papers to return, had newspaper routes, pumped gas, and washed cars. All had egg routes. When William was "up the line" on the railroad, he would bring back eggs, which he got wholesale, for the children to sell. Records were kept of their money. Half went to their parents, a quarter into savings, and a quarter for "mad money" – whatever they wished or needed to buy. The children worked hard. At one point Ray bought himself a bicycle and Virginia bought a wristwatch.

The Scott ethos was somewhat ambivalently religious. Wilma's mother was and is a Lutheran and active in the congregation. During their stay in Ferndale, they lived three miles from the nearest church and usually walked both ways every Sunday. After they moved to Connellsville, Ada was more directly active in church affairs, and Wilma later became involved also. Her father, however, was a questioner and what he called a "shopper," exploring and evaluating different organizations. He explored Catholicism and Christian Science as well as the many Protestant denominations. Wilma recalled his praying while fishing: "To Whom It May Concern – If Anybody."

Although skeptical intellectually, he communicated to Wilma an awareness of a spiritual depth to life. Particularly when he was fishing, he seemed to be in communion with a reality with which he felt at peace.

In racial attitudes also, the family ethos was ambivalent. Wilma received the message that "Negroes are all right – in their place – and some are as good as we are." Further, her father's concept of fairness demanded a higher standard of behavior toward Black people than many other whites employed. Her father argued that "the Negro problem had to be addressed," as "the problem" was viewed at that time. Similarly, she learned that "they couldn't help being Negroes"; they were not to be blamed for their situation.

At the same time, Wilma sensed that race was a taboo subject – not to be talked about, along with cancer, tuberculosis and children who had lice. There was something humiliating about people who had any of these, and specifically something unclean. "I think I accepted that; I believed in cleanliness. You know, 'no matter how poor you are, you can always get a bar of soap'."

This, then, was something of the pattern of values, practices and expectations in which Wilma grew up. Her response to them was both increasingly complex and increasingly consistent, and in her response there emerged a sense of herself.

Her own earliest memories were miscellaneous, but perhaps significant. She recalls, for instance, going to have her picture taken; a small figure, she was dressed up with a Dutch Boy hair cut and wearing new patent leather shoes, and she wanted the world to know about those shoes. She wanted to communicate something of importance to her. It may, however, have been the first and last time that what was important to her was an article of clothing. Her mother recalled her preferring a tricycle to dolls and becoming more and more of a tomboy.

During her first years in school, she received confusing messages about race and poverty. In kindergarten, she became aware that the black children were not treated in the same way as the white ones, and Wilma thought that was not fair. She had a Black playmate named Sissy (a nickname for Sister) and the two youngsters were discouraged from playing with each other. On one occasion, they were sent together to the cloakroom in punishment for playing together, where, of course, they continued to stay and play together. In recalling that incident, Wilma commented, "It's a wonder children trust adults at all; I suppose it's the need for survival that makes them do it."

In the Ferndale school, children were ranked by their grades and assigned seats accordingly. Wilma was consistently aware that those who were close to the bottom of the hierarchy were often poor and Black. Again she felt that there was something wrong about the way they were being treated, for among her own friends, poverty and Blackness did not mean intellectual slowness.

Wilma was also puzzled by sexuality – both in terms of gender and behavior. She was very much aware that she was a girl and that people responded to her differently from the way they responded to boys. "You have your daddy's brains," they said; "It's too bad you're a girl." She does not recall wishing to be a boy, but she saw that boys had more freedom than girls did and she envied them that. She consistently chose to wear slacks instead of dresses whenever she could. She did not like housework responsibilities, which were assigned mostly along traditional gender-role lines. According to her sister Virginia, Wilma managed to get out of doing them much more effectively than Virginia could.

As a child Wilma talked with her father about many of the inconsistencies and contradictions in her ethos and in the lives of people around her, particularly the economic dimensions of poverty and injustice. Occasionally, librarian Margaret McVicker, relative of the neighboring Hays' family, visited the Hays. Wilma would go next door to talk with her. "She let me talk, she listened to me, and she encouraged me. She took seriously the fact that I wanted to know." Apparently Margaret McVicker was something of an exception, for Wilma generally was told from adults and peers, "Oh, Wilma, why bring that up again?" and "Well that's just the way it is."

But Wilma, even then, was persistent. When she did not receive a satisfactory answer, she sought other means of finding out. One day she decided to ask her mother about sex. Ada was preparing the family for a trip to Johnstown and answered, "Not now." But it seemed to Wilma always to be "not now." So she listened to her sister's conversations with her friends about what they had read in a medical book, information that struck Wilma as puzzling and somewhat frightening. Still not satisfied, she decided to walk into her parents' room when she was sure they were having intercourse. She knew, even as she decided, that she was breaking a boundary and that she would have to pay the consequences of her action. Nevertheless, in she walked. After an initial moment of stunned silence, she was ordered out. She sensed that she had embarrassed and even humiliated her parents and later had to deal with their anger. She tried to justify her action with the statement, "Well, you won't tell me anything, so I have to find out someway." Her parents did not punish her, but they still did not talk with her about sex.

As a child Wilma frequently tested limits and in the process, tested and discovered herself. Loving the idea of flying, she decided to see if she could fly. She jumped out a second story window with a parachute made out of an umbrella with a sheet fastened to it. She sensed that the umbrella was insufficient alone, so she tied the ends of a sheet to the handle to make contact with more air. Since she had been forbidden to do this at home, she went to the house next door and jumped. The parachute did not work, and she fell, badly bruising an arm. Apparently, her parents were so relieved that she was not more seriously hurt that she escaped punishment.

Other efforts were more successful. She learned to ride her brother's bicycle standing up on the seat. She pretended the grape arbor was a tight rope and learned to walk across it. And she experimented with smoking dried pods hanging from one of the trees in the yard, which she and her friends called "Indian tobies."

At this time, she was not particularly influenced by books. She read, but apparently did not find what she was looking for. As she grew older, she read some of the Harvard Classics on her father's book shelves. Still she did not find them especially enlightening. Yet, she persisted in wanting to learn, wanting an education, and as a child she enjoyed school. Perhaps that too was a part of a child's need to trust the adult world.

But even as she was asking others for direction and clarity, she was also listening to herself. She knew that she was "different" in significant ways from many of those around her. She asked questions others seemed uninterested in, and her persistence was often greeted with exasperation and even ridicule. Her recollection of conversations with the librarian is revealing, because the librarian is one of the few people that Wilma can remember who did take her seriously. "She didn't encourage me by saying anything, but she listened without putting me down, being disparaging, or calling me names."

Perhaps what is more significant about Wilma's sense of being different was that she accepted it without feeling that something was terribly wrong with her. She had some support in her father's response to life, but beyond that, she seemed to have trusted herself.

She also accepted her sense of being different without feeling thoroughly alienated from others. As a child, she did not attribute malice to those around her; she was trusting and omnivorous for whatever anyone could teach her. As she grew older and more aware of the depths of injustice, she continued to trust the fundamental goodness of people. She realized that relatively little is done to one another out of deliberate ill-will. It is, rather, the limitations of values and perceptions that make one's actions destructive and oppressive rather than conscious intention – although as Wilma rather ruefully observed, "it would be easier sometimes if I could feel 'that people are out to get you.'"

After the Scotts moved to Connellsville and Wilma moved into junior high and high school, she became a leader in athletics, educational and church activities. Wilma loved athletics. She played basketball, tennis, football, and softball. The high school had no varsity sports for women. There was, however, a basketball tournament at the end of the year, called the Yale-Princeton (neither of which school admitted women at that time) Tournament. Wilma was consistently on one of the teams playing in the

Fayette Shamrocks at Armory in Connellsville, PA, about 1938. Left to right: Wilma, Polly McGrath, Pep Conner, Flo Phillips, Edith Tully, Dorothy Rowe, Isabel Metzgar.

tournament and captained her team in her senior year.

In addition to high school athletics, Wilma played for two and a half years with a local semi-professional basketball team called the Fayette Shamrocks, named for the county and the Irish background of a couple of team members. Each woman on the team was paid about enough to cover expenses, and they played other teams throughout the country whenever they could. Since travel funds were minimal, they played with other teams as the latter were visiting in the tri-state region of Pennsylvania, West Virginia and Ohio. On some occasions, the Shamrocks played two or three games an evening.

The Shamrocks held their own against many of the teams, including a strong one from New Washington, Pennsylvania, called the Hazel-Atlas team, sponsored by the Hazel-Atlas Glass Factory. They also played – and always lost to – one of the best teams in the country at that time – the Goldenson Vanities from Chicago.

Wilma was quite small – about 5′1″ and 100 pounds. She was the shortest and youngest member of the team. The others tended to be larger working women of second and third generation immigrant families. But Wilma was fast and quick. She played forward and was an excellent shot, darting in and out under the arms of the opposing guards.

The Shamrocks practiced with local men's teams, played "men's rules," and were coached by two men – Fred Snell and Emmett Hicks, one white and the other Black. Although Wilma heard the inevitable innuendoes about why a Black man would want to "hang around" primarily white kids, the team loved and respected him. He, in turn, gave hours of his time and even some of the little money he had to them. Wilma recalled he gave of himself, and many a teenager cried on Hicks' shoulder while dealing with one crisis or another.

During those years, Wilma was also active in other school and community activities and in the church. In junior high, along with seven other youngsters, she was started on a "college track" taking Latin, science, math, and social sciences, in addition to the standard English and history courses. She did particularly well in social sciences, and her teacher, Beulah Gilmore, encouraged her to pursue them. In high school, she was on the editorial staff of the school paper and the yearbook; she was elected president of the Leaders' Club and made a member of the National Honor Society and the Quill and Scroll, a national honor journalistic society. In the community, she and her sister Ginny became members of Gradale, a social and service organization.

In church, she was active in Luther League, taught Vacation Bible School, and attended Wednesday night prayer meetings. At one of the Wednesday sessions, she experienced a call to become a minister in the Lutheran Church. With characteristic thoroughness and logic, she began seriously to set about it. Since no Lutheran body permitted women to be ordained in 1936 however, her parents became concerned and spoke to the minister. He and his wife talked to Wilma: ordination was impossible, and she could not have been called to the ministry.

Wilma was stunned. Embarrassed and hurt, she had come up against a limit that could not be transcended. Why could she not be a minister? Had she been wrong in the believing that God had called her? As she tried to sort out such questions, others began to surface – what kind of faith was it that barred women just because they were women? Did she really believe the doctrines she had been taught? She knew that she did not. As Wilma began to articulate doubts that had been latent to that point, she did not persist in seeking ordination, as other women were to do, but rather simply walked away from the institution.

During high school, in spite of her involvement in sports and school activities, Wilma found time to enjoy many friends. Her closest friend was Sara Belle Seese, also from a railroad family. Sara Belle was a bit taller than Wilma, but thin with a long face and naturally curly brown hair. The two youngsters spent long hours exploring economic and political questions, with Wilma tending to be more optimistic about the possibilities of change and Sara Belle more suspicious of affluent people and aware of snobbery and hypocrisy. One summer Wilma and Sara Belle traveled with Sara Belle's mother and aunt on the train to California. Wilma left with $10 and returned with some of it, living primarily on ice cream cones.

Another close friend was Rena Moore. Reared by a grandmother and an aunt, Rena also knew something of poverty and "being different." She and Wilma shared out-of-door activities – biking and camping and Girl Scouts.

Her other friends included her professional basketball colleagues and peers in her college preparation classes. "Pep" Connors and Polly McGrath were two of her basketball friends. In her classes were three young women who, with Wilma, were among those at the top of the honor roll – Mary Ellen Shives, Edith Mitchell, and Anna Mary Evans.

Wilma found in Mary Ellen someone who shared some of her interest in learning and pursuit of questions of social change and justice. They talked together and participated together in school activities. But Mary Ellen Shives recalls Wilma as being both more of a loner and more of a leader than she was.

At one point during high school, some of these friends and Wilma formed a club they called the Ten Deuces. It was dedicated to their individual improvement. They were to criticize one another, and each was expected to work on changing the faults which had been drawn to her attention. The club did not endure for long. As Wilma observed with the advantage of hindsight, "It was a naive and sincere effort, and what we ignored was the importance of supporting one another in addition to criticizing one another."

At this time in her life, she was not particularly close to her sister. Virginia was about four years older than Wilma and had her own friends, and their interests were quite different. Virginia had learned to play bridge, enjoyed shopping and participation in the Gradale sorority. She liked clothes and took care of them – something Wilma did not do even when she borrowed Virginia's.

Wilma, tomboy that she continued to be, was often unfavorably compared to her sister, "Why can't you be more like Virginia?" Virginia was not only more accepting of expectations on her as a girl, but also she had to assume more responsibility for the family than did Wilma. When their father had a job away from home and was absent for long periods of time, their mother sometimes also left to spend some time with him. Virginia was left in charge of the other children, with a neighbor to "look in." "Mother set me up on a pedestal," Virginia recalled "and that didn't help relations between Wilma and me."

Virginia, in part by inclination and in part by the responsibilities imposed on her as the oldest, tended to identify with a traditional adult female role. Wilma did not, and was somewhat freer not to. Instead, Wilma shared the athletic interests of her brothers. Both Ray and Hal were interested in sports, although Wilma was a better athlete than either and actually participated more often in organized sports. She was closest to Hal at that time. They both enjoyed ideas, and Wilma sensed that their values were similar.

High school came to an end, and Wilma was ready to leave. Only basketball held any great appeal for her in Connellsville. In June, 1938, she graduated with honors and was offered a partial scholarship to Seton Hall, a Catholic Women's College about 20 miles away. Her parents refused to let her go, although she was willing to work to earn the rest of the cost. But her parents argued that it was not fair for one to spend one's money primarily on oneself while the others had to help support the family. Hal was still in high school, but both Virginia and Ray were working full-time, Virginia in the telephone company and Ray with a radio station. Wilma felt the decision somewhat unfair since she thought she was the only one interested in going to college (although Virginia has indicated in more recent years that she too had wanted to go).

Nevertheless, college was denied her, at least for the time being. She was not interested in marriage; other options were unclear. Loyalty to and sense of responsibility for her family demanded that she get a job and her own being demanded that she continue to participate in sports. She postponed a decision to leave, found work, and continued to play basketball with the Shamrocks. She ventured into pingpong and became the city champion. None of these activities either satisfied or subdued her longing for something else. Her willingness to test and protest limits and her capacity for leadership were about to take a new direction.

3

A SENSE OF VOCATION

I felt as if I were carrying the whole world on my shoulders, and I couldn't get a handle on how to change things.

– Wilma Scott Heide

The metaphor in the quotation is mixed, but the meaning is clear. The years between 1938 and 1948 were among the most difficult and crucial ones for Wilma. They were years of insight and growth, of acting and testing. They were also years of frustration and near despair. But through them a pattern began to emerge, a pattern that would offer understanding and direction.

Wilma's inability to attend college was a keen disappointment and she refused to accept the situation, although she could not see how to change it. She looked to her older sister and brother but received little guidance from them. Virginia, four years older, had found a job with the telephone company. It was, people agreed, a good job for a woman. She was also dating and seemed to accept her life. Wilma, too, could have had a job with the telephone company, but she sensed that to take it would be to fall into a trap that could be devastating, at least for her:

I wanted more education, and I sensed – with my father – that there was more to life than what I saw around me.

Women who had jobs at the telephone company, she perceived, did not move on to something else. Perhaps because it paid relatively well and offered security, it could lull one's restless spirit, dull other yearnings within. However inchoately, Wilma knew that she did not wish to silence those yearnings. Quiet meant hollowness and entrapment rather than well-being. Frustration was preferable to economic security.

Ray, two years older, at age sixteen had known what he wanted – a life as a broadcaster, and he had left home to pursue it. But such a course did not seem a model for Wilma. What a boy could do, she knew, was irrelevant, although Ray's singlemindedness of purpose impressed her.

Wilma knew that she too had to leave. She had to reject her sister's alternative. She did not see her way as clearly as Ray had. An education cost money, and there was no money. Further, what kind of education and what she wanted beyond an education she could not yet name, since it had not yet emerged. What she eventually was going to discover was that instead of a career she had a vocation – a still largely unseen configuration of loyalties for which she would hold herself responsible and which would, in turn, offer her meaning and worth, deep travail and great joy.

Nevertheless, even then vision and vocation and practical reality were not wholly divorced from one another, however separate they sometimes appeared. Even as Wilma was exploring the immediate concerns of providing for herself, contributing to the family, and gaining psychological and economic independence, she was aware of something more – something for which available alternatives could provide the occasion, but never the condition, of finding.

The ten-year period from the time Wilma left high school until she enrolled in sociology at the University of Pittsburgh was a time when vision and vocation began to emerge. From 1938 to 1947, Wilma learned that she could take care of herself financially even though she experienced more severe poverty than she had as a child. She became a registered nurse, discovered something of the depth of resistance to social change, and began to integrate her own life around a center of value.

Those years included war years. War meant both loss and gain for Wilma. She lost friends killed in battle, including a young man to whom she was engaged. But in those years women were needed for jobs, and opportunities opened that previously did not exist. Wilma took advantage of them, both in education and in jobs.

Initially, after graduating from Connellsville High, Wilma stayed at home. It was cheaper, and she had no particular place to go. She worked in a department store selling jewelry and cosmetics. She sold products door-to-door for four or five companies at a time – cards, pots and pans, and paper products. She continued to play basketball, "certainly the lowest paid profession in the world." Sometimes, indeed, the pay was little more than a milkshake after a game. But she loved it.

She was briefly engaged to a Connellsville man, Bill Stevens. He had been in Ray's class and an occasional friend of her brother's. Bill played the violin, and he and Wilma attended some concerts together. He was thoughtful and rather serious, and Wilma cared for him. But as with the telephone company, she sensed that marriage was not yet appropriate for her, that it would be a trap, and she called off the engagement. Bill was hurt and responded with, "I'd like

Taken by a street photographer about 1938, when Wilma was a clerk at a department store in Connellsville.

to turn you over my knee." Furious, Wilma flung back, "Don't you dare touch me! Don't you or any other man ever lay a hand on me!" and the tentative consideration of male physical force was ended.

In 1940, Wilma left Connellsville, never to return except to visit her family and friends. As a part of a "Problems in Democracy" course she had taken in high school, the class had visited the state mental hospital at Torrance, about 50 miles from Connellsville. Now an acquaintance was working there and suggested that Wilma apply for a job. She did and was hired as an attendant for $55.00 a month, plus room and board.

In the early 1940's, conditions in publicly-funded mental hospitals were often only a little more humane than conditions in jails, and the situation at Torrance was no different from others. Funding was inadequate; qualified medical help was scarce because of a combination of low pay and the growing need for doctors in the war effort; tranquilizers and other medications were extremely limited and ineffective; many people were simply ill-informed about mental/emotional disturbance; and much of the staff was untrained with little more than a high school education.

Patients received little more than custodial care. They were physically restrained, placed in canvas-like bags and strapped to beds, sometimes for hours at a time. They were wrapped in cold sheets, which had the effect of weakening them. Attendants worked twelve hours a day, six days one week and five days the second. There was little incentive – except as individuals cared enough to take the initiative – to view their work as anything other than a routine and repetitive job.

As a result, violence – psychological and physical – was sometimes the rule rather than the exception. Patients were violent, in part because they were disoriented, and appropriate medication and counseling were unavailable. But they were violent also because of the conditions – fear of being restrained for long periods of time, fear of one another, fear of attendants who took advantage of the conditions to be brutal. Patients ate their meals together, for instance, and the stronger and larger ones grabbed most of the food, leaving the old and sick and more passive to fare as best they could. Attendants carried large rings of keys and some would swing and rattle them as if it were a jail; custodians had terrifying power over the patients.

Wilma was nineteen when she encountered Torrance. It was a nightmare for her. It also became a test of a different order from trying to fly or walking the grape arbor lattice, but a test nevertheless. As an attendant, Wilma's responsibilities included seeing that the patients were clothed, fed and cleaned; that they kept appointments for treatment; that they were released from restraints and got some exercise each day; and that they took their medicine. She was also expected to help with intake procedures, to supervise the work patients did, and to break up fights.

The entire experience was traumatic for Wilma. She was often terrified. She dreaded going to work. She hated what she saw and was unable to adjust to it. In retrospect, she thinks that she was able to survive as well as she did in part because her mind refused to grasp all of what was happening to people there – staff as well as patients. It was a snake-pit experience; ignorance, indifference, and lack of money made it one of nearly unrelieved brutality and dehumanization.

But what she grasped she passionately wanted to change. Soon after arriving, she discovered that a few staff members were trying to organize a union to improve working conditions and pay and hoping thereby to attract more skilled employees. Wilma joined and worked with them the two years she was there. This activity marked her immediately as "different" and someone to be watched warily.

Wilma eventually found support and even some direction there. After nearly a year, she was assigned to a large ward of physically and mentally ill patients supervised by Marie Fagan, who, in turn, had wanted to bring about change when she had been assigned to that ward. Fagan recalled:

> The conditions of the ward were deplorable when I was put in charge. I was a strict disciplinarian and insisted changes had to be made to improve the care of the patients. I knew I wanted things done in only one way – the right way.[1]

Fagan found Wilma a willing colleague and learner. Wilma watched and questioned constantly. "She [Wilma] kept me on my toes because I knew her powers of observation were always working overtime."[1] From the older woman, Wilma learned basic procedures of nursing and ways of interpreting symptoms.

Wilma was conscientious in her work. Considered by some as naive and too idealistic, she demonstrated a commitment to the patients' welfare; she learned what she could; and she tried to change what she could.

The result was often frustration and near collapse for herself. Wilma had become a particularly close friend with another attendant, Peg Smith, a woman about seven years older than Wilma. To Peg, Wilma turned for reassurance and emotional support. Shortly after arriving at Torrance, she began telling Peg about a woman who was following her with the apparent intention of killing her. At first, Peg believed Wilma but then understood that the woman was a product of fear, and finally said, "This woman won't bother you any more." That ended the incident, which itself was a consequence of the combination of terror, frustration, and despair Wilma was already beginning to feel.[2]

Marie Fagan and another supervisory nurse, Mary Helen Fisher, realized that if Wilma did not move on, she would explode. They saw to it that she was given as many opportunities for learning as they could. On days off, they took her into Pittsburgh for testing and inquiries about school, and they continued to encourage her to go on to nursing school.

On other days off, since no one had much money to spend, the attendants sat around and talked, hiked or visited one another's families. Gathering in one of the women's rooms, they endlessly explored philosophical, social, and personal questions, sorting out beliefs and values and feelings. During one of these sessions, Wilma talked Peg into becoming an agnostic.

> Scotty [Wilma] was very persuasive in her logic. She was atheistic in her belief and had me almost convinced to her point of view. At the time I was on the fence about religion and it took Scotty's nudge to direct me toward agnosticism. Many years later I returned to my belief in God.[3]

Often, when they had a day off, Wilma and Peg, along with other friends went to Peg's home to get away from the hospital and to visit Peg's mother and sister. They talked, played cards, and ate baked beans and french fried potatoes – their favorite Depression meal.

Peg's family was open and warm. They welcomed Wilma and loved her. They provided her with a much needed context of support and closeness while she was away from her own family. Wilma needed to be away from her family, she needed to establish her own identity as an independent individual, redefining, in the process, her loyalty to her family. At the same time, she needed support and encouragement and a safe context in which to work through frustration and lack of clarity. Peg and her family provided much of this.

In turn, Wilma pushed Peg and her sister Hon (for Helen) to go beyond where they were. She encouraged Peg to take chemistry in preparation for college and Hon to pursue interior decorating, although she had not finished school. Hon did become a decorator and then finally a realtor.

As it became clear to Wilma and Peg that they still could not afford a college education, they thought more and more of nursing school. On one occasion Marie Fagan and Mary Helen Fisher drove them down to Greystone State Hospital in New Jersey for admissions and aptitude tests.

But the expense of nursing school remained an obstacle even though it was less than college. The tuition at that time at Greystone, for instance, was $170.00 for the three years. Finally, in the summer of 1942, the two decided to leave Torrance and go to Cleveland where Hon lived. They worked in an electrical instrument factory, manufacturing gauges for air force planes. They lived with Hon, paid her $6.00 a week for room and board, and helped with household chores and maintenance, including scrubbing the old wooden floor of the house on hands and knees, a task Wilma protested – futilely.

In September they left Cleveland for nursing school. Friends told them they were fools to abandon good paying jobs in the defense industry for nursing school. But in part because of what Mary Helen Fisher and Marie Fagan had invested in them, they felt committed. Since Greystone State Hospital had closed in the interim, they went to Brooklyn State Hospital in Brooklyn, New York, primarily because it paid them a token wage for the work they would do in addition to their studies. Wilma was more than ready to go. Peg was willing but more reluctant:

> Scotty was aggressive and seemed to have no qualms about leaving home. She was determined to get ahead. I was more retiring and in considerable conflict over leaving my family and the necessity of advancing myself. However, the leaving was made bearable because I was with my trusted friend.[2]

Brooklyn State Hospital occupied a block of red brick buildings. One big building contained both rooms for patients and a residence for students. They lived, worked and studied all in the same place.

Just before I left for Nursing School

W.S.

Mother
Ada Loughy Scott

Sister
Virginia

kept to first time in Connellsville, Pa.

Sept. 1942

Wilma and Peg spent their first year there. For the second year they transferred to Morrisania City Hospital in the Bronx, where they could receive additional clinical experience in surgery, gynecology, obstetrics and pediatrics. They returned to Brooklyn for the first half of their third year. Both were accepted as cadet nurses, and Wilma spent her last six months at a military hospital on Staten Island.

Wilma arrived in New York with high expectations. The three years, however, proved to be more of an ordeal to be survived than the fruition of hopes. On their very first day, students were told to write an essay on why they wanted to be nurses. Since they had already answered that question when applying to enroll, Wilma treated the request as a joke. She wrote that during a blackout, she had stepped into a nurses' home and later discovered she had signed up for school. She added that she had run away from home because she hated to make beds. The next day she was ordered to make seventy-six empty beds. It was the beginning of a regimen to turn young women into nurses. In Wilma's eyes then and also now, in retrospect, it was designed to make them conform to the medical heirarchy, "to take the wind out of the sails of anyone with any gumption."

The ethos was rigid and quasi-military; Wilma resented all of it. The students wore black shoes and stockings and blue uniforms. Doctors, not atypically, asked for nurses who had, as Wilma said, "a strong back and weak mind." Students were expected to stand up when doctors entered a room and to open doors for them. They worked forty-eight hours a week and on top of that had classes and homework. They had a half hour for lunch which included the ten to fifteen minute walk of getting to and from the dining room. Wilma found courses boring and poorly taught. When lectures were dull, she sat in class, wrote letters and essays, and designed projects for improving nursing and the world. In physiotherapy and massage classes, she outlined those courses as she would have taught them.

She found the character of the hospital dehumanizing. On one occasion as a new student she was particularly nervous and spilled some water on a patient who was a physician. The supervisor did not attempt to discover why Wilma was nervous but simply castigated her, making her, of course, more nervous than before.

The more she learned, the more discerning and critical she became about the quality of nursing care and the nurse's responsibility for the patient. In her mind, quality care preempted bureaucracy and rules. But when she protested or suggested alternatives, she was consistently brought up short by custom, hierarchy, and legalities. Wilma pointed out that patients needed room in their beds to move their feet and that sheets should not be tucked in so tightly. She protested using nurses' time to clean classrooms and dust the head nurse's desk. She protested the rules that governed students' lives. She initiated a patient health teaching program, enlisting patients in taking some responsibility for their own care, instead of learning to play the sick role and then being rewarded with care from someone else.

Such activities earned her the reputation of being both intelligent and impertinent. A few of her teachers and many of her colleagues recognized her critical and imaginative capability. One of the former was a physician – teacher of neurology, Dr. Tamarin. He saw Wilma, Peg, and two other students – Celia Leeds and Florence Hager – as serious students, women who wanted to learn rather than simply as obstreperous. Wilma found his classes interesting and applied herself, asking questions and pushing for more information and insight. He told them, according to Wilma, that they made him a much better teacher.

Florence Unwin, the director of the school, gave Wilma as much support as she could. When someone would march Wilma into Unwin's office with a grievance, the director dismissed the supervisor and then turned to Wilma: "Tell me, Miss Scott, about your ideas."

Many, however, saw her as a troublemaker. When she was honest about staying out later than the rules allowed, she was declared impertinent. When an unauthorized change occurred in a nurse's responsibilities or in the approach to health care, she was blamed. She was generally considered insubordinate, and only the facts that Miss Unwin supported her, that her grades were good, and that she had not given a wrong treatment, prevented her from being expelled.

At Morrisania during her second year, Wilma helped deliver a baby for the first time. The baby's mother and Wilma were trapped in an elevator. The mother asked Wilma if this were her first time, and Wilma responded "Yes." The mother – a poor, Black woman – said, 'This is my ninth. I'll tell you what to do." She coached Wilma throughout the delivery. They used sheets to wrap the baby and a shoestring to clamp the umbilical cord, but left it uncut until they were in safer and more sanitary quarters. After the baby was born and was taken care of as well as possible, the two women sang spirituals until they were freed.

The action was contrary to hospital expectations and even rules. Although taught in classes not to try to stop the delivery, Wilma was also firmly impressed with ensuring that the baby was born in the delivery room with a doctor present. She was also told that a cardinal rule of nursing behavior was to "exude confidence." "There was no way I could pretend confidence or get to the delivery room," recalled Wilma. "Under the circumstances, I think we did the only intelligent thing."

The last six months of her third year of nursing school at the army hospital on Staten Island were more endurable. The work week was forty hours, and Wilma had more time for courses she wanted to take. She took classes in photography, pottery, public speaking, and even flying lessons. The cadet nurses were neither strictly military nor civilian, and since the hospital was staffed for the periodic loads of wounded that would come in, it was often overstaffed. As a result, Wilma and her friends were able to turn many events to their advantage.

They were always available when they were needed, working with the rest of the staff long and continuous hours in surgery and at bedsides. But when there were few patients and an overload of staff, Wilma and others simply disappeared. They went for walks, read, rested, talked. Their supervisor, an Irish nurse named Captain Harrigan, understood what was happening, and although she could not condone their actions officially she supported the errant cadets as much as she could.

Similarly, they played much of the military procedure "for laughs" and got away with it. At drill, for instance, when they were ordered to go right, they went left. Sometimes, being mistaken for officers, they were saluted, and they responded with a salute. In short, they clowned as much as they dared, and Captain Harrigan protected them. Wilma recalls that Captain Harrigan once said to them, "There's no question but that I earned my pay."

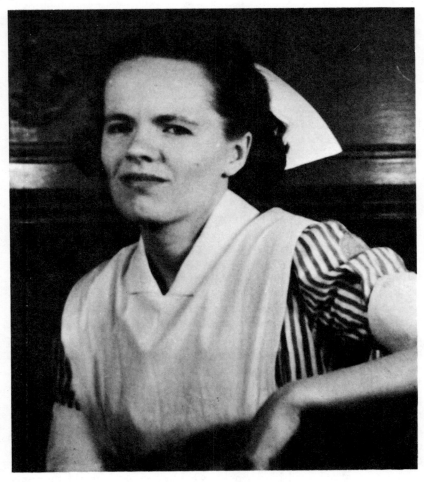

Wilma as Senior Cadet Nurse, 1945

They clowned for survival. They also clowned because they cared about the patients. The casualties had not only physical wounds, they also had emotional ones and sometimes the latter were harder to care for than the former. Indifference, lack of a will to live, and bitterness inevitably complicated the treatment the cadet nurses were responsible for. So Wilma and the others began deliberately doing things to stimulate a reaction, such as putting cornflakes in paraplegics' beds. Wilma was captain of a softball team that spent as much time joking, protesting calls, and generally exaggerating the game as actually playing. On one occasion, dissatisfied with the calls, they literally carried the umpire off the field. The wounded spectators laughed at and often felt superior to what was happening on the field, and the team felt it had accomplished its primary purpose of taking the patients' attention off themselves and giving them something positive to respond to.

While still a cadet nurse, the tragedies of war touched Wilma in another, much more intimate way. She had met a young serviceman, Lee Worthington. He was small – about 5'10" and thin with an angular face, blond hair, and sensitive features. They dated and within a couple of months, were engaged, deeply in love. Not long after their engagement, he was sent overseas and was killed. Wilma did not reveal much of how she felt, but within she was torn with grief. For several years afterward, she maintained a protective wall of casualness toward men.

Among all the frustration and pain of those three years, Wilma had an opportunity to meet and talk with Eleanor Roosevelt, an experience that she treasured deeply. One day the director at Brooklyn State, Florence Unwin, had asked Wilma whom she admired, particularly women. Wilma had included Eleanor Roosevelt high on her list. Then on another day, Unwin asked Wilma if she would like to meet Eleanor Roosevelt. Apparently Unwin and Roosevelt had known each other and the First Lady was speaking in the city at that time. A meeting was arranged. For the first couple of minutes Wilma couldn't quite believe what was happening, but she was soon put at ease and they talked for about an hour on issues of justice and social change.

The three years of nursing school and work were hard ones for Wilma, but she had begun to gain insights that she found invaluable. Her contact with patients helped her begin to make some connections between the larger society and the illnesses represented in the hospital. Malnutrition among poor patients and the diseases accompanying it could be better healed by a change in social and economic structure than by medical care. Stress and poor interpersonal relationships in people's lives outside the hospital put many inside just as much as accidents, germs and viruses did.

The quality of care within the hospital was also a complex factor in healing. It was important, for instance, that the patient take as much responsibility for her/his own healing as possible and of minimizing the differences of power in that environment. Wilma was beginning to see that nursing involved much more than knowledge about diseases and sanitation and following orders; it involved care for and with the human beings lying in the beds.

As grueling as the three years had been, Wilma did survive and did so in part because of her friendships. She and Peg remained together except for the last six months of their stay in New York. Although there were marked differences and sometimes tension between the two, there was also an abiding loyalty and affection. While Wilma redesigned the world in class, Peg carefully took notes on the course content, then lent them to Wilma to study the night before an examination. Wilma often stayed up late, talking and reading, while Peg tried to sleep. Then fearful of oversleeping, Wilma occasionally set the alarm two hours in advance of when she needed to get up; when the alarm sounded, she quickly went back to sleep in the cheerful knowledge that she had another

Peg Smith, Wilma and Ceil Leeds on the steps of Morrisania City Hospital in Bronx, NY, 1943.

couple hours, while Peg lay there wide awake.

Wilma supported Peg's growing independence of spirit. After Wilma had gone to the army hospital on Staten Island, Peg discovered that she was being paid less than she should be. After several futile efforts to change the situation, Peg finally wrote state officials in Albany and immediately her stipend was increased. In her letter to me, Peg writes that it was Wilma's influence that enabled her to take that action.

Another friend, whom Wilma met in New York, was Celia "Ceil" Leeds. Ceil was a very bright Jewish woman who had been orphaned as a child and had been responsible, as the oldest sister, for rearing her younger siblings. She too had the intellectual interests manifested in Wilma and Peg. Together they worked, studied, and challenged their instructors.

Friends also helped to ameliorate a continuing strained financial situation. Friends from Torrance who had gone into war-time factory jobs sent Wilma and Peg towels and other gifts. One friend at an army hospital sent them cigarettes. Peg's mother sent them food, and her sister occasionally sent money. Once when Peg's mother came to visit, she bought each a pair of slacks, the first new clothes they had had in three years other than their nursing uniforms.

Finally the three years came to an end, and it was time to graduate. Wilma left nursing school qualified to work in a profession she had serious questions about. But they were questions not about her own ability or interest so much as about the values that shaped the profession. Many of her insights and convictions generated at Torrance had now been reinforced. Specifically, she believed that one's primary responsibility as a nurse was to the patient and that responsibility was defined in terms of the patient's comfort and opportunity to experience as normal a life as possible while in the hospital. Responsibilities for one's own advancement and to the institution and its regulations were secondary.

These convictions were not a result simply of youthful idealism but rather a combination of the legacy of her childhood yearnings and values and the repudiation of much of what she had experienced at Torrance and in New York, a radicalizing of her relationship to the profession. "I felt," she recalled of that period, "that I was carrying the whole world on my shoulders, but I couldn't get a handle on how to change things."

Wilma and Peg decided to return to Pennsylvania and practiced there for three years. On two occasions, they risked their professional standing. One of their patients was the sister-in-law of a friend, Nell Long from Torrance. The sister-in-law was seriously ill in a homeopathic hospital, a place that made minimal use of medicines and general hospital technical resources and maximum use of massage and chiropractic.

The sister-in-law needed oxygen, and Wilma and Peg were appalled at the minimal supply of extra tanks at the hospital. The sister-in-law also seemed to be in a good deal of pain. They tried to get more oxygen supplies through the hospital, but when this effort did not prove quickly successful they went directly to an oxygen company. They had become friends with the resident in the hospital and with his assistance secured some relief from the pain. Technically, their New York licenses could have been revoked for allegedly practicing medicine without a doctor's license. They were considered insubordinate for not leaving the situation to a doctor and for not waiting until the bureaucratic process worked itself out.

A second occasion also occurred in response to a request from Nell. Another friend, Annie, was in a barbiturate coma from an attempted suicide. Wanting to protect Annie, since she had taken the pills from the hospital, and unable to enlist any doctor into working under those conditions, they in effect became their own doctors and worked with Annie for two days and nights until she regained consciousness, then took her to the hospital. Annie lived, but wished she had not and later tried suicide again. That time she succeeded.

During this period Wilma found that doctors were doing pre-frontal lobotomies (severing key motor nerves in the brain to help render patients less "intractable"). The operation was held to be part of a therapeutic process, which supposedly included the regeneration of those nerves. But Wilma saw no nerves regenerated and knew there was no clear evidence that they could be. Wilma protested the practice, futilely so.

When Wilma and Peg returned to Torrance to work as nurses they found that conditions had, if anything, deteriorated there during the war. The staff still worked a twelve-hour shift, six days one week and five another. Patients were illegally restrained for hours and even days at a time. At meals patients literally ran to the dining room and the stronger ones continued to get most of the food. Wilma was put in charge of Building Five, which contained all women, some of whom were considered among the "most disturbed." She immediately set to work and helped to reduce staff working time to an eight hour day with two days off a week. She refused to sign statements that were untrue. She refused, for instance, to state that a patient had been freed from restraints for the period of time prescribed by the Welfare Department, when the patient had not been. She refused to continue to allow attendants to assume more responsibility than she felt was appropriate for them.

At times, she was simply insubordinate. She staggered meal times, contrary to the rules, so that all had a more equal chance of eating. She refused to dress patients up in gingham clothes for visiting day; she felt family and friends should see them as they were most of the time.

The results of these actions were varied. Conditions for patients and staff did improve, but resentment also mounted. Marie Fagan and Mary Helen Fisher were back at Torrance from a stint with the Army Nurse Corps, and Fisher was sent to Building Five to "get Wilma under control." It was an order which put the supervisor in an awkward position, because she agreed with Wilma's intentions although she disagreed with some of her means. Many attendants objected. They continued to see Wilma as an attendant who had become too feisty and was, in some instances, jeopardizing their own power. The supervisor's office did not like it; Wilma's actions were an affront and some of them expensive to implement.

Eventually, in anger and desperation, Wilma reported the hospital's non-compliance with health regulations to a representative from the Welfare Department. Wilma observed in retrospect, "I may have been wrong, but I didn't see that the administration would bring about change, and I felt someone should know."

While Wilma and Peg were trying to improve patient care and working conditions at Torrance, they were also trying to complete their college education. To work full time and go to school full time meant that shifts and course time had to mesh. As Wilma became more insistent about changing conditions at the hospital, her hours were changed and her use of the hospital's library was prohibited. Both actions increased the difficulties of scheduling time for courses and of obtaining necessary books and resources.

Wilma both overestimated and underestimated her power at Torrance. She originally assumed that her status as a registered nurse would give her more authority than in fact it did. She underestimated the resentment generated by a young, ambitious woman with a thirst for learning; she was resented for wanting to get ahead as well as for challenging practices. And in resentment and defensiveness, the institution responded – devastatingly so.

In the midst of this increasingly tense situation, Wilma borrowed $50.00 from Peg to complete paying for an old Nash which they used to drive back and forth between Pittsburgh and Torrance. One day, returning from school, Wilma was arrested by two plain-clothes State Police for allegedly stealing and cashing pay checks. Wilma was fingerprinted, taken down to the county jail and locked in a cell.

The experience was a nightmare for Wilma. She could not believe it was happening to her. She knew she was innocent and knew, therefore, that either there was some crazy misunderstanding or it was political – a deliberate act to embarrass and discredit her. For a twenty-six year old idealistic woman, in the days before civil rights marchers made it acceptable to go to jail, it was bizarre and humiliating. And Wilma felt that there was no misunderstanding, that it was indeed political, and her body responded with nausea and headaches.

When Peg discovered that Wilma had been arrested, she tried to raise money for the $500 bail. She did not have the money herself, and she tried unsuccessfully to borrow it from a pharmacy in Blairsville, where they had a checking account. Finally, their friends Nell and June were able to raise the money. When Peg went to the jail to tell Wilma the good news, Peg found Wilma reading poetry to the other women prisoners in the cell.

After Wilma was released on bail, her sister Virginia and brother Ray visited her. Ray told her that this incident would hurt his career and Virginia that it would hurt the family. Wilma was shocked and further demoralized by what seemed to her to be lack of support – financial or emotional – from her own family.

Wilma was called into the superintendent's office and was asked to resign. She refused to do so until further change occurred. She went to the Chairman (sic) of the Board of Trustees and demanded that "either you have these illegal and inhumane practices stopped or I'll do an exposé you won't believe! And I won't resign until my name is cleared." She was not forced to resign.

Instead, the charges were dropped; checks indeed had been stolen, but there was no evidence pointing to Wilma. The Welfare Department was persuaded to change some of the practices at the hospital that Wilma had challenged. Nevertheless, after several months of shock, depression, frustration, and conflict, both Wilma and Peg resigned.

They found work elsewhere – first at Mayview State Hospital, then at Pennsylvania College for Women (now Chatham Hall). Wilma was becoming more and more interested in her studies. She had shifted from a pre-medical program into sociology – not simply to gain a second career but to find resources for understanding personal and institutional behavior and for bringing about change.

NOTES

1. Letter to me from Marie Fagan, July 10, 1977.
2. Letter to me from Peg Smith, Summer, 1977.
3. In Peg's letter to me, she referred to Wilma as "Scotty." All the Scott children were called Scotty at one time or another. Wilma went through at least three nicknames before she was thirty. In her childhood, she was "Serious," in her adolescence "Scotty," and in her young adulthood – particularly while she was working with the National School of Girl Scout Leaders – "Skip."

4

WOMEN'S PLACE:
AT HOME IN THE WORLD

To date, we have raised men to be brave and women to care. Our expectations have been sex-stereotyped more often than not. Now, we must raise boys and men to be brave enough to care about the quality and equality of our common lives. Likewise we must expect women to care enough to bravely assert our deep concerns and exercise our talents in all aspects of society.

– Wilma Scott Heide[1]

Caring and courage are two of the more dominant motifs in Wilma's ethics. In the years between 1947 and 1969, she was able to weave them into a pattern that gave her life both direction and congruence. In 1947, she was stunned and humiliated by the violent response to some of her idealistic efforts at change. By 1969, she had become a powerful, competent, and inspiring leader very much cognizant of the depths of resistance to change and more than ever committed to change.

We *become* in at least three different ways. We *become* in a chronological fashion; we are born, most of us mature, each of us dies. In the course of that journey, we make choices, and in so doing, to some extent, make ourselves.

We also *become* in a generational and cultural fashion; we are daughters and sons and may be parents and grandparents. We are first – or fifth – generation Americans. We are bearers and creators of particular religious, racial, class and ethnic heritages and values.

We also *become* in a generative fashion; we move closer to the creative well-springs of our lives. We experience the reality of "coming to ourselves." We *see*. We *become* by coming-to-be at home in ourselves and in the world. We are not only sojourners and witnesses; we are also residents and actors.

It is this process of coming-to-be at home with ourselves and in the world that I wish to explore, for I think Wilma's movement toward it is critical for understanding her ethics. It enables her to hold together caring and courage, commitment to principles and to human beings, creativity and careful analysis, pragmatism and formalism. The sense of self and the sense of vocation that Wilma already had were necessary but insufficient for emerging as a powerful, stern, and compassionate woman of later years. Her sense of self and sense of vocation had to be transcended into a new unity and a new identity of self and world.

The wide-ranging variety of activities, causes, and projects she engaged in from 1947 to 1969 provided the occasion for this new unity and identity to emerge. She continued to pursue her yearning for further education and began to establish herself as a health educator. She became friends with women who were strong and caring people. She married, and she became a mother. When her husband was drafted, she went south with him and plunged into activities for racial justice. Returning north, she confronted competing and often frustrating demands on her energy. Tension and stress increased until a crisis provided a break-through to a new integration of self and responsibilities.

From 1948-1950, Wilma was a nurse at Pennsylvania College for Women (now Chatham College) in Pittsburgh. In 1951 she went to Oswego, New York, to teach health education and be a nurse at the campus elementary school there. While in Oswego, she became involved in community activities that addressed issues of racism and what was later called sexism. She found, for instance, that there were few opportunities for women in sports and no YWCA there. She became the first woman to serve on the Board of the local YMCA and worked to provide more activities for women.

She encountered blatant examples of racial prejudice. When Wilma and a Black friend ate out, they were served but consistently their dishes were broken after they had finished and in full view of the diners. "It was," Wilma observed, "their way of showing how they felt." She never returned to those restaurants a second time; she also publicized their policies and practices.

At the same time, she was enlarging her sphere of friends and her contacts with strong, competent, and caring women. The summers of those years were spent as a camp nurse at Red Wing Girl Scout Camp in southwestern Pennsylvania and then as a health consultant at the Edith Macy Training School for Girl Scout Leaders, a national center to train Scout staff and administrators. For the first time, she experienced creative, sharing women working together, not bound by authoritarian and political considerations, and Wilma thrived in that environment. Her own ideas and her own person were taken seriously by others; she was free to learn as much as she could.

Wilma became close friends with some of the other resource people. Mary Helen Keating was one. She was a guidance counselor and older woman – a wise woman, whom Wilma described as a "dear, dear woman." She and Wilma emotionally adopted one another.

Another was Helen "Nele" Cuyjet, a resource person in crafts. Nele had grown up in Philadelphia with a passion for crafts. Like Wilma's, her family was not affluent; unlike Wilma's, hers was Black, and she had to work hard to establish herself in crafts.

Nele and Wilma met at a staff meeting. Nele recalled that "Skip [a nickname for Wilma] made it very clear that she was not 'just a nurse'," that is, that she was interested in people and their ideas, and Nele responded warmly.[2] "Wilma could talk all night – about philosophy and things going on in the world," she recalled, and added, "There was a great mental attraction. You know, it's a great privilege one has to choose friends who aren't boring."

Nele did not hesitate to tease her friend, however, particularly about her vocabulary if she thought Wilma was being unnecessarily abstruse. "Skip!" she would exclaim, "What words! All those words – to say this ...?" and she would repeat the idea very simply.

A third person was not so much a close friend but an example of administrative leadership that Wilma had not really experienced before. This was Clara M. "Polly" Allen, Director of Edith Macy. She was firm and could be tough, in Wilma's perception, but it was also clear that she genuinely cared for individuals. She developed lines of communication with others in ways that incorporated respect and interest and compassion. She was also skilled at bringing together high-powered and talented women of varying temperaments, into a working whole. Wilma was impressed and excited by what she saw. Some alternative to the prevailing models of leadership and decision-making was possible.

Confronting justice issues and finding new resources were two directions of *becoming* for Wilma. During this same period, she continued her educational work and decided to marry. In 1950, while still at Pennsylvania College for Women, Wilma finished her undergraduate degree in sociology at the University of Pittsburgh and continued to work on a master's degree. In one of her classes, she met Eugene Heide, who was to become her husband. Gene had grown up in a multi-ethnic area of Pittsburgh. His family was German, devoutly Lutheran, and working class.

At an early age, Gene expressed an artistic interest and ability. He recalls being taken to a different church in Pittsburgh occasionally and preferring that one to his own congregation because it had more aesthetic appeal to him. His artistic interests, however, were not particularly encouraged, and he went to the University of Pittsburgh on a track scholarship. He continued his art as a hobby, enjoying carving and carpentry, decorating and designing. After Wilma and Gene were married, he made most of their furniture, using dark wood, with primarily square or rectangular shapes, but finishing the pieces in glowing, almost sensuous tones.

Wilma was seven years older than Gene, and he was attracted to her independence, maturity, and what he called her "feisty" character. In turn, she liked his sense of humor, his aesthetic appreciation, the creative and sure use of his hands, and his intelligence. In other words, their mutual attraction was based in part on the way Wilma expressed many of what were considered more "masculine" characteristics and Gene more "feminine" ones, without denying each one's own femaleness and maleness.

When they met, neither had much money or time for dating. Wilma was still working at Pennsylvania College for Women and in addition to her own responsibilities accepted many of those of the head nurse, who was terminally ill with cancer. At the same time, she was a full-time student at the University of Pittsburgh. Gene was both a graduate student and a lecturer. They combined visiting with lunch between classes and occasionally attended something that was free – the planetarium, radio shows with live audiences, and a few concerts.

They were engaged in December 1950, and married on May 27, 1951. Wilma was thirty years old and accustomed to an independent existence. She thought a good bit about the coming marriage, and she and Gene discussed its implications for their lives. Indeed, her decision to teach in Oswego, New York for a year was based in part on her desire to test their relationship by spending a year apart. In their discussion, she expressed reluctance to change her name but finally agreed to because they both felt their parents simply would not understand her keeping her own name. They agreed to a joint bank account and to continue to pursue their own separate interests. They also agreed that Gene would have the first chance to finish his education. Wilma actually did not agree to the principle that the husband should go first, but she accepted what seemed to her at the time the reality of expectations on them. Wilma told Gene that if he ever laid a hand on her in anger, that would automatically end the marriage. Gene, gentle as he was, was shocked at the thought. They also agreed that they would have children and decided on four.

The wedding was a small one, held in Trinity Lutheran Church in Connellsville. According to Wilma, half the faculty at Oswego heaved a sigh of relief when she bought a suit for the occasion instead of wearing slacks. She bought an expensive beige suit and hat. "After all," she recalled, "I figured I'd get married only once, so I might as well do it up right." Since her father had died, Ray gave her away. Virginia served as matron of honor. Hal ushered. William Heide, Gene's older brother, was best man.

Both Wilma and Gene were relaxed about their marriage and were in fact, almost late for the wedding. Both had separately drifted off to sleep just before the ceremony. They were not, however, quite as relaxed as they thought, as they discovered after Wilma had driven fifty miles the wrong way on the turnpike as they headed for a brief honeymoon.

Wilma had to return to Oswego to finish the school year and Gene accompanied her. He soon became Mr. Scott to the children at the campus school, and she remained Miss Scott. After her marriage, Wilma continued to work outside the home, and both Wilma and Gene continued studies in sociology at the University of Pittsburgh.

In 1953, Gene was drafted and sent to the south. When she could, Wilma joined him, at first in South Carolina and then in Georgia. Gene was part of a human research team. Its task was to determine a way of motivating soldiers to kill, a goal which Gene and many of the others did not accept. Wilma found a job as Educational Director in the School of Nursing at the Orangeburg Regional Hospital in Orangeburg, South Carolina. She turned down an offer to be the Educational Director at a Columbia, South Carolina hospital because it admitted white students only. When Gene was transferred to Fort Benning, Georgia, she worked in the Phoenix City Hospital in Pheonix City, Alabama, as night supervisor and sociology researcher.

In addition to employment, Wilma plunged into the growing but still rather quiet movement for racial justice. She helped to register voters for the League of Women Voters and was active in the National Association for the Advancement of Colored People (NAACP). Contrary to local League policy, she registered Black voters as well as white ones. She edited the League newsletter and soon became visible on both a local and state level as sympathetic to "Negro rights," as they were then called. She also had a radio show, "Time for Living," and on this program consistently introduced questions of justice through reviewing books, providing background information about the songs she played, and talking with visitors to the area.

She and Gene lived on the second floor of a privately-owned home. They had many Black visitors, including two men in Gene's research unit. Although the owners, who lived below, did not entertain Black people at all, they remained on cordial terms with the Heides. For some reason, they simply overlooked the liberal convictions of their tenants.

But others were not so sanguine. Wilma received hate mail and threatening telephone calls. She was labeled a "nigger lover" and "white trash." On occasion people spat on the sidewalk as she passed or crossed to the other side of the street to avoid her. Wilma watched them cross and then return to the original side when they had passed her. One evening she and a Black man were walking along on their way to a meeting. A shot was fired, and her companion fell on the sidewalk, dead. Wilma thought then and continues to think now, that the shot had been intended for her. For a long time afterward, she carried a large burden of guilt for the man's death.

As she became more involved in civil rights in the south, she also became more aware of white patriarchy. White patriarchal patterns had existed in the north, of course, but perhaps because she was an outsider and unable to take the southern ethos for granted, it seemed to jump out at her. Here, it seemed to be a stark, unrelenting reality. White men were very much in control, and there were fewer token exceptions. White middle class women were treated with great politeness, and it was quite clear that white women did not do many of the things Wilma took for granted. She was acutely aware of the difference in the way she was treated and the way a white man was treated, just as she was aware of the difference in the way she was treated and a Black woman or man was treated. In her writing during this period, Wilma recalls, she began using the phrases "white male dictatorship" and "white male patterns of dominance."

She pondered the significance of the question that she heard over and over again in conversations with white people opposed to integration: "But would you want your daughter to marry one?" Why, she wondered, was it not of much concern if "your son married one?" The answer she discovered was simply another bit of evidence for her growing awareness of what later was to be called *sexism*; for a white woman to marry a Black man was considered terrible because of the assumption that the man was the one in authority and power, regardless of race. She found sex to be as significant a variable as race in determining one's position in the hierarchical structure of values.

After Gene was released from the army in 1955, they returned to Pennsylvania, where they followed Gene's employment opportunities in the state university system. Finally, in 1958, they moved to New Kensington, Pennsylvania, where Gene initiated and directed a new branch of the university system. Between July and September with Wilma's help, he literally put together a college, cleaning out an old school building, painting it, hiring faculty, and recruiting students. There they remained until they moved to Connecticut in 1971.

During this period, the two Heide children were born, Terry Lynne in 1956 and Tamara Lee in 1959. If the time in the south was one of expanding insights and action, these were years of personal struggle, focused on integrating family responsibilities with public ones, maintaining a separate identity from Gene's and a fuller identity than wife and mother, and seeking more power over her own life and ways to influence the larger community and society.

During these years, Wilma had a variety of occupational positions. She was a night supervisor at Lankenau Hospital. She taught sociology, she coordinated nursing education. She administered various programs for Penn State, including Headstart Staff Training Programs.

Wilma enjoyed much of married life and parenthood. She and Gene designed their own house and then talked with builders and worked out compromises with them. They liked to ride through the city streets identifying "junk" other people had thrown away and turned the objects into a lamp or a piece of art. On weekends, the whole family explored zoos and parks and shared house and yard work.

They shared many values, which brought them into community activities together, particularly those concerning racial and economic justice. In New Kensington, where they spent ten years of their married life, they were both a part of the civil rights efforts in the community, Wilma the more active and Gene the more supporting. Similarly Wilma was active in the PTA and chaired the Home Health Care Advisory Committee of the Miners Clinics, a part of the federal anti-poverty program. Gene participated less, but consistently supported Wilma's activity.

Wilma and Marge Stratman became friends and saw each other about every day. They worked together on PTA and school affairs, drank endless cups of coffee, shared the joys and difficulties and boredoms of being parents and homemakers, and discussed the state of the world.

> We worked together in the PTA; the year Wilma was president was probably the most interesting one we ever had. We had cooperation from all the parents because she dared to have speakers come in who were somewhat controversial. We worked on getting the curriculum up to date and new things introduced into the schools.[3]

With Wilma's growing involvement in civil rights activities, Marge participated less with her, but she supported her friend in any way she could: "I used to help her by taking care of her children and doing some typing for her – that sort of thing. I'm not much of a 'do it' kind of person. I was much better at helping her doing the kinds of things she wanted to do."[3]

Other friends and colleagues included Anita and Dan Fine, Charles and Mary Andrews, Lester and Marian Knapp, Jane and Paul Vosberg, Jane and Jim Glenn, Gene and Libby Simon, Evelyn Silvus, Ruby White, and Magnolia Garner. Anita Fine was a social worker and Dan a physician. Charles Andrews worked in industry and was president of the local chapter of the NAACP of which Wilma was a member. Mary Andrews was a teacher in the public schools and quite active in the NAACP. Lester Knapp was a chemist with Alcoa and Marian a homemaker and active in the PTA. Jane Vosberg was a homemaker and an active Republican, and Paul was an Alcoa executive and an influential Republican. Jane Glenn was a homemaker and Jim had the local Buick agency. Gene Simon was a publisher of several newspapers in the area and owner of others in Arizona. Wilma wrote several articles for him, which he referred to as "think pieces" and "striking a blow for freedom!" Libby Simon was a homemaker and active in community affairs. Both were supporters of liberal causes. Evelyn Silvus was a homemaker and active in the PTA. Ruby White was a domestic worker and a community organizer, working in civil rights and child care issues. Magnolia Garner was a homemaker and a close family friend.

While in New Kensington, Wilma became ill and needed a gall stone operation. Dan Fine was her doctor. According to him, she should have been operated on immediately, but she postponed it for a week until she had more time.[4] Then a day or two after the operation, she was sitting up and working full time in the hospital. Dan recalls, "She was never a passive patient. She would take advice but she had the final say." She was indeed simply putting into practice for herself what she had encouraged others to do some twenty years earlier.

For all the activities, values and interests the Heides shared, however, there were increasing difficulties and conflicts that could not seem to be resolved. In spite of going into her marriage with its terms carefully defined, she found the consequences of that decision extremely complicated, frustrating, and difficult to sort out. She began to be treated as Gene's wife rather than as an independent person in her own right. She felt blocked in her efforts to pursue a career of her own in the state university structure. She resented and protested being taken for granted as an appendage to Gene. On one occasion in 1955 when they were both being interviewed for a position for Gene, she asked the interviewer how much her salary would be if she were to do what was expected of her as Gene's wife.

Although they both enjoyed many dimensions of parenting, primary responsibility was Wilma's. Since Gene travelled a good deal in the university system, Wilma was often alone with the children for days at a time, particularly when they had first moved to a new area and she had not made friends or found sitters. On one occasion Terry was ill for a week. Doctors were unable to diagnose the disease, and nothing seemed to help the child except reading "Mary had a little lamb" to her, singing Brahms' Lullaby, playing records, or holding her. At the end of the week, Wilma was exhausted and finally called her husband to come home or both she and Terry would be in the hospital. Eventually, doctors determined that Terry had a form of blood poisoning and that she was also allergic to the antibiotic they had been giving her. Once Terry's illness was correctly diagnosed, they were able to give her medication to clear it up quickly.

Wilma's emptiness and lack of public influence became so severe that once when she was referred to as Mrs. Gene Heide by the local newspaper, she burst into angry tears and exclaimed to Gene, "I'm a wife, a mother and a nurse, but I'm more than that. My life means more than that!"

She thought about her obituary – and could think of nothing she had done or was doing that would be considered important enough to include. Nothing at all counted, she felt, even though her community leadership and contributions to nursing care and education, to civil rights, and to voter education were considerable.

While Wilma was pregnant with her second daughter, Tami, the feelings of frustration and being blocked came to a head, and she went into a deep depression for about two months. "Oh God," she thought, "six more years to truncate things." The sense that she was not doing things that she needed to do weighed her down. She was not clear about what she needed to do, and she had no one she could talk with; there was simply a great sense of emptiness, insignificance and desperation. She finally decided to take her life with an overdose of anti-allergy pills that had been prescribed for Gene. Appalled at the realization that she was seriously considering taking her own life, and feeling responsible for Terry, she decided to see a psychiatrist. That one visit was radicalizing. He told her she wanted to be a man. Furious, she left, but the visit did force her to confront her own growing feminism.

She concluded that what was wrong with her was the result of an ethos that insisted on trying to make her conform to predetermined notions of what it meant to be a woman. The growing realization that it was not she but a patriarchal culture that was sick helped her to move beyond her depression, and specifically to move beyond the guilt she was experiencing in longing to live a life that included but also transcended being a wife and a mother. "And I'm sure I made the right decision [to trust her own insight] then, even though there are times still when I do things that would be regarded as compensatory. It's [the guilt's] so deep that I doubt if any woman completely erases it."

Perhaps ironically, she also found support and resource in teaching a community course on mental health at Penn State. Although she had attended courses and had worked in a mental health hospital, she brought a new depth of awareness to her research and teaching. It provided her with an opportunity to bring together her intellectual insights and her emotional insights, and to clarify how and why she was feeling as she did. She also began to share some of those insights with the women and men taking the course. Inevitably, she rediscovered that she was not alone. Soon after this, she applied for a position as Executive Director of the Pennsylvania Mental Health Association but was informed that she had been denied the position because she was a woman. No civil rights laws forbade such sex discrimination then.

She became a free-lance journalist for the *Valley Daily News* and *Daily Dispatch* (newspapers published by Gene Simon) that covered an eight-county area of southwestern Pennsylvania. She was asked to write about civil rights in the lives of Black people in the region, and wrote her findings in an eight-part series for the paper.[5] Reluctant to do the series as a white person, she agreed only with the understanding that she was writing the Black peoples' stories as they wanted these told. She won a state award for the series, and at the ceremony, some other publishers reportedly said to Gene Simon, "I wish we'd had the guts to do that."

In 1965, Wilma wrote a twelve part series called "Poverty is Expensive," bringing to bear her talents as a sociologist, journalist, and community activist. That same year, she and Gene were invited for a week's vacation in Laurel, Mississippi, by the Laurel Rotary Club, other service clubs and Chambers of Commerce, in an effort to counter some of the negative publicity Mississippi had been receiving over civil rights demonstrations and the resulting threats, bombings and killings. Nineteen other couples were also chosen by service clubs to participate in what was called "V.I.M.: Vacation in Mississippi." Wilma and Gene were selected by the New Kensington Rotary Club as the most "interested." There was an official itinerary, but the Heides created their own unofficial one before and after they arrived, since Wilma knew several Mississippi civil rights leaders. They wrote an eight part newspaper series, exploring many dimensions of race relations in Laurel, talking with civic club members and families, police, clergy, FBI, citizens, educators, maids, laborers, welfare workers, white citizens' councils and NAACP, rich and poor, CORE and segregationists, business people and employees and communications media people.

In the next-to-last article, Wilma and Gene shifted to a brief discussion of the role of women there:

> One courageous lady who lost a surprisingly close election for mayor of Laurel recently, reminded us that in Mississippi,

"criminal, the insane and women" are not eligible to serve on juries. Given that attitude toward the place of women in public affairs, it's not surprising that the female member of your reporting team was considered bold by some Laurel residents. This position of women is not uniquely Southern. It's simply more pronounced there.[6,p.2]

Wilma wrote often for the paper. In the following couple of years, she did a five-part series entitled "Someone Lit a Candle," co-authored with a Black minister. She interviewed people nationally prominent in civil rights, human rights, and anti-poverty concerns. In whatever way she could think of, she continued to bring to the attention of the reading public and her sociology classes at Penn State University issues of social, legal and economic justice.

In 1965, a group of people, many of them poor, approached Wilma about starting a pre-school program. She agreed and together they formed the Community Enrichment Association, which in turn, developed a pre-school educational program that was community supported. Pre-dating Headstart, it sought to recognize both the needs of "disadvantaged" children and their own creative talents that are often used to survive in a classist and racist society. There were two half-day programs and fees were based on a sliding income scale. Wilma was the original director, a position she quickly relinquished to someone better qualified.

From that, she became vice chair of the Allegheny County Civil Rights Council and vice chair of the Westmoreland County Economic Opportunities Program, which was responsible primarily for health and legal education and employment programs. Through such activities, plus her teaching and involvement in the schools, Wilma was becoming known in the region for herself. In January 1969, she was appointed to the Pennsylvania State Human Relations Commission.

The Commission had many responsibilities. It heard individual complaints and what it called "pattern and practice" complaints, ie, systemic ones. The Commission investigated school populations, policies and practices and where necessary, held public hearings. It educated employees and employers and the public about desegregation in all areas – housing, employment, education, public accommodations.

Much of this work was done by a staff of over one hundred people throughout the state. The Commissioners devoted their time to policy formulation, hearing of complaints, and then taking the initiative of developing systemic policy orders, educating the public, and lobbying to ensure that the Commission would not be eliminated or weakened.

As the only woman on the Commission, Wilma spent some of her time and energy educating the other Commissioners on issues of sexism. Shortly after her appointment, prohibition of sex discrimination was added to its responsibilities as a result of the work of the National Organization for Women (NOW), of which Wilma was a state, national and local leader. Some folks viewed Wilma's human rights activities and her Commissioner role as "conflicts of interest." Apparently they thought that absence of such activity led to a "more objective" stance as a Commissioner. Wilma successfully insisted that her activist commitments better qualified her to be a Commissioner. When feminist organizations, as well as civil rights organizations, expressed dissatisfaction over the Commission, Wilma encouraged them to protest publicly or demonstrate, putting pressure on the Commission. "No group likes to be embarrassed," she reflected.

With growing recognition came increasing harassment and once again danger. She received threatening phone calls. "I'll get you," some said to her. She was taunted with the usual epithet of "nigger lover" and sent anonymous mail. On one occasion her car was forced off the road.

As if to symbolize the growing recognition of her own self, she left Penn State and secured a position with the American Institutes for Research in Pittsburgh as an associate research scientist. Once again, she found herself confronting racist and sexist assumptions and practices – in definitions of mental health, in salary difference, and in job opportunities. While others on the staff documented discrimination but were reluctant to sign a complaint, Wilma agreed to using her name. Investigators found probable cause, and the Institute was forced to change some of it policies and practices.

At the Institute, Wilma met Evelyn Perloff. They developed an abiding friendship, sharing professional interests and mutual concern about women's issues. Evelyn Perloff had come to Pittsburgh from Indiana where she had been a member of the Indiana Commission on the Status of Women. The first time Wilma walked into Perloff's office, she stopped, surprised and delighted. Row on row of books by and about women greeted her. Wilma had never seen such a collection among her acquaintances and she was enchanted.

They also shared more personal concerns. Wilma was able to talk with her about her harassment as a member of the Human Relations Commission, even exploring with her the possibility of carrying a gun for protection. As Wilma became more involved in NOW, she was able to share her frustration and pride. Evelyn Perloff did not join NOW; she thought the strain on her family commitments would be too severe. She was able, however, to listen to Wilma and provide safe space for her.[7]

With the variety of activities that Wilma had undertaken, she was extremely busy and away from home much of the time. When she and Gene both had to be away, they turned to babysitters, often to neighbor Marie Katusin; between those sitters and the Heides strong bonds developed.

Terry and Tami accepted their mother's growing reputation and involvement matter-of-factly. Both remember watching her on TV while they were young. The children, Gene and Wilma were all queried about Wilma's absence from home and they developed some stock replies. Wilma's was that "I spare them my constant presence," which was true and helped raise the consciousness of the inquirer. Terry's was, thinking of babysitters among others, "I am loved by many people."

Both children sensed that their parents were "different" and Terry added "better than other people." For Terry a part of this difference had to do with discipline. She felt that she "got away with" more than other children did, that her mother found it difficult to say "no." "I can remember when I got glasses that I wasn't supposed to use them for anything but school work. I read my books too, and my mother found it hard to tell me not to. She wasn't always bothering us, and we could also put off chores."

Similarly, Tami thought that perhaps they were a bit spoiled. "Mother wouldn't make me do things – like try out food. I was a picky eater, and sometimes she would make something special for me."

When the children were young, there were always animals around – turtles and ducks; a dog named Boots, who adopted baby rabbits; a rabbit that chased dogs. With their father, they took long walks in the woods, gardened, and learned to identify plants, flowers and birds. With both parents, they went to museums and zoos. Gene built things for and with the children. One of the most memorable for the two daughters was a tree house.

Opportunity was available for music, swimming, and other lessons, and Terry took advantage of them for a while, but neither child was strongly urged. Tami felt, in her words, too shy to participate in such activities. Neither daughter saw herself as particularly aggressive or desiring to star. They felt free to pursue their own interests and friendships.

Nevertheless, there were rules and expectations. As they grew older they were not given a curfew, but they were expected to be responsible and to call and inform their parents of their whereabouts. They were expected to tell the truth, and Terry, particularly, felt on occasion that the truth imposed some unnecessary hardships on her. On other occasions they felt called upon to defend their parents' values and beliefs to others, and both daughters found that their own sensitivities and behaviors reflected their parents', at least in part. "One thing I think I learned," reflected Tami, "was not to have prejudices, or at least to be aware of them and try to overcome them. I think I'm sensitive to other people's feelings, and that's partly from my mother." Terry saw a significant difference between her and many of her peers because she was not disagreeing much with her parents' values.

Yet, conflicts inevitably arose. "Like over shaving legs," recalled Terry. And, as a child, Tami recalled wanting long hair and new dresses, but in her memory, at least, always wore "short hair, pants, and hand-me-downs."

It is during this period that Wilma gained much more weight than she had previously. At age 22 she had weighed 98 pounds. She put on some weight during her two pregnancies. She not only did not take that off, but during the next decade, continued to add more. Some of it reflected her indifference to conventional appearance; some of it reflected a response to frustration, and as she became a more and more public figure, to the controversial and even hostile contexts within which she acted. A larger woman, psychologically and sometimes literally, conveys more power and authority than a tiny one.

But it also reflected her perceptions of and response to her husband. Gene continued to want women to be sexually attractive as well as aesthetically so. According to Wilma, he acknowledged a pull toward the James Bond fantasies and Playboy images of manhood and womanhood. He also seemed to prefer a wife who was more interested than Wilma was in a family life together, shared projects and vacations, time for one another.

Those preferences on Gene's part could only accentuate the growing awareness Wilma experienced, that there was a reservoir of herself that she could not share with her husband. Those feelings were still further intensified by her perception of his involvement in the women's movement; she saw him participating not so much because he believed in it but for her sake, derivatively, as it were, and she longed for a fuller commitment from him.

> While it was good to be involved in some things together – homebuilding and family – there was still a whole reservoir of me I couldn't communicate with him. The more I realized that, there just wasn't that much going for us – what we wanted for the rest of our lives wasn't the same thing.[8]

Wilma was becoming more aware of and involved in feminism, and she felt Gene found it too threatening. He had taken stands at some risk to his career. He had made his opposition to Vietnam known; he had tried futilely to have the president and the board of the university respond more understandingly and compassionately to the possibility of student riots on campus. He grew a beard and refused to shave it. Wilma's growing public activity was a continuing source of harassment for him, both from colleagues of Wilma's and from those who were opposed to what she was about. He was on occasion referred to as ''hen pecked;'' and on one radio interview he was asked why he allowed his wife to do all the things she did. He replied, ''I 'allow' her to do all these things like I 'allow' her to breathe, to eat and sleep.''

But at some point he stopped; he was unable to go further. Gene expressed it this way: ''We could share more of ourselves when we were working for civil rights because neither one of us was Black; we were both outsiders. But in the women's movement, Wilma became an insider, and I remained an outsider.'' He felt she was hearing a different drummer, one that he simply did not hear. He did not see how he could become an insider.

> I had a lot of pride in what she was doing ... but could never see myself doing it. I have in some ways a more fatalistic historical sense; movements have a natural history, and this one is now past the peak of public awareness. Now whatever will occur is going to be tough and slow – I don't have that kind of personal commitment ... Most other people important in the movement did their own thing also, but her rise was by virtue of almost total commitment. That isolated her; her family and mine didn't understand her; they tolerated her but used conventional arguments against her.[9]

It was not two careers that separated them so much as two worlds, not diverse obligations pulling them in different directions but two centers of value. Wilma's world was the future, what was possible and ought to be; Gene's was the present, however critical he also was of it. Wilma was loyal to a vocation, a call, as it were, like a religious commitment; Gene's loyalties were more pluralistic, more diverse. Wilma's spirit was restless, craving, anguishing, demanding, serving; Gene's asked to be allowed to enjoy the grain of wood, the smell of dirt and forest, family vacations and leisure time. This divergence of interests and values was expressed also in practice. Gene began seeing other women and bringing them home for supper.

Finally, they agreed to a divorce, and told their children. Tami recalled her mother telling them about it and their father's plans to marry someone else. However, before Wilma was able to tell anyone else, including her family of origin and NOW (of which she was then president), the news broke. One morning early the doorbell rang. When Wilma answered it, light bulbs flashed, and a reporter began asking questions. The news media made the most of it, and a story went on the wires and all over the country and in 22 other countries. Faith Middleton, a local reporter, recalls:

> In the newsroom reporters were being instructed to call various countries in an attempt to locate Eugene Heide, rumored to be off somewhere with another woman. Writers and photographers were dispatched to Wilma's house, where they harassed her, using the worst journalistic techniques. The scene bordered on the bizarre ... The paper received an award from the wire service ... [for] such a national "beauty" of a story.[10]

And then she added:

> I can't help thinking of Emma Goldman now, and how the press treated her. They either attacked her personally or treated her humorously, thereby trivializing her every move. As you can see, I'm still disgusted. A year after the event I wrote Wilma a letter saying how disgusted many of us were with what had gone on. And that I hoped she'd continue to be angry for all the right reasons ... And suddenly it's clear how our finest revolutionaries become lost in even their time.[10]

The divorce itself occurred in 1972 after Wilma's identity of self and vocation were formed. It was a normal and predictable but not natural consequence of the events traced here. From 1947 to the late 60's, Wilma was developing a clear inclusive identity around a center that put her outside the area of preoccupation with both career and family. Her long-standing commitment to issues of justice had matured into a clear perception that her *work* and her *being* were the same.

Both in the south and again in the north, Wilma had discovered patterns of discrimination against her because she was a woman. She had been treated differently from the way white men were treated in the south, and she, like other white women there, simply did not have access to the power and privileges and responsibilities that white men had. She began to perceive something of the patterns of domination and subordination of society, patterns that put minority men and women of all racial backgrounds in the position of subordinates, however different those positions might also be. As a married woman, in spite of her efforts, she found herself identified by others in ways that did not fit with her own perceptions of herself. She became primarily wife and mother, whether she wanted to or not, and indeed to some extent, in spite of herself, she internalized some of that definition. An acute depression was the consequence.

But depression was not the answer. She had learned from her father a strong sense of justice as fairness, and she had acted since childhood to correct what in her perception was not fair. As she became older, she had more direct contact with people who were hurt, vulnerable, powerless, victimized. She saw patients strapped to their beds. She and other students of nursing suffered the often unthinking, sometimes malicious use of power their superiors had and used over them. She saw and tried to stop some of the patterns of relationships that robbed Black people of their dignity and very lives, and white people of their sense of either justice or compassion. She knew the frustration of finding the space and direction to develop and express what she knew was in her, even as she did not know clearly what that was. She watched Gene carefully give form to a piece of wood, cherishing its texture and grain as if he were making love to it, but yet trying to make the center of his life an administrative and academic one.

What she saw and experienced made her angry; but it also gave her a sense, an intuition of both the vulnerability of and resources in the individual human being. People, individuals, were to be cherished and nurtured. They were not means to some further end – the triumph of Christianity or communism or the American way of life. The person, as a unity of body and spirit, was to be cared for in concrete, specific ways.

With these insights, Wilma was able to name her vocation – to make her life one of action "in the human interest," as she described it. She had a center, a center of value, around which to integrate, evaluate, and organize her life. A career was not of highest priority, and indeed a career stood judged by that principle. Responsibility for her family was not of the highest priority. Instead, it was included within and given direction by this center. Now it had become clear; such responsibility included intrinsically working to provide her daughters with a more humane society within which to live. A particular role, therefore, had to fit in with, be consistent with that principle; it was defined by the principle, not by custom or tradition or even personal preference.

Naming what is most important, what gives meaning and purpose to life not only clarified the complicated choices she had to make. It also helped her further identify who she was.

From the beginning, Wilma had a sense of who she was and trusted that sense, although it was largely unarticulated. She knew and had accepted that she was a woman, but she was unable to accept certain role expectations on her as a woman. If those roles were invalid for her, what then did it mean to be a woman? Similarly, as an adolescent, she had aspired to the ministry, only to find that she was rejected from that role and in turn she refused membership in that community. Yet many of the values that had been communicated to her through that institution remained. If not in the church, how could she minister? What did it mean to minister? Wilma knew also that she was creative and intelligent; she was a competent administrator, careful researcher, and inspiring teacher. She had worked in many different areas, from producing radio programs to investigative reporting to administering pre-school staff training, nursing education and administration. She had even worked with investments, and she could do all of these well. But either the opportunity to make of those activities something more enduring did not materialize, or they did not finally sustain her. What then, was she? What was *she* about?

She was a woman; she was a wife and mother; she was a professional sociologist, nurse, administrator, and change agent; she was white, she was angry and sometimes depressed and tired and frustrated. But beneath and embracing all of these identities, she was a moral self. It was finally her moral identity that gave meaning and direction and unity to all the other. To say *I am* was to say *I am responsible,* and if Wilma were somehow to deny being responsible and responsible being, she would cease to *be:* "You can never forget, no matter how comfortable you might be, no matter how much you might rationalize; it's as if it's seared on your consciousness." With her growing identity, Wilma's leadership abilities, her intellect, and her energy were being woven together into a strong and compelling personality.

"You know, I think she could pick up a piece of clay and talk it into doing something," her friend Marge Stratman observed of Wilma as she emerged from this period of her life. She was now ready to become a major spokesperson for the cause that was most clearly and profoundly named in her own journey – the cause of feminism.

NOTES

1. Wilma Scott Heide speech. Fargo, North Dakota, December, 1975.
2. Interview with Helen Cuyjet, November, 1977.
3. Interview with Marge Stratman, June, 1977.
4. Interview with Dan Fine, September, 1977.
5. Published in both papers, Spring, 1964.
6. Heide, Eugene and Wilma Scott: "A Working Vacation in Mississippi." *The Valley Daily News* and *Daily Dispatch.* June, 1965.
7. Interview with Evelyn Perloff, February, 1980.
8. Conversation with Wilma, January, 1977.
9. Interview with Gene Heide, Fall, 1977.
10. Personal letter to me from Faith Middleton, November 9, 1977.

5

PITTSBURGH NOW!

I don't enjoy criticism, for heaven's sake. But we simply can't afford to wait until everyone agrees, and the very fact of demonstrating communicates our values.

– Wilma Scott Heide

By November 1967, Wilma had organized and become president of a strong Pittsburgh area chapter of NOW, was the Pennsylvania coordinator and on NOW's national board. In February 1968, she became National Membership Coordinator, whose responsibilities included chapter development. In 1970, she was elected to chair the national board of NOW. She was also working full-time at the American Institutes for Research (AIR), participating in the New Kensington chapter of the NAACP, working on her doctorate, and with her husband, maintaining a home and rearing two children. In January 1969, she was appointed to the Pennsylvania Human Relations Commission, on which she served until 1971, when the family moved to Connecticut. All of these commitments were important to Wilma, but she increasingly focused her time and energy on NOW, a commitment that was to last for the next several years – through a two-term presidency, which ended in the spring of 1974. The time had come: NOW provided the institutional means through which her vocation could be directed on a national and international level. In turn, she gave NOW years of dedication and leadership. NOW and Wilma brought together the passion, creativity, and intellect, on the one hand, and the organization, support and power, on the other, to be a major voice in the second wave of feminism.

In this collaboration, Wilma and her many colleagues in and out of NOW developed a distinctive approach to social change. Some would call it a *feminist-humanist* approach; she prefers simply to call it *feminist*, since, for her, *humanist* is included in her understanding of feminism. Significant concepts of ethics emerged from Wilma's activity in NOW.

The early 60's were times of ferment, confusion, confrontation, and examination of personal and national conscience. The movement for racial justice (generally known as the Civil Rights Movement) was continually front page news. Tremendous energies, kindled by anger, frustrations, and idealism, soared into demonstrations, boycotts, marches, sit-ins, and freedom rides. In hot summer months, some of those energies erupted into riots. The government responded – with tanks and the National Guard but also with legislation. In legislation, attention was focused on efforts to overcome racial discrimination and poverty. In 1964 Congress passed a major Civil Rights bill, including Title VII, prohibiting discrimination in employment on the basis of race, religion, national origin and sex. The prohibition of sex discrimination was apparently added as a ploy to weaken the bill, introduced by Howard W. Smith from Virginia. [1]

> If it were rejected, the ancient tensions between blacks and women might be rekindled in time to split the bill's supporters. If it were accepted, it would saddle the bill's proponents in the Senate … with a totally unwanted burden … [1,p.415]

When it was debated in the Senate, the provision of sex was hardly mentioned, apparently because issues of race were uppermost in senators' minds. As the debate wore on, however, more and more women began to lobby. Betty Friedan was a major voice. The Women's International League for Peace and Freedom was another. The bill passed the Senate. At the signing ceremony, many civil rights leaders were present.

> But neither Griffiths[2] nor any other feminist leader was there. And the president, in his remarks, made no reference to the guarantees for women. [1,p.420]

National attention began to focus on poverty since racial minorities were disproportionately included among the poor. At the same time a few people were examining the roles of women in American society. In 1961, Eleanor Roosevelt helped persuade President Kennedy to establish a National Commission on the Status of Women. Esther Peterson, then Director of the Women's Bureau of the Labor Department, became its first staff person. The Commission was charged with the responsibility to study education, employment, insurance, and the law as they affected women. As the Commission studied, however, its members became increasingly and dismayingly aware of the pervasiveness of discrimination on the basis of sex as well as the general indifference of public officials toward seeking to remedy the situation by enforcing Title VII.

Meanwhile, in 1963, *The Feminine Mystique* by Betty Friedan was published, a book which put into words what many, many middle class women had been feeling – their entrapment and isolation as suburban homemakers, the superficiality of women's lives after an expensive and sophisticated education at eastern women's colleges, and the ethos of a country that encouraged isolation and boredom in the measuring out of lives in coffee spoons, tea cups, or glasses of gin and tonic.[3]

After the publication of that book, Friedan began research on a second one. While in Washington one evening in 1966, she had dinner with Catherine East and Mary Eastwood. East worked with the Women's Bureau, Eastwood as an attorney in the U.S. Department of Justice. They urged Friedan to start an organization for women, gave her a list of names of women attending a June conference on the status of women, and helped her gain entry to it as a writer covering the conference for her book.[4]

The conference was an annual one, convened by the National Commission on the Status of Women. Women from all over the country were there. On this occasion, however, it took an unprecedented turn. On the last night of the conference, Friedan invited several participants to her room to discuss organizing.[5] According to Friedan, there were about fifteen women, including Pauli Murray, a Black lawyer; Kathryn (Kay) Clarenbach, a white faculty member from the University of Wisconsin; and Dorothy Haener, a white woman with the United Auto Workers.[5,pp.81-2] One of the reasons for the meeting was the failure of Richard Graham's reappointment to the Equal Opportunities Employment Commission (EEOC). The EEOC had been established to help monitor compliance with antidiscriminatory legislation. Initially its real interest was with charges of racial discrimination, and its awareness of sex discrimination was low. According to Aileen Hernandez, who is Black and female and was the only woman on the five-member Commission, "a major meeting with employees in California was arranged in a private club which barred women – even though I was scheduled to accompany the Chairman [sic] to the meeting."[6]

Richard Graham, one of the male commissioners, was an exception. He was sensitive to sex discrimination and committed to eliminating it. But his term had ended, and he was not being reappointed. The women who met in Friedan's room were angry over this, but they did not agree to organizing.

The next morning, however, Kay Clarenbach tried to introduce a resolution calling for the reappointment of Richard Graham. She was reminded that the group had no such power; its charge was only to study. She was outraged, as were many others. So a second meeting of the women who had met the evening before was held over lunch. Another woman, a furniture merchant and chair of a Wisconsin municipal Commission on the Status of Women, Gene Boyer, was sitting at a table next to the one where Betty Friedan, Kay Clarenbach and some others were seated. Boyer saw them writing and talking and was filled with a sense of both frustration and excitement. She knew something was happening but was not sure what. After lunch, Clarenbach invited Boyer to come again to Friedan's room, and twenty-eight women each contributed five dollars to form The National Organization for Women.[7] In reflecting on that day, Gene Boyer said, "I knew we were involved in something very exciting, something that would have a tremendous impact on the country!"[8]

The group chose a coordinator, Kathryn Clarenbach, and a steering committee to implement the program sketched by the founders: recruit new members and plan the first annual conference.[9] On October 29-30, 1966, the conference was held in Washington and a statement of purpose adopted. It included:

> We, men and women who hereby constitute ourselves as the National Organization for Women, believe that the time has come for a new movement toward true equality for all women in America, and toward a fully equal partnership of the sexes ...
>
> The purpose of NOW is to take action to bring women into full participation in the mainstream of American society now, exercising all the privileges and responsibilities thereof and in truly equal participation with men ...
>
> NOW is dedicated to the proposition that women, first and foremost, are human beings ...
>
> We ...[are] convinced that human rights for all are indivisible [and] we expect to give active support to the common cause of equal rights for all those who suffer discrimination and deprivation ...[5,p.5]

Betty Friedan became the first president; Kathryn Clarenbach chair (then a chairman) of the Board; Richard Graham, the former EEOC Commissioner, vice-president; Caroline Davis of the United Auto Workers secretary-treasurer; and twenty women and men were elected to the first board.

NOW did not grow out of liberation movements in this country and around the world. Its immediate roots were anger, awareness of discrimination, and the assumption that something should and could be done. Its theoretical heritage was not Marxist so much as libertarian – the eighteenth century and American revolution rather than the twentieth century, Chinese and third-world. Its goal was completing unfinished work initiated by the Declaration of Independence and continued by waves of movements in this country for legal, economic and political change. Its language spoke of discrimination rather than oppression, of the indivisibility of human rights rather than liberation from oppression, and bringing women into the mainstream of American culture rather than the creation of a new state or culture.

Soon, of course, it was to encounter and enlist other women and men also seeking change but inspired by and using the tools of Marxist and anti-colonialist philosophies. The tensions in the two traditions created both confusion and creativity. A part of Wilma's task, one that emerged more clearly in the next decade, was to articulate a new starting point for examining both traditions – that of feminism.

NOW grew phenomenally. Between June 30th and October 30th, 1966, more than 300 people joined. Within another year, membership had risen to over 1200. [9,p.6-7] It grew so rapidly because it provided a means of action for many American women and some men who already had experienced the frustrations of sex-role stereotyping. Many had read *The Feminine Mystique*, and agreed, "Yes, that's the story of my life." A fairly typical response is found in the frank statement of Jacqui Ceballos, a New York member:

> After reading Friedan's book, I read that NOW had been formed, and I managed to get back here [from Colombia, South America] with the main purpose of working for NOW and feminism until the end of my life![10]

The work of NOW was structured around task forces and committees. Initially the task forces included equal opportunity in employment, legal and political rights, women in poverty, education, image of women, the family, women and religion. The committees were finance, membership, legal, public relations, and constitutional protection of equality for women.

NOW was first and foremost an action organization. Among its first actions was putting pressure on the EEOC to reappoint Richard Graham, to enforce legislation prohibiting sex discrimination, and to rescind discriminatory guidelines on "help wanted" advertising. Indeed, on one occasion, the first Board decided it wished to meet with the EEOC, and within twelve hours the members had shifted their schedules around and were present at the agency's office.[11] Similarly, it put pressure on the U.S. president to amend Executive Order 11246 to include sex in the list of discriminations banned by institutions having government contracts.[9,p.6-7] As the years progressed, NOW added action to end discrimination against women airline attendants, it supported equality for women in opportunities for jury service, and it became a participant in four legal cases: Row vs Colgate-Palmolive Company, Weeks vs Southern Bell Telephone and Telegraph, Daniel vs Pennsylvania, and Menglekoch vs Southern District of California. Row vs Colgate-Palmolive Company involved job assignments and seniority lines that discriminated against women. Weeks vs Southern Bell Telephone and Telegraph involved weight-lifting restrictions on women. Daniel vs Pennsylvania involved a state law giving women a longer sentence than men for the same robbery offense. Menglekoch vs Southern District of California involved issues of state protective legislation, which resulted in loss of wages and promotional opportunities.[12]

The actions almost immediately began to bear fruit. Judith Hole and Ellen Levine, for instance, write:

> The impact of NOW during those initial months was enormous, largely because nothing like it had ever happened before. "NOW scared the wits out of the government," according to one founding member.[13,p.97]

The effectiveness of NOW's actions was immeasurably enhanced by the fact that many women working in significant areas for the government knew and were often friends with NOW members. At that time, they themselves did not think they could become members, but they were sympathetic to what NOW was doing, and they were able to alert the organization to upcoming legislation and provide it with information about research and contacts. Women in the Women's Bureau of the Labor Department were particularly helpful in this way, although employees of countless other arms of the government also provided assistance as they could.

At the second national convention, held in Washington on November 18-19, 1967, NOW pledged to support and work for the passage of the Equal Rights Amendment. It also took a stand in support of repealing existing abortion legislation, the first national organization to do so. Both of these stands were controversial, much more so than the actions taken earlier. Dorothy Haener, for instance, one of the founders and a strong union member, opposed the ERA because the United Auto Workers (UAW) did not support it yet, and UAW was then providing office support for NOW. Other members resigned as a result of the stands on the ERA and abortion, some for reasons of principle, others for considerations of implementation and political sensitivity.

Wilma found out about NOW from her husband in 1967. He showed her a newspaper article about the organization, commenting, "Here is something that may interest you." Wilma immediately called Betty Friedan and Kay Clarenbach and made two decisions – to attend the next Board meeting in September, 1967, in Madison, Wisconsin, and to start a Pittsburgh chapter. She called Kay Clarenbach again, who paused when Wilma invited herself to the meeting, but then agreed that she could come. She arrived without her luggage, mislaid by the airline, and tried to be inconspicuous. Her memory of her first impressions of the group was that: "God, that is a group of smart women. Why haven't we met before? I've got to get them organized."

At the meeting, the Board appointed Wilma the Pennsylvania convener, and in two months, she was elected to the Board. Twelve names were required to receive a charter for a chapter. Wilma found them, and the NOW Chapter of the Greater Pittsburgh Area was officially established in November 1967. According to Dan Fine, Wilma called him and Anita Fine about 3:00 a.m. When he sleepily answered the phone, she announced:

> This is Wilma. There's a new women's organization, and it needs members. I want you and Anita to join. This is the most important movement of the century; I've been waiting for it all my life.

Dan replied: "If you'll let me go back to sleep, I'll do anything!"[14] Wilma denies that she called him at three in the morning or that she called NOW a women's organization instead of a feminist organization.

In addition to Wilma, the members of the Pittsburgh chapter were:

Charlotte Coe – nurse educator who had preceeded Wilma as project director at the American Institutes for Research (AIR). One day they had lunch together and waited a long time to be served. Charlotte Coe observed that if Wilma thought they would be served before all the men were, she could forget it. Wilma responded, "Charlotte, yes we will." Wilma demanded and received service, and Coe became the second member of Pittsburgh NOW.

Cindy Judd Hill – teacher near Pittsburgh, who was bringing a suit against the school for refusing her a sabbatical leave while she was pregnant.

Ruth Heimbuecher – reporter for *The Pittsburgh Press.*

Anita and Dan Fine – social worker and physician.

Anne and Bob Mast – sociologists.

Daryl and Sandy Bem – psychologists and co-authors of one of the early classics of the Movement, "Training the Woman to Know Her Place."

Ann Heuer – homemaker.

Virginia Harrington – one of the few lawyers accepting sex discrimination cases at the time.

Wilma was elected president, Anne Mast Vice-president, Virginia Harrington treasurer, and Ann Heuer secretary. The chapter in many ways mirrored the national organization. Its membership grew rapidly. In an undated letter to Kay Clarenbach (probably early 1967) Wilma wrote that there were now forty members and eighty more people on a mailing list.[15]

Pittsburgh NOW was also structured around task forces: employment, legal and political rights, image of women in the media, family, and education. The chapter established a speaker's bureau. As on the national level, the focus was action. Some of the most significant actions were:

- adding sex discrimination to the prohibitions in the Pittsburgh City Ordinance;
- ending sex-segregated want ads:
- boycotting of Colgate-Palmolive Corporation and products:
- advocating for the ERA.

The successful action to add sex discrimination to the prohibitions in the Pittsburgh City Ordinance was due primarily to Wilma's efforts. On October 23, 1968, she spoke to the City Commission on Human Relations. In a moving presentation, she urged the Commission to amend Pittsburgh Ordinance #75 to prohibit sex discrimination in the same way it prohibited racial and other forms of discrimination. After a description of NOW in terms of the people who made it up nationally and locally, Wilma cited examples of the effects of discrimination on women and men. Then she appealed to the Commission, not to its self-interest, but to human well-being. She concluded with the by-now famous challenge:

> Men have always been taught to be brave, and women have always been taught to care. Now, men must be brave enough to care

about the total quality, the interpersonal quality of our lives without fear of being called soft or effeminate. Women need to care enough to bravely assert our concerns about the quality of our common lives without fear of being called too aggressive.[15]

The Commission agreed unanimously with Wilma and NOW. It recommended adding sex discrimination to the other prohibitions listed in the Ordinance, and the amendment became state law on July 3, 1969.

This enactment made easier the task of desegregating the want-ads. On the national level, NOW had been challenging practices by newspapers of listing jobs by sex, for instance, in the "Help Wanted – Male" and "Help Wanted – Female" columns.

According to Aileen Hernandez, in 1965, lawyer Pauli Murray "blasted the EEOC and the New York State Commission on Human Rights for permitting segregated employment advertising for male and female help." [6,p.12] New York and Los Angeles chapters had challenged the *Times* of those cities, and the Pittsburgh chapter decided that the *Pittsburgh Press* and *Post Gazette* should be similarly challenged. At a Pittsburgh NOW meeting, one of the members, Gerald Gardner, voiced some skepticism about the significance of such action. There seemed, he thought, more important things to do. Wilma suggested he read them from the standpoint of a woman in a non-traditional field looking for employment. The following Sunday morning, breakfasting in bed and lounging with the Sunday paper, Gardner did that. Since he was a mathematician, he examined them as a woman mathematician might. He was appalled. All the relevant jobs were listed under "Male – Help Wanted."[16,p.8]

Gardner became one of the more active members in NOW's campaign to eliminate segregated listings.[17] He and other participants wrote letters, met with publishers, and finally picketed. Letters and meetings elicited no positive response. The *Press* offered the picketers coffee and doughnuts, a move which struck the NOW people as a further sign that the issue was not being taken seriously.[18] Although it was bitterly cold, they refused the refreshments and strengthened their efforts. The *Press* refused to change its policy, claiming that it was a service to advertisers and readers.

NOW filed a formal complaint with the City Commission on Human Relations, claiming that the paper's policy violated the city ordinance which prohibited discrimination on the basis of sex. The *Press* responded by agreeing to eliminate words like 'salesman' or 'lineman' and change the headings to "Jobs – Male Interest" and "Jobs – Female Interest" and added a note:

Notice to Job Seekers

Jobs are arranged under Male and Female classifications for the convenience of our readers. This is done because most jobs generally appeal more to persons of one sex than the other. Various laws and ordinances – local, state, and federal – prohibit discrimination in employment because of sex unless sex is a bona fide occupational requirement. Unless the advertisement itself specifies one sex or the other, job seekers should assume that the advertiser will consider applicants of either sex in compliance with the laws against discrimination.[16,p.8]

After several months of hearings and various delays, the Commission ordered the *Press* to eliminate classification by sex within a month (by August 23, 1970). The *Press* appealed, and the case was heard by the Court of Common Pleas of Allegheny County. The reasoning given by the paper's attorney was interesting. It included the same kind of arguments used since against the ERA – fear of desegregated bathrooms, private schools, housing, prisons, and clothing. The underlying point was that the analogy between race and sex was often an invalid one, that women and men were different:

and these differences, physical, cultural and psychological, manifest themselves in job preferences and in statistical differences in job occupancy ... Women comprise not 10% of the population as Negroes do but fully one-half. Are we to expect one-half of the truck drivers, laborers, policemen, firemen, ironworkers, plumbers, engineers, lawyers and seamen to be women? Of course not. Common sense screams – no ... [16,p.11,13]

And in a perceptive insight, the testimony of the paper's lawyer added:

The National Organization for Women, through its testimony, particularly the testimony of Dr. Sandra Bem, Mrs. Heide, and Mrs. East, has shown that its primary desire is not to eliminate discrimination against women but to change cultural patterns of our country concerning women.[16,p.11,13]

The *Press* lost again, and again appealed. This time it was heard by the U.S. Supreme Court. The *Press* actually based its case on First Amendment rights more than Civil Rights legislation. In opposition was the Pittsburgh Commission on Human Relations, to which NOW had turned for further resources. ACLU lawyer Marjory Matson argued the case for the Commission. Again the *Press* lost, this time finally. The want ads were duly integrated.

In another instance, desegregation occurred smoothly. Wilma simply went to Gene Simon, publisher of the papers she was writing for. She asked him to examine the want-ads as a woman with non-traditional competencies. He did so and acknowledged the legitimacy of NOW's position. The want ad columns of Simon's papers were desegregated.

A third action was Pittsburgh NOW's participation with other chapters in pressing Colgate-Palmolive to change sex-discriminatory policies, including a weight-restriction one, which in effect barred women from certain promotions. A woman employee had been denied promotion because the job required her to lift packages of over 30 pounds and would violate the company's "protective policies" for women. The courts had ordered the company to change, but it seemed reluctant to move. The NOW Board picked a day for chapters around the country to pressure publicly the soap company to obey the law and court order. On the selected day, Wilma walked with others around the block, carrying signs explaining this action. Wilma's read "Colgate-Palmolive is a sex offender." A white man in his late 30's came up to her with a grin and asked "what have they thought of that I haven't?" Wilma was not fazed. She proceeded to tell him and also asked him to hold her sign while she handed out leaflets. He did and began listening to her. They walked along, taking turns holding the sign and handing out information sheets. This continued for about fifteen minutes. Suddenly the man slapped his forehead and exclaimed, "Oh my God, I'm involved! And in only fifteen minutes!"

A fourth action was Pittsburgh NOW's work for the ERA. Wilma returned from the national conference in November to inform the chapter of NOW's support of the ERA and also the plan to hold the January national board meeting in Pittsburgh. At that time plans were to be made for action around the country to get the Amendment out of the Senate sub-committee, where it had been, in one form or another, since 1923.[19]

For two years NOW worked on getting the ERA out of a sub-committee on Constitutional Amendments. Pittsburgh NOW took an active role, and one member in particular became so active that her life was transformed. Her name is Jean Witter, and her story is typical of how intensely people became involved in NOW's activities during this period. Although a college graduate with a degree in chemistry and aspirations of being a crystalographer, Jean was at that time a homemaker and a librarian. She knew little about legislation, but she began to read the *New York Times* for information about bills of interest to women and particularly to see which ones Martha Griffiths was supporting. Within a couple of months, she was chairing the legislation task force.

By 1970, according to NOW's analysis, over 80 senators supported the ERA; but the Amendment was still in committee. Jean proposed and was made coordinator of a large demonstration in Washington to dramatize the issue of constitutional equality for women. Jean went to Washington to organize the demonstration, press conferences, and meet with Senators and Congress people. While there, she found that the Senate sub-committee on constitutional amendments responsible for the ERA was holding hearings on the eighteen-year-old vote and called Wilma to that effect.

On February 17, 1970, the day of the demonstration, Wilma and about twenty other members of Pittsburgh NOW went to Washington. Before she left, Wilma told her family that she did not know when she would return. She felt that 47 years was long enough to wait and she intended to stay there until action occurred on the ERA.

After duly participating in the demonstrations, meetings, and press conferences, Wilma proposed that Pittsburgh NOW go to where the subcommittee was in session. Wilma said to the others:

> You don't owe me a thing. I realize this is new to most of you, but I
> am going over there and interrupt that hearing, and it's an
> arrestable offense. If I must, I'll do it alone, but I'd love to have
> somebody else with me.

Jean; her young son Ray; Barbara Evans Crawford, a nurse; and Jo Ann
Evans Gardner, a psychologist, immediately volunteered. Since signs or
placards at the hearings were prohibited, they each took a manila folder and on
the inside wrote their ERA messages. They tucked the folders under their
arms along with other papers and purses.

As they entered, Ramsey Clark, former Attorney General, was testifying.
When he finished, Wilma, Jean, Ray and Barbara stood up. The rest of the
group, sitting on the rows behind them, immediately stood up also. Together
they opened up the manila folders and held them up above their heads.

The media were there, covering the hearings, and quickly the TV cameras
swung to the women. Wilma spoke. She identified them only as Pennsylvania
NOW members without giving individual names. Security guards started to
move forward, but retreated on a signal from one of the senators, and Wilma
knew then they would not be arrested and would be heard. Wilma recalls:

> We all stood up; we were all scared to death. Security guards
> started to move forward, but at a signal from one of the senators,
> did not do anything. At that moment I knew we could do almost
> anything and get away with it. Our case was so strong they didn't
> want to make martyrs out of us. I didn't either.

Wilma said to the committee that the ERA had been bottled up in subcommittee too long, that this was a new breed of women who were changing
their behavior to assure that Congress took them seriously. It did not matter
how much the senators sponsored and supported the Amendment; if the
Senators did not act effectively after forty-seven years and with 80 Senators
claiming to support the ERA, then obviously women would have to be more
insistent and not be turned aside.

Birch Bayh and others protested that they were friends of the ERA and that
they should not be alienated, and Bayh said, "Well, ladies, now that you've got
yourselves on TV are you satisfied?"

Wilma recalls her response:

> That is an insensitive remark, no friend would make it, and
> nobody who really understands would make it. We're not seeking
> publicity, we didn't give our names. The issue is change, not
> personal publicity.

The group was then informed that they were delaying the hearings and that
one who was to testify would be an hour late and miss a plane.

Barbara Evans Crawford, Jean Witter, and Wilma, identifying themselves only as NOW members, interrupt Senate hearings to urge action on the ERA, February 17, 1970.

Wilma again spoke:

> I find it difficult to be sympathetic about an hour's delay on this issue of the 18-year-old vote – which has gotten very quick action – when I'm talking about several centuries' delay and it needs to be seen in that context. My sympathies lie with the majority of the population on this fundamental issue of being included in the Constitution, the basic legal document of this alleged democracy. That's the issue. We've not only waited long enough, we've waited too long, and we're not going to wait any longer. What are you planning to do, Senator? What are your plans? You're the chair of this sub-committee, and I'd like to know.

Bayh said that he would meet with them later. But Wilma was not to be stopped. "We're here now." But Bayh would not be more specific. Finally, Wilma said, "This man will not give us the time of day – when he'll meet. We are going now, but we will be back."

Leaving one NOW member there, the rest visited some other legislators, then returned. After the hearing finished for the day, Bayh did meet with them and said that he planned to announce hearings on the ERA. Wilma concluded that his decision was reached after the interruption since there would have been little reason not to announce it in response to her question. Wilma continued to press: "When will you announce it?"

Bayh responded only that it would be announced at a Business and Professional Women's convention later in the spring, and it was.

The act was effective. According to Hole and Levine, Bayh acknowledged that the ERA hearings were a result of the February interruptions. [13,pp.55-6] Senator Marlow Cook also acknowledged to Wilma that their action had made the difference.[20]

After two further years, the proposed Amendment finally passed Congress on March 22, 1972. NOW then started to work in state coalitions for ratification. Jean Witter continued to play a significant role in that activity. As soon as the Amendment was sent to the states, she attended law school and received her degree. Then she applied her legal skills to the long and still unfinished efforts for ratification. Traveling to unratified states, she worked there for a week or so at a time with pro-ERA groups. She also prepared the basic research and legal rationale for NOW in support of extending the time of ratification. And when the Illinois Legislature passed a law requiring a three-fifths majority rather than the traditional two-thirds majority for passing the ERA, she wrote an article challenging it. In light of Jean's continuing work for the ERA, Nancy Bowdler, another Pittsburgh member, referred to the Amendment as "Jean's Amendment."[21]

As Wilma and the NOW chapter were involved in direct action and confrontation, they were also involved in an on-going process of consciousness raising and education. Through speeches, conferences, and hearings, they challenged and clarified and explored implications of feminism. There was hardly a night Wilma did not speak somewhere.[22] She addressed community, professional, and government groups, including churches, schools and colleges, a United Nations association, civil rights groups, business and professional women, service clubs, the Industrial Health Foundation, PTA's, a U.S. Mines conference, and a conference of priests. She spoke in the neighboring states of Ohio and West Virginia as well as in Pennsylvania. Usually she was invited because of her work with NOW, but also because of her work at AIR, her appointment to the Pennsylvania Human Relations Commission, her position on the State Board of the ACLU, and her involvement in and writing about economic and racial justice.

The consciousness-raising often began with rewording the topic she had been asked to address. In 1969, for instance, she addressed the American Psychological Association. The theme given her had the improbable but thoroughly academic title of "What can the behavioral sciences do to modify the world so that women who want to participate meaningfully are not regarded as and are not, in fact, deviant?" She turned the question around and challenged her hearers to change their *psychology* – the sexist values implicit in the discipline – rather than try to apply it to the situation of women.

Similarly, when she was asked to address the Pittsburgh Personnel Association on "Creative Use of Woman Power as a Means to Improve Profit," she suggested that the best way to use "woman power" was to erase sex-role stereotyping and discrimination against women in the work force by educating employers, remembering that "brain has no sex," providing child care, ending sex-segregated want-ads, employing and promoting women on the basis of ability, and adapting jobs to women's commitments rather than the reverse. She urged values other than economic profits.

A continuing characteristic theme in her speeches was the necessity of feminism. She stressed the necessity that lay particularly in its values – its emphasis on nurture and care and humaneness – to the well being of personal and global health.

In May, 1969, Pittsburgh NOW, United Mental Health of Pittsburgh, the Pittsburgh Psychological Association, and Chatham College sponsored a conference on the double standard in mental health. The conference was generated by a study done by Inge and Don Broverman and colleagues that found that the criteria which mental health workers used to determine adult mental health were applied only to men. For women, they had a second set of criteria, which made "mentally healthy" women unhealthy adults.[23] The study was not published until after the conference, but pre-publication copies were available, and NOW found the results so significant that they persuaded the other institutions to collaborate on a conference exploring implications and alternatives. Presentations were made by Donald Broverman and Paul Rosencranz on the study itself, by Catherine East on employment consequences, by psychiatrist Natalie Shairness on images of women through time, and by Wilma on the "Reality and Challenge of the Double Standard in Mental Health Practice." In her address, she compared the situation of women with that of racial minorities in terms of their roles and expectations as subordinates in a society, in a way that anticipated Jean Baker Miller's analysis in a later book.[24] Wilma also pointed out ways in which parallels between racism and sexism did not apply. She then suggested that violence, alcoholism, and mental ill-health all were rooted in part in sexism, because of the ways women and men were denied the expression of their whole humanity. She closed with a paragraph that had already become a hallmark of hers and has been quoted from her talk to the Pittsburgh City Council – that men need to be brave enough to care about the quality of our lives and women to care enough to assert ourselves.

With all her other responsibilities in addition to those related to NOW, Wilma nevertheless also found time and energy to fulfill her national Board responsibilities. She became chair of the membership committee and made a particularly concerted effort to remain in contact with chapters through letters, telephoning, and visits.

The visits were usually combined with speaking engagements in nearby areas of family trips. In the summer of 1968, for instance, the Heides planned an automobile trip to California, visiting members and chapters going and returning. It was a multi-purpose trip. It enabled Wilma to visit NOW chapters. It enabled Gene to do original research for his doctoral dissertation.

It was to be a family vacation that included visits with friends and relatives around the country. The trip, however, was ended about half-way through when their car was hit by another and demolished. Gene spent time in the hospital, but Wilma and the girls were not seriously injured. In spite of such events, Board minutes of that time reveal that Wilma was as much in touch with chapters as anyone else on the board, if not more so.[15]

Wilma, Pittsburgh NOW, and National NOW were action-oriented. But it was not to action of a well-seasoned guerrilla cadre. It was action by people not particularly used to that kind of action; it was action by professional and lay people who had careers and reputations to lose, spouses and lovers to live with and sometimes to lose; it was action by people who often had few financial resources to work with; it was action, in short, that challenged the very identities of the actors.

As their action challenged their identities, it changed them and in some instances transformed them, a process in which Wilma often played a critical role. There was more than enough to do for anyone who was willing to work and Wilma encouraged women to pursue their interests and to take more and more responsibility. Jean Witter, who became active with the ERA, was one who was radically changed. Jo Ann Evans Gardner was another. A psychologist, she became an activist and a political figure in the Pittsburgh area. Later, she became a founder of KNOW, Inc. Ellie Smeal was still another. A rather quiet homemaker and political science doctoral student in Pittsburgh, she later became the fifth national president of NOW. In addition to these are many women and men who spoke out, stood up, and picketed for the first time in their lives, who in Wilma's words, "demonstrated their values," and their lives were never to be the same.

There were many people outside the Pittsburgh area who were in contact with Wilma, who had significant positions in government and industry. Of particular importance at this period were three women in government – Mary Eastwood, Catherine East and Elizabeth Duncan Koontz. Mary Eastwood worked in the Justice Department, Catherine East worked in the Women's Bureau of the Labor Department, and Elizabeth Duncan Koontz was Director of the Women's Bureau. All exchanged valuable information with NOW and other activists and anticipated moves on the part of the government. Catherine East, whom Friedan calls "the pivot of the feminist underground in Washington," had come to Washington from West Virginia to work for the government in 1939, where she continued for twenty-three years. [5,p.77] She held various positions, and after 1963 worked full time on issues involving the status of women. She, as so many others, was shocked at the discrimination she found in Washington and even more so at the facts and figures being compiled about discrimination against women on a nation-wide basis. Convinced something should be done and feeling unable to do it herself, she sought to persuade Betty Friedan to begin an organization. Even after NOW was formed, she did not think that she could join; it would jeopardize her opportunities to pass along information to the organization, she felt. She did contribute financially to the Women's Party. In the early 70's she joined NOW and also became the first vice president of the National Women's Party. Later she served on the Staff of the 1975 Commission for International Women's Year.

Similarly, Mary Eastwood was involved in issues concerning the political and legal status of women. She collaborated with Pauli Murray on another classic of the Movement – a legal analysis entitled "Jane Doe and the Law." An attorney, she was also an early member of NOW. She did much legal work for the organization, including the Colgate-Palmolive case.

Elizabeth (Libby) Duncan Koontz was another significant "behind the scenes" contact and friend from the Labor Department. In 1969, she succeeded Mary Keyserling as Director of the Women's Bureau. Keyserling had been opposed to the ERA, and Wilma and NOW were uncertain about where Koontz stood. So Wilma, Betty Friedan, and Marguerite Rawalt, another lawyer who did much legal work for NOW, came into Koontz's office to find out. Koontz recalls:

> ...They came to find out what this new director was like, where she was coming from, and most of all, where she stood. I admired the women greatly, and as they began their questioning, I stopped one of them ...and said, "Look, you don't have to persuade me. I'm already committed to the same things you are. I expect through my leadership at the Bureau not only to support but to work hand in hand with your efforts to improve things for women." They went away fairly well satisfied, but I am sure if I had been in their place, I would have followed up to see whether this woman was just giving me some more verbiage or whether she actually meant what she said.[25]

Koontz came to the position with the conviction that this was one part of the government that could be an advocate for women. A Black woman herself, she brought together minority and white women, poor and affluent women. Under her leadership, the Women's Bureau revised its former position and openly supported the ERA.

Prior to establishing the Pittsburgh Chapter of NOW, Wilma had acted primarily on an individual basis or as a member of an organization, often in secondary roles in male-dominated organizations. Now, she had become a leader – a strong and effective one. Through NOW, she generated an incredible amount of activity that took many forms, but was focused on a single end – freedom from pre-determined expectations about what it means to be a woman or a man, freedom to develop one's own gifts and resources.

Wilma's leadership was grounded in understanding the complexities of patriarchy and in her own maturity. Libby Koontz said of her at this period:

It took a couple of meetings to realize this was a woman who had looked much, much deeper into underlying causes, such as philosophies, canons, tenets – all kinds of underlying basic beliefs that women are indeed inferior, which were causing the problems women were facing in this century ... She is a courageous person, nervy, self-confident, intelligent, worldly – she knows the real world, and I don't know that she will ever change.[25]

This kind of groundedness helped generate trust among chapter members. They knew Wilma had thought about, analyzed, and experienced what she discussed with them. So they were willing to risk, to transcend whatever inexperience or timidity that might otherwise have stood in their way.

With the self-confidence came authority – not authoritarianism, but authority; not simply facilitation, much less leaderlessness – but authority. Wilma led, indeed pushed, almost any group beyond where it usually wanted to go. Her presence could be very uncomfortable and disconcerting and embarrassing at times. The exasperation voiced by one colleague was echoed many times. When Wilma refused to accept *no* for an answer and continued to insist on a particular course of action, her colleague said: "Wilma, sometimes I think you think you are God." Wilma's characteristic reply was, "No, but I think I'm right." And she persisted until the others agreed with her or until she had gone as far as she knew how to go.

The authority is based in part on her having "done her homework." She was well informed both from study and experience. But the authority was based in part also on her charisma. She not only generated trust; she inspired. It was not accidental that twenty women accompanied her to the Senate chamber and stood with her, or that the Pittsburgh City Council voted unanimously to add the category of sex to the list of prohibited discriminations in the city ordinance.

Wilma's authority was clearly without interest in personal aggrandizement. She was generous – non-competitive and sharing. Jacqui Ceballos wrote of both Wilma and Aileen Hernandez, the second president of NOW, that while many "clung to non-feminist ways ... it was a marvel to witness two brilliant women create space for everyone to contribute."[10]

The result of those qualities in contact with others was synergistic – the energy and power of the whole was more than the sum of the parts.[26] Like an electrical circuit, energy and power flowed, ideas were sparked, and everyone felt more oneself and more competent than before. Theodora Wells described it as the sense of "being turned on, being tuned in, in focus," and she added, "And that's the kind of power I think it takes to bring about change."[26] For the next several years, at least, that current was not to be turned off.

NOTES

1. Robinson, Donald Allen: "Two Movements in Pursuit of Equal Employment Opportunity." *Signs*, Spring, 1979, 4:3, pp. 413-455.
2. Martha Griffiths was a Congresswoman from Michigan who was active in women's rights legislation. For documentation of Griffiths role in bringing the ERA out of the House Judiciary Committee, see Hole and Levine (note #13), p.56.
3. Friedan, Betty: *The Feminine Mystique*. W.W. Norton, New York, 1963.
4. Telephone conversation with Catherine East, January, 1978.
5. Friedan, Betty: *It Changed My Life: Writings on the Women's Movement*. Random House, New York, 1976.
6. Hernandez, Aileen: "The Women's Movement: 1965-1975." Symposium on the Tenth Anniversary of the United States Equal Employment Opportunities Commission, Rutgers University, Law School (unpublished).
7. They were Ada Allness, Mary Benbow, Gene Boyer, Analoyce Clapp, Kathryn Clarenbach, Catherine Conroy, Caroline Davis, Mary Eastwood, Edith Finlayson, Betty Friedan, Dorothy Haener, Anna R. Halsted, Lorene Harrington, Mary Lou Hill, Esther Johnson, Nancy Knaak, Min L. Matheson, Helen Moreland, Pauli Murray, Ruth Murray, Inka O'Hanrahan, Pauline Parish, Eve P. Purvis, Edna Schwartz, Mary Jane Snyder, Gretchen Squires, Betty Talkington, Caroline Ware. (From *NOW: The First Five Years, 1966-1971*, prepared by Aileen C. Hernandez and Letitia P. Sommers, p. 2)
8. Telephone conversation with Gene Boyer, November, 1979.
9. *NOW: The First Five Years, 1966-1971*. Prepared by Aileen C. Hernandez and Letitia P. Sommers.
10. Letter from Jacqui Ceballos, June 28, 1977.
11. Telephone interview with Kathryn Clarenbach, April, 1980.
12. Among the early lawyers who worked with NOW in such actions were Marguerite Rawalt, Carruthers Burger, Mary Eastwood, Phineas Indretz, and Sylvia Roberts.
13. Hole, Judith and Ellen Levine: *The Rebirth of Feminism*. Quandrangle Books, New York, 1971.
14. Interview with Dan Fine, October, 1977.
15. NOW files, Schlesinger Library, Cambridge, Massachusetts.
16. Gardner, Gerald: NOW vs. *The Pittsburgh Press*. KNOW, Inc., Pittsburgh, 1971.
17. NOW was not alone in the endeavor in Pittsburgh or the nation. The American Civil Liberties Union, Women's Equity Action League, National Association of Women Lawyers, and other organizations participated at NOW's invitation and urging.
18. Letter of September 28, 1977, from Ruth Heimbuecher, feature writer for the *Press*.
19. On August 26, 1920, the Nineteenth Amendment was included in the Constitution and gave women the right to vote. In 1921 Alice Paul reorganized the National Women's Party and focused its attention on a sweeping end to discriminatory legislation rather than a step-by-step approach. Paul wrote and introduced a federal Equal Rights Amendment into Congress in December 1923. It was reintroduced every new session until 1970. Each time it was sent to committee and in effect died there. NOW decided it was past time to get it out, so Congress could vote and send it to the states for ratification.

20. Reported to me by Wilma in conversation, January, 1977.

21. Hundreds, even thousands of people from NOW and elsewhere lobbied Congress during those two years. Congress received more mail on the ERA than on any other proposed legislation.

22. A partial list of Wilma's publications and published speeches can be found in Appendix B.

23. Broverman, Inge, and others: "Sex Role Stereotypes and Clinical Judgments of Mental Health." *Journal of Consulting and Clinical Psychology*, February, 1970.

24. Miller, Jean Baker: *Toward a New Psychology of Women.* Beacon Press, Boston, 1976.

25. Interview with Elizabeth Duncan Koontz, Winter, 1977-78.

26. Tape from Theodora Wells, Spring, 1977. Ms. Wells is a communications management consultant and an author.

6

REVOLUTION:
TOMMOROW IS NOW!

What we are about is a profound universal behavioral Revolution: Tomorrow is NOW! Men are demonstrably unable, without the full partnership of women at every level of public life, to fully conceptualize, let alone solve our deepest problems that have their roots in sexism, racism, poverty and organized violence. Indeed, the very absence of women may *be the problem* itself. Even more than the brotherhood of all men we need the sisterhood of all women and together create the integrated humane family. •

– Wilma Scott Heide[1]

Aileen Hernandez succeeded Betty Friedan as president of NOW. Aileen had been an early Equal Employment Opportunities Commission (EEOC) commissioner and an advocate of women's and minorities' rights and had on occasion put her job on the line in an effort to gain a hearing for women from a reluctant EEOC. At the first national conference of NOW in 1966, she was elected executive vice president in the west. In 1970, she became president.

During Aileen's presidency, Wilma chaired the NOW Board. At the national conference in 1971, Wilma became president, a position she held until the 1974 conference in Houston.

During those years, NOW moved from a nascent movement into a major force for social change. In 1970, membership in the organization was 3,000 and the budget $28,000. In 1974, the membership was over 50,000 and the budget was over $750,000. NOW had become the world's largest feminist organization. Hundreds of thousands of individual lives were touched and changed directly and millions indirectly, painfully even traumatically, but also exhilaratingly. Laws were changed and procedures of enforcement established. Major economic, political, social, religious, health and communications institutions were confronted, and however reluctantly, to one degree or another, they too were changed. At the same time, the ethos that had sanctioned and reinforced "manly" and "masculine" values as the central ethos of society was being re-evaluated, found wanting, and challenged. The ethos began changing, slowly, often reluctantly, but perhaps most enduringly.

Organization of NOW

NOW's policy is determined by the membership at national conferences, usually held every twelve to eighteen months. Workshops on many topics and issues are conducted; participants formulate resolutions for action by the conference body. The resolutions that pass then become the basis for planning and actions during the ensuing months. In addition, officers are elected and other business conducted.

During Wilma's presidency, the national Board convened four times a year to interpret and implement policy and address intervening issues. The Executive Committee of the Board met before each Board meeting and sometimes again afterward. The responsibility of committee and task forces was to carry out policies. The task forces and their respective coordinators included:

Coordinator for Task Forces: Mary Jean Collins-Robson
Women and the Arts: Suzanne Benton
Child Care: Tery Zimmerman
Compliance: Lynne Darcy
Higher Education: Ellen Morgan
Credit: Sharyn Campbell
Education: Ann Grant
Broadcasting and FCC: Whitney Adams
Fund-Raising: Gene Boyer
Women and Health: Joan Goldstein
Legislation: Ann Scott
State Legislation: Mary Samis
Labor Unions: Marjorie Stern
Marriage, Divorce, Family Relations: Elizabeth Core Spaulding
Masculine Mystique: Warren Farrell
Minority Women and Women's Rights: Aileen Hernandez, Ellie Spikes
Older Women: Tish Somers
Politics: Karen DeCrow
Women and Poverty: Dorothy Haener
Image of Women: Joan Nicholson
Women and Religion: Joyce Slayton Mitchell
Rape: Mary Ann Largen
Reproduction and Population: Jan Liebman
Sexuality and Lesbianism: Sidney Abbott, H. Jayne Vogan
Women and Sports: Judy Wenning
Stockholder Action and Insurance: Betty Harris
Taxes: Dorothy Amdur
Volunteerism: Pat McCormick

Some coordinators were elected National Board members or officers; some were not. Ideally, each chapter also had each task force, although that actuality depended upon size, interest, and perceived urgency by the chapters. One person from the chapter task force was chosen to be a part of the national one.

The chapters and task forces were the heart of NOW, its means of acting and of coordinating actions locally and nationally. Most Board meetings included discussions of understanding the organizational structure in terms of chapters and task forces. There were also discussions of how the chapters and the Board should and could pay for operating expenses of the task forces. In general, the Board allocated funds for the task forces, the amount depending on priorities set by the national conference and the practical needs and resources of the task forces. The chapters made their own decisions about funding chapter task forces.

In addition to NOW the membership organization, was the NOW Legal, Defense and Education Fund (NOW-LDEF). Legally the LDEF is both a part of NOW and also separate from NOW. Its membership consists of the NOW Board and its own officers and Board. It is responsible to the NOW membership through NOW's Board. It is not, therefore, a grass roots membership organization; and it is an entity of its own. NOW-LDEF was formed in 1968 and in contrast to NOW, it is a tax-deductible organization. Its purposes are education about issues, legal defense in cases involving sex discrimination, and other kinds of support for such cases.

NOW, in the early 70's, appeared to be a structural organization with many features that looked traditional on paper. In practice it did not function using the top-down organization of the stereotypical corporate model. Some members sometimes expressed the feeling that they were being dictated to or that NOW was too hierarchical for a feminist organization. However, any real movement in the direction of consolidation of power "at the top" was hampered or even prevented by decisions made at national conferences, sheer lack of finances, lack of day to day contact, and the fact that it was mostly an organization of volunteers who could always quit. Task force members and coordinators, many of whom were operating in what one member, sociologist Sally Hacker, has called "structural isolation," were scattered all over the country. [2] NOW's successes depended to an enormous extent on the energy and commitment of individuals who could also generate similar energy and commitment from others.

That energy and commitment was, it seems in retrospect, almost miraculously generated. What is perhaps less obvious are some of the sources of the energy and commitment - particularly the reality of anger and the discovery of power. Through consciousness-raising groups; confrontations with discriminatory practices affecting women's own lives; increased knowledge of the institutionalization of sexism and of data on sexual harassment, rape and other realities; increased awareness of the absence of women's story in school, college, and the general culture - through all of these and more, anger mounted and mounted. People had to find both release and effective ways of overcoming its causes. Finding release and effective ways to overcome the causes of sexism led to the discovery of power. The news media tended to focus on some of the more overtly angry expressions, even perpetuating stories that did not happen, such as the famous "bra burning" non-episode. But the anger was much more pervasive than was reported. More important, the anger was channeled into many, many constructive directions.

The anger did not remain individual or isolated. Like NOW, hundreds of groups and organizations emerged spontaneously throughout the country. Jo Freeman cites, for instance, the nearly simultaneous founding of five different groups scattered over the country.[3,p.59] The reasons for this are multiple. Certainly the American tradition of volunteerism played a role; more specifically, the grass roots organizing of the civil rights workers, war protestors, and the "New Left" played an extremely significant role. In 1970, a directory called "The Mushroom Effect" listed several hundred such women's groups and organizations. As Freeman observes: "It was outdated the day it was printed."[3,p.147] Three years later there were several thousand. But whatever the reasons for the proliferation, the consequence was that women discovered power.[4]

In NOW, the anger and the discovery of power led to significant challenging of traditionally powerful institutions and organizations. NOW's drive to eliminate sexual and racial discrimination in AT&T, the push to ratify the ERA, and action to eliminate discrimination and stereotyping in the broadcast media are three significant activities that represent major investments of NOW's energy, time and money. These actions continue to represent significant change for both women's and men's lives.

American Telephone and Telegraph Company
In 1970 the AT&T conglomerate, with over 700,000 employees, was the largest private employer in the country. It owned or had a controlling interest in Western Electric, a manufacturing and supply corporation; Bell Telephone laboratories, research and development agencies; and "associated" telephone companies, those that provide customer service, and what most of us probably think of when we speak of "the telephone company" – Southern Bell, Northwest Bell, Pennsylvania Bell, etc.[5]

NOW initially became involved with AT&T through a suit brought by an employee against Southern Bell. Lorena Weeks had worked for the telephone company since 1947. In 1966 she bid for a vacant switchman's (sic) job and was refused. The company had a policy prohibiting women from positions which included lifting equipment weighing over thirty pounds. Although Weeks was familiar with the equipment, easily capable of handling it and knowledgeable about the procedures of the job, she was turned down. She took the matter to court and turned to NOW for help. On behalf of NOW, Sylvia Roberts argued the case. As she made her points in court, Attorney

Roberts (five feet tall and weighing about 100 pounds) easily carried with one hand all the equipment the position required. In 1969, the court ruled in Weeks' favor, establishing the principle that an employer must consider women applicants unless it can prove substantially that all women could not carry out the job requirements. However, it was not until after NOW and other organizations demonstrated around the country that Southern Bell actually carried out the court order.

In 1970, within one year of the court decision in the Weeks case, AT&T petitioned the Federal Communications Commission (FCC) for a rate increase. The corporation cited increased expenses because of high employee turnover and attorneys' fees from complaints and suits brought by women and racial minorities, along with other reasons. NOW was incensed, filed a petition to deny the request, and created a task force to work on the action. The task force was coordinated by Sally Hacker, a sociologist at Drake University in Iowa. NOW was not alone. The National Association of Colored People (NAACP), American Civil Liberties Union (ACLU), the Mexican-American Legal Defense Fund, and California Rural Legal Assistance also filed against the rate increase.

Locally, chapters filed complaints about specific telephone companies and collected material to substantiate charges of sex and race discrimination. The Seattle chapter was particularly active. Delores Doninger, a telephone employee, risked her job on several occassions to supply evidence to the task forces.

NOW brought AT&T to the attention of the EEOC and urged it to take AT&T as a "track case;" that is, to do a systematic investigation of policy and practice with respect to both sex and race. The Commission agreed and also asked the FCC to deny the rate increase until the company ended what the EEOC described as its "callous indifference" to the law.[6] The EEOC then assigned the tasks of preparing a case to two lawyers, David Copus and Lawrence Gartner.

NOW and the lawyers worked together. In one conversation with Wilma, Copus asked Wilma whether he should push for integration of men into the still traditionally female jobs in the companies.[7] Wilma's response was immediately, "Of course." She continued that it was important to be clear about the principle. Getting women into higher paying jobs and equalizing pay among jobs of equal responsibility regardless of the sex and/or race of the incumbent were only examples of the principle. The principle itself was eliminating sex-based stereotyping. Copus agreed, and EEOC sought for the first time to apply the principle to their task:

> ...we were advancing the really revolutionary view of sex discrimination. We took more or less hook, line and sinker the feminist view as espoused by the National Organization for Women – their view of institutionalized sex discrimination – and we said we wanted to attack it at its roots in the Bell System. Not

just equal pay for equal work, etc. We wanted to present the whole sociology and psychology of sexual stereotypes as it was inculcated into the Bell System structure.[8,p.189]

The EEOC investigation was limited to the AT&T companies supplying customer service. It did not include Bell Laboratories or Western Electric, not, in NOW's words, for lack of discrimination but for reasons of simplicity.[9] After over a year of work, the investigation was completed, and a report was issued in December 1971. Entitled "A Unique Competence," it was over 22,000 pages long. A summary report of 300 pages was also prepared. Both documented instances and patterns of sex and race discrimination. The EEOC findings included:

- one out of every four employees was classified as management (which included a range from president, chauffeur, and secretarial stenographer);
- ninety-four percent of women "managers" were in the lowest level of management ranks, compared to 50% of men managers;
- the plant department was 85.5% male and the traffic department (telephone operators) 97.3% female;
- "operator" was the lowest paying major job in the system;
- in the areas studied, 54% of all employees in major job classifications were in totally sex-segregated jobs;
- Eighty percent of the women were in positions with maximum annual wage of less than $7,000, whereas only 4% of the men were in that classification;
- a woman in first level management (the lowest level) averaged 79% of what a man was paid at that level.[9]

The Report estimated that because women were not distributed evenly throughout the range of available jobs, they lost 422 million dollars every year. In short, "all low-paying, high-turnover, dead-end jobs are female. High-paying, desirable jobs with substantial chances for promotion to middle and upper management are male."[9]

In addition to wages, promotions, and job opportunities, the Summary Report described the working conditions of the operators as "horrendous." Strict discipline and regimentation were the rule, tardiness and absenteeism "sternly punished," and work hours constantly shifted.

Not only were inequities documented, but systemic patterns which perpetuated the inequities were addressed. Manuals were written with information on how to discourage women from applying for certain jobs. Different tests were used for women and men to determine qualifications, so no comparative judgment could be made about whether an individual was qualified for non-traditional jobs.[10] In summary, the Commission described the Bell System as being "the largest oppressor of women workers in the United States."[9]

In the summer of 1972, Whitney Adams called Wilma about an affirmative action plan that AT&T had submitted to the General Services Administration

(GSA) which, in turn, had accepted the plan. NOW regarded the steps outlined in the plan to remedy the situation as meaningless.

NOW members again met with Bell people on both local and national levels. In October, Wilma, Sally Hacker, Joan Hull and Ann Scott met with AT&T President Robert Lilley and David Easlick, Vice President for Human Resources development. At that meeting, Easlick acknowledged that he had not read the summary of the EEOC report.[11] Wilma demanded his resignation for his obvious lack of concern and competence.

The purpose of the meeting was two-fold – to make clear just why NOW had challenged AT&T's affirmative action plan and to try to develop a working relationship with the corporation in establishing alternatives. Clarifying NOW's action was done primarily by Wilma in a point-by-point content analysis of AT&T's so-called affirmative action plan. She stated that the provision for back pay was inadequate, that there was no provision for maternity leaves, that the company should state goals and timetables for correcting abuses and for placing women in positions of higher-level management, and that all job opportunities should be made clearly available to employees of both sexes, all races, and all religions. To this analysis Wilma added a critique of the process by which the content was determined. AT&T's approach:

> itself perpetuates the traditional role of male dictation of "what women need" and is the opposite of feminist thinking in which women define themselves and must be given an active part in designing programs for their own welfare.[12]

After the analyses of the weaknesses of the plan, Sally Hacker and Joan Hull submitted their requirements of a good affirmative action plan, which included four billion dollars in back pay, meaningful and concrete goals and timetables, adequate maternity leave policies, clearly visible job posting, policy level participation by feminist-oriented women, distribution of the summary report among Bell employees, and an analysis of the effect on women and minorities of continuing technological change at the telephone company. This last was a particular concern to Sally. Based on independent research she had done, Sally feared that whatever gains might be secured for women would only be destroyed by increased automation, since women would still be in those positions most likely to be automated.

Beyond what the corporation could do within its companies, NOW representatives insisted that AT&T had a responsibility to effect change in other areas – in the civic organizations, for instance, to which AT&T executives belonged. "Waiting for society to change is an evasive technique. AT&T *is* society, and it must take a leadership role in corporate responsibility."[13]

Apparently Lilley expressed sympathy with NOW's intentions, and the meeting ended on a rather cordial note. As the NOW representatives left,

Lilley told Wilma that he would be glad to be of help to NOW if he could.

Following the October meeting, negotiations between AT&T and EEOC continued. In January, 1973, NOW held a Board meeting in New York the same weekend as an AT&T Board meeting. NOW members decided to present a bill to the AT&T Board for four billion dollars in back pay. Posters and leaflets were designed. Then NOW discovered that the AT&T Board had at the last minute switched to Chicago for its meeting. Evidence from inside the AT&T corporate world led NOW members to the conclusion that the AT&T Board meeting was moved to Chicago to avoid another confrontation with NOW.[14]

On the 18th of January, 1973, a settlement was reached between AT&T, EEOC and other government agencies. Under the category of a consent decree (a mechanism whereby the defendant does not have to acknowledge violation of law but nevertheless agrees to certain terms), AT&T agreed:

- to pay an estimated $15 million in back pay and compensation to women and minority employees,
- to adjust wage and promotion pay for an estimated $23 million per year increase in the wages of women and minority employees,
- to submit an affirmative action plan acceptable to the EEOC,
- to provide significant opportunities for promotion and advancement for women and minorities.[15]

After the agreement was reached, NOW continued contact with AT&T, monitoring compliance and exploring, without success, other avenues of action. Wilma wrote an article on feminism for the Bell *Magazine*, which the editor rejected. Similarly, discussion about a proposal from NOW for AT&T to fund a TV presentation on child care proved so frustrating that NOW decided to scrap it.

Nevertheless, important changes had been made. The largest civilian employer in this country had to *redirect* its policies away from those that reinforced structural sexism and racism and toward those that reflected equality. AT&T did not suddenly eliminate racism and sexism in structure, much less in individual attitudes and practices; but the direction of policy and behavior had changed. Actually, the 53 million dollar price tag – the largest settlement to that date – and the rest of the consent decree were a message to other employers, which was what NOW had originally intended.

Further, enforcement of laws prohibiting sexism had become a significant priority for the EEOC, one of the reasons for which NOW had been founded just seven years earlier. William Brown, the director of EEOC, had become committed to that task, and EEOC lawyers had gained sophistication and insight about the pervasiveness of sexism in business and industry.

It is important to bear in mind that NOW was not the only human rights organization to challenge AT&T, and that NOW criticized AT&T on grounds of racism as well as sexism. The result of the AT&T case was a single but inclusive determination about discriminatory practice that did not reflect, suggest or foster competition among organizations seeking justice for workers. According to Jo Freeman, the EEOC learned that:

> efforts to secure an end to race and sex discrimination do not necessarily have to compete with each other. A concerted attack on the elimination of both in the same companies can be mutually reinforcing.[3,p.190]

Though NOW members knew that AT&T employees were entitled to much more back pay, they were nevertheless reinforced and further empowered to continue their work. They had become actors, influencing important areas of government and business.

NOW members were also gaining more insights into what I call a "principled pragmatism," which is typical of Wilma's way of bringing about social change. "Principled pragmatism" is a willingness to push at whatever point seems vulnerable as well as a willingness to cooperate. Wilma and other NOW members involved worked with people at all levels of government and industry. They worked with people "inside" the establishment and also pushed them from the outside. At the same time, Wilma and other NOW members did not hesitate to turn away from established institutions and develop or encourage the development of alternatives. The principles were clear: the elimination of racism and sexism and the establishment of feminist-humanist alternatives. Whether these conditions were to be achieved by working "within" or "without" the "system" depended on opportunity, energy, resources, and some probability of success.

To act, holding onto both humaneness and fundamental change, is difficult at best. In acting on the AT&T case, some of the experiential basis for both humaneness and change was being formed and tested. Sally Hacker, reflecting on Wilma's leadership and her own skepticism at times, commented:

> I don't really expect corporations to do much of anything, especially if it costs them money, but Wilma has more faith and hope in the human spirit ... [she] is more willing to see people, even in positions of power, as more capable of voluntary action toward change.[16]

There is still another footnote to the AT&T story. One day in 1977, four and a half years after the settlement, Wilma received a letter indicating that she had been randomly selected among AT&T stockholders for a management visit. She had bought a modest amount of stock earlier as another means of monitoring the company, but so far as she can tell, the people who had selected her had no idea who she was. She arranged for Sally to be present, and on the appointed day a man arrived, who proceeded to inform them about how new technologies would eliminate more and more workers and thus improve profit – one of Sally's earlier fears.

According to Sally:

> Wilma said that as a stockholder, she would be willing to see profits decline if women and minorities would have more job opportunities ... social factors should take precedence over profit. I thought the guy was going to have a stroke. His eyes got bigger and bigger. He extracted himself from the position and promised to send a report to headquarters, but no ... he would not give her a copy. [16]

So Wilma wrote up the meeting and made her suggestions directly to the AT&T Board. The response she received was that:

> We don't believe we can or should stop the introduction of new technology which cuts costs and improves productivity. To do so would be a disservice ... to ... investors ... [and] to our customers. While it is difficult at times to balance the interests of all those involved ... we don't believe meeting our social responsibilities ... is contrary to the long-term interests of our shareowners.[17]

Sally's fears of automation's replacing personnel, still primarily women and minorities, were in the process of being vindicated, and the gains that had been won seemed, once again, about to be lost – or at least challenged.

Broadcast Media

A second major focus of action by NOW was the broadcast media. A task force on the image of women, which included images of women in the broadcast media, had been a part of NOW since its inception. During Wilma's presidency, at least three different task forces – Broadcasting, Legislation, and Image of Women, on both national and local levels – worked on issues related to broadcasting and women.

The broadcast media, primarily television, were an obvious although rather monumental object of concern to NOW. The communications media in general have become a permanent and pervasive part of our lives. Movies, books, magazines, newspapers, radio, and television continually offer both entertainment and "news." In so doing these media, to a greater or lesser extent, help select the information people work with in decision-making and help shape our very perception of reality. This kind of power is preeminently true of television. NOW took direct action in relation to television stations and the industry's regulatory and policy-making bodies – the Federal Communications Commission (FCC) and the National Association of Broadcasters (NAB).[18]

According to a report on television by the U.S. Commission on Civil Rights:

> audiences place a higher value on television as a source of information and entertainment than on other media ... It receives

the highest marks for providing the fairest and least biased news coverage ...It confers status on those individuals and groups it selects for placement in the public eye, telling the viewer who and what is important to know about, think about, and have feelings about. Those who are made visible through television become worthy of attention and concern; those whom television ignores remain invisible. [19,p.1]

Blacks, Native Americans, and other racial minorities have tended to be invisible or presented as whites saw them. White women have not been invisible in entertainment programs, but they have been portrayed in stereotypical ways. White women have been practically invisible in news reporting and making, and have continued to be absent from policy-level positions within the industry. A study of station WRC by the Washington, DC, chapter of NOW, Women's Equity Action League (WEAL), and others in 1972 found that women's rights and changing roles received the least emphasis of twenty-one topics; women were "10 percent of all newsmakers and 6.5 percent of all reporters."[19,p.2]

Such a situation was obviously intolerable to feminists, and it had to be challenged and changed. NOW's action was two-fold – legal and educational. Legal action included suits, petitions, and out-of-court settlements; the educational action included an ad campaign.

The FCC regulates specific broadcast stations and not a network, since the stations make so many decisions about programming and personnel. NOW, through the work of Whitney Adams and others, prepared kits for chapters to monitor local stations and submit evidence on behalf of or in protest of renewing a station's license.

Before the chapters were busy monitoring, first Aileen Hernandez and Lucy Komisar, and then Wilma, Whitney, and others submitted a petition to the FCC to enforce its prohibition of sex discrimination. In 1969, the FCC had adopted a non-discriminatory rule that included race, color, religion, and national origin. In 1970, the rule was amended to include women, but still excluded them as a class in need of affirmative action including active recruitment and promotion. NOW submitted a petition to amend this latter rule, along with the support of 30 other national civil rights and other organizations. In May, 1971, the rule was finally amended.

After Wilma became president, she and the task forces began to push first for the adoption of the amended rule and then for compliance. As with AT&T personnel, NOW members sought and achieved meetings with FCC and local broadcasting people. NOW members phoned, they wrote, they phoned again. Like mosquitoes, buzzing and buzzing around one's head, they refused to go away, to be lady-like, to be appeased. And so they met; they spoke at conventions and workshops; they presented evidence of stereotyping and discrimination; they demanded goals and timetables.

A coalition of ten organizations in the Washington area began monitoring WRC-TV. The coalition found that news about the movement was ignored or distorted, women were limited primarily to entertainment roles and/or primarily in stereotypical roles. The coalition charged that the failure to provide fuller and fairer programming for women was in effect a violation of the fairness doctrine.[19,p.63] The fairness doctrine stated that if there was a presentation of controversial matter of public importance, a station was obliged to afford opportunity for presentation of contrasting views. NOW claimed that the question of appropriate women's roles and characteristics was a controversial issue and that only one side was being aired.[19]

Simultaneously in New York, a NOW chapter had been monitoring WABC-TV for a year and a half. The work was coordinated by Judith Hennessee and Joan Nicholson, and the chapter was assisted by lawyers from the Center for Constitutional Rights. Again, the charges were similar to those made in Washington. WABC-TV did not assess the needs and interests of the audience it served. It did not even report that the ERA had been passed by Congress and was being sent to the states for ratification. It did not have equal opportunity in employment. It stereotyped; in 1,241 commercials examined, women were primarily in two roles – those of sex objects and homemakers-mothers.[19,p.12] The station consistently portrayed women as unintelligent, irresponsible, and dominated by men.

With this mass of evidence, NOW and other organizations petitioned the FCC, but the agency rejected the petitions. NOW appealed the WRC case to the U.S. Court of Appeals for Washington, DC, and again it was rejected. The court concluded that WRC was "responsive to the needs and interests of women;" nevertheless it also found that there appeared to be "an industry-wide problem" with respect to women.[19,p.65]

The WRC and WABC challenges were followed by others in Columbia, Detroit, New Orleans, Syracuse, Pittsburgh, and elsewhere. Several challenges were settled out of court, including those in Detroit, New Orleans, Syracuse and Pittsburgh.

The Detroit negotiations serve as an example of what could be accomplished. The Detroit petition was filed against WXYZ-TV by Detroit NOW in a coalition with other agencies. The legal work was handled by the United Church of Christ, Office of Communications. In August, 1973, NOW and WXYZ-TV reached an agreement that provided for goals to increase women in official, managerial and technical positions; a training program for women interested in becoming camerapeople, soundpeople, or electricians; advertising of positions in feminist literature; a maternity policy that conformed to EEOC regulations; the establishment of a Woman's Advisory Committee; and a small amount of feminist programming each year. The agreement was submitted to the FCC and approved, and NOW did not further challenge the local ABC license.

As local chapters and the national task forces worked together on petitions to deny license renewal and/or negotiations with stations, other NOW members were in conversation with the National Association of Broadcasters (NAB) in an effort to affect broadcast policy. In 1971, while she was still Chair of the Board, Wilma was invited to speak and lead workshops at a Broadcasting Industry Symposium. Later, in 1973, Toni Carabillo, NOW Vice President for Public Relations, spoke at least twice to the NAB, proposing changes in the Code and a statement of ethics for broadcasters. Essentially, the changes she proposed would require broadcasters to show "special sensitivity" to material in non-stereotyping ways. Afterward, Toni wrote Wilma, stating that she thought the effort was probably a waste of time, but the NAB did respond to the effect that it would work harder on implementing what was already in the Code, that it would disseminate highlights of Toni's speech to other broadcasters, and that NOW was invited to contribute a guest column to the monthly Code News.[20]

In addition to actions that sought to end stereotypical programming and discrimination in the television industry, NOW developed a novel means of educating the public about some feminist goals – the public service ad campaign. One day in 1972 while Wilma was in New York on NOW business, Midge Kovacs, a New York NOW member who worked in advertising, approached Wilma with an idea – to create and run a series of ads in magazines and newspapers, on radio and television, to dramatize inequities with a light touch to demonstrate how ridiculous they were. Wilma's response was immediate. "It's a terrific idea! How can we [national NOW] help?"

The New York Image Task Force and Wilma met with the president of Westinghouse Broadcasting Corporation, who was also the head of the Advertising Council of America, about running public service ads. He agreed to look into it but made no commitment at the time.

In the meantime, Midge and New York NOW secured the cooperation of four people in advertising – Anne Tolstoi Foster, Vice President of William Esty Company; Jeanne Harrison of Harrison Productions; John de Garmo of de Garmo, Inc.; and Seth Tobias of Savitt Tobias Balk. CBS supplied studio facilities. They put together ten public service announcements for broadcast – eight for radio and two for TV. They also created about 40 print ads for newspapers and magazines.

Ms. Magazine was the first to run them. Probably the most well-known is the cartoon of a man holding up his pants legs and exposing knobby knees, with the caption "Hire him. He's got great legs."

Then the ads began to appear in magazines, on the radio, and on TV around the country. According to Midge, TV stations provided $1,323,934 worth of air time for the ads, newspapers $141,883, radios $126,264, and magazines $99,713. [21] Time, Newsweek, and Business Week continued to run the ads beyond the date for which those figures were computed. In a note to Wilma asking her to send a letter of appreciation to Jean R. Groesi of Time, who was responsible for the ads there, Midge indicated that Time had contributed $94,265 in free space.[21]

In the course of planning for the ads, the NOW Board decided that when pictures were used, the people represented should not be only white; women and girls of color should also be pictured. Those in advertising objected. Their position was that an ad could make only one point and that to add the dimension of race would confuse and dilute the issue. NOW and Wilma insisted. In spite of that, however, the ads portrayed only white people. Wilma and others were furious and would have tried to stop the campaign had they known what was going to happen. Why did it happen? "I'm not sure," Wilma said; "Someone didn't get back to me about the decision in New York, and I didn't have the time to monitor the follow-up." In a letter to Midge, after the campaign, she congratulated the New Yorker warmly, but also stated that NOW had to stand by principle; it could not afford to compromise on an issue that involved all women and girls, and not only white women:

> My position on inclusion of minority females is unequivocal, unchangeable. To the extent that what I have communicated is in any way deemed unfair, belated, non-constructive, I am genuinely sorry ...Meantime, the Ad Campaign is a stunning project of incalculable value for NOW, LDEF, feminism and society. [22]

Midge responded that there had been no intent to exclude minority women, and that the Ad Council absolutely refused to approve ads which included "black and Chicano [sic] problems."[23]

The Board also brought the matter up, and there were conflicting views on it. Mary Jean Tully, representing NOW-LDEF, was upset as was Aileen Hernandez. And Wilma stated bluntly that while it was important to receive professional advice, that advice should not take precedence over NOW's principles. There was some criticism that Wilma was being anti-professional, but Wilma remained adamant. She felt strongly that the ads should not have appeared as they did, and although there was nothing she could do about it then, she continued to feel some responsibility for what happened.

Like AT&T, the broadcast industry is a powerful force in American society. When one sees, still in the 1980's, the sexism and racism of TV and other media, one is aware of how slowly such giants change. Yet NOW, often in coalition with other organizations, did make changes in the media and at least pointed it toward a new direction. More women are appearing on the screen, particularly as reporters and newscasters. More women are being employed in non-traditional positions behind the screen. Competent, mature, realistic women are beginning at least to compete with more stereotypical images.

As with the action toward AT&T, Wilma's "principled pragmatism" was at work in action toward the media. In the case of the public service ads, principles had priority for Wilma. In other cases, where principles were not in question, a variety of means were employed to press the media toward more responsible positions on issues of sexism and racism.

Equal Rights Amendment

The Equal Rights Amendment (ERA) was approved by Congress on March 22, 1972, and sent to the states for ratification. Three-fourths of the states, or thirty-eight, were needed if the ERA were to be included in the Constitution. Seven years were provided for the process, a number settled on by Congress based on some precedents and not on any Constitutional or legally binding mandate.

Between March and December 1972, twenty-one states had ratified the Amendment. In January, 1973, opposition was observed to be increasing by the *New York Times*, which reported that well organized and seemingly well financed opposition had appeared and were making arguments against the amendment.[24]

The drive to ratify the ERA was an organized part of NOW's activity during Wilma's presidency. Hundreds of thousands of hours of work were spent by members locally and nationally. Money had to be raised, mailings sent to citizens and politicians, the composition of state governments had to be analyzed, intensive and prolonged lobbying done, and special direct actions and demonstrations had to be planned and executed.

Ann Scott assumed a major responsibility for coordinating this drive. As Vice President for Legislation and Director of NOW's legislative office until May 1974, she was familiar with the legislative processes and with people from all the states who had made ERA Congressional passage and state ratifications their major commitments.

The summer and fall of 1973 were designated research time for the chapters – identifying politicians and their positions on the ERA, getting to know office staff, analyzing state laws and local ordinances that could be affected by the ERA, raising money, and publicizing the need for ratification.

In January 1974, fifteen legislatures in unratified states were scheduled to convene. NOW called for daily lobbying, picketing of the headquarters of those who were opposed and keeping favorable news about the ERA before the public. Montana, Maine, and Ohio voted in favor of ratification.[25] In early 1975 North Dakota followed suit, and then in early 1977 Indiana did also.

While grass-roots and state-wide action was occurring, NOW conducted two nation-wide fund raising campaigns. One was both symbolically and literally to give their life's blood for the ERA. Members poured into commercial blood banks and sold their blood pint by pint, and contributed the money to the organization for use in ratification activities. The second project was the ERA Emergency Fund. NOW sent out extensive mailings to people all over the country requesting donations. Within two months, over fourteen thousand dollars had been raised.

NOW also sought support from and coalition with other national organizations in favor of the Amendment, or potentially so. Wilma took an active role in this process and was able to use many contacts she made through her involvement in the struggle for human rights. In 1970, for instance, the ACLU was on record in opposition to the ERA on the grounds that the

Fourteenth Amendment included women and that the ERA was therefore unnecessary. NOW's position, in contrast, was that since much of American legislation is based on English common law, in which the legal concept of "person" excluded women, a specific amendment directed to women was indeed necessary. After all, if the 14th amendment included women as legal persons, the 75 year struggle to have women's right to vote *acknowledged* in the Constitution would not have been necessary.

Wilma met with other feminists in the ACLU, particularly Louise Noun from Iowa and Pauli Murray, faculty member at Brandeis and a founder of NOW. Together, they urged the ACLU Board to change its position, which it did.

Common Cause, another major organization that stated it was for human rights and citizen lobbying, had not yet taken a position on the ERA and other women's rights issues as of August 1971, although NOW had been pressing it to do so. Wilma, Aileen Hernandez, Ann Scott, and Carol Burris, NOW ERA co-coordinator, had urged NOW members to return promotional material they received from Common Cause with a note indicating that they would not join until the organization realized that feminism was the common cause and, specifically, until it had taken a position supporting the ERA. Finally, a meeting was arranged between John Gardner, then head of the organization, and Wilma, Aileen, Ann and Carol. In reflecting on the event, Wilma said, "We wanted it that way, four women and one man, not because we needed four of us to talk with one man, but because we wanted him to have no one to talk with except us. Gardner had been listening to the unions, and we wanted him to hear feminists." (The AFL-CIO, for instance, was still opposing the Amendment.) At the meeting, Wilma cited aspects of his career and, in the effort to establish common ground between them indicated that in many ways his interests could be called feminist and humane. At one point she asked him, "Am I communicating?" And according to Wilma, he responded softly, "Oh, yes; oh, yes." They left him some literature and in early 1972 sent him Wilma's speech to the American College Personnel Association entitled: "The Feminist Cause is the Common Cause." Common Cause soon came out with a position of support for the ERA and developed lobbying contributing to its passage in the Congress.

Another organization from which Wilma sought support was the League of Women Voters (LWV). From the time she was engaged in voter registration for the League in the south in the 50's, Wilma had urged support of the ERA, but then "no one wanted to talk about it." In 1971, Mary Jean Tully, president of NOW-LDEF, suggested to Wilma that she meet with Lucy Wilson Benson, president of the League and also on the Common Cause Board. Since at that time, Wilma was living in Vernon, Connecticut, and Ms. Benson in Amherst, Massachusetts, they arranged a meeting half way between at a restaurant. They talked for several hours. Benson joined NOW, and then asked Wilma, "What else can I do?" Wilma asked to meet with the League's Board and explore ways of cooperating. Benson agreed, and a meeting was scheduled. Wilma talked with them about citizens' rights and the ERA, and they set up a liaison committee of women members of both NOW and LWV. The League subsequently invited Gloria Steinem to speak at their national conference in April 1972, at which time they announced their support of the ERA.

Similar efforts occupied Wilma's time in enlisting the support of the American Nurses Association (ANA). One day Barbara Schutt, then editor of the *American Journal of Nursing,* and a woman Wilma had known from Pennsylvania nursing days, called Wilma for a short, quick statement to include in the *Journal* on the women's movement. Wilma followed up that contact with lunch with Barbara Schutt. Schutt joined NOW, and they explored the ANA's opposition to the ERA and how they might help the organization find a graceful way to change its position. The opposition was based, at least in part, on a reluctance to give up what had been considered "protective legislation" for women. Again through personal contact, information, and discussion, the ANA changed its position in 1971 to one of support for the ERA.

With respect to the American Federation of Labor-Congress of Industrial Organizations (AFL-CIO), Wilma worked with union people in NOW. They sought to show the union leadership that it needed to re-think its opposition when its position was one shared by the John Birch Society, the Communist Party USA, the Ku Klux Klan, and the fundamentalist, anti-Communist Christian Crusade. They continued to send AFL-CIO lists of other unions that did support the Amendment. They also demonstrated that opposition helped continue to make available a pool of cheap labor (ie, women) in the work force, and that therefore the union's stand was part of the problem of resistance to unionization. Finally, on October 22, 1973, George Meany (then president) announced the union's unanimous support of the ERA.

Wilma approached other organizations in a similar way. About 130 organizations had entered into a coalition called the Leadership Conference on Civil Rights, of which NOW was also a member. In January 1973, the Conference sponsored a five dollar a person banquet to honor Emmanuel Cellar (Representative from New York) and William McCulloch (former Representative from Ohio) for their work in civil rights. Cellar had prevented committee hearings on the ERA for 21 years, and McCulloch had opposed including the prohibition against sex discrimination in the 1964 Civil Rights Act. Wilma wrote to Roy Wilkins, then Executive Director of the NAACP, who was sympathetic, that NOW "vigorously protests the selection of these two stalwart opponents of women's rights for honors."[26]

Nevertheless, NOW and Wilma continued their efforts within the Leadership Conference, bringing up the issue whenever possible. Wilma talked particularly with women and men she had known through her own participation in the movement for racial justice. And in 1973, the Conference also switched its position in favor of support for the ERA.

In her work for ratification, Wilma often appeared in public with Phyllis Schlafly, ERA opponent. In such encounters, Wilma showed the audience why many organizations and individuals throughout the country found it imperative to support the ERA. She did this by pointing to ways the Amendment would, could and ought to benefit women and also men, while Schlafly focused on claims of its destructiveness. Wilma met Schlafly's charges in several ways. In some instances, she simply reminded the audience that some states already had what Schlafly was afraid of – state ERAs. None of Schlafly's predictions had come true and indeed homemakers' legal position and economic value were already improved by state ERAs. When Schlafly tried to scare with the prediction that the ERA meant that women would be drafted along with men, Wilma pointed out that Congress has had the power to draft women since 1947 without the ERA. Similarly, when Schlafly argued that the ERA would exempt divorced men from paying alimony and/or child support, Wilma pointed to the small percentage of those who pay now. But she also went beyond that response. Judges, she explained, are guided in their decisions by legislative history; that is, they seek to determine the intent of the framers of a piece of legislation as well as the substance of it. And the intent of the framers of the ERA was a matter of public record, which stated very clearly that the Amendment was to eliminate legal double standards, and not to penalize further women who chose to work at home and who were, therefore, unable to build up independent financial security.

Wilma also did not hesitate to challenge Schlafly's veracity. Wilma heard Schlafly taking quotations out of context and twisting their meaning. She also heard Schlafly contradicting herself from one speech to another. Wilma refused to allow those practices to pass in silence and on each occasion that she could, she pointed them out to the audience. Indeed, one way Wilma developed to refute Schlafly's claim of concern for women, especially homemakers, was to quote Schlafly's own publications. On one occasion, Wilma defined misogyny (woman-hating) and asked the audience to examine the quotations from Schlafly's writing for evidence of misogyny.[27] Schlafly was momentarily flustered, and then ignored questions of the audience about her writings. After several encounters like this, some of Schlafly's former supporters were persuaded that she was a political opportunist and no friend of women or men. They reported to Wilma that she was the ERA proponent that Schlafly least wanted to encounter again.

Wilma's appeal, in short, was to reason and fact. It was designed to allay fears and at the same time, to acknowledge that real change would result when the ERA is ratified, changes that she saw meant a fairer and freer life for all. Wilma's appeal had the effect of challenging Schlafly with accuracy and straightforwardness.

In a few short years from its founding, NOW, a volunteer organization composed of many who had little political experience as well as some with considerable experience and without a well-recorded history of protest, challenged not only two giant institutions – AT&T and the broadcast industry with all their power, financial resources and prestige – but also all other institutions of society. In addition, after 200 years of women's virtual absence from the Constitution, NOW began the process to include women in the Constitution by shepherding the ERA to the states and working at a grass roots level for ratification.

A variety of means were used – negotiation and direct action, careful fact-finding and persuasion, court action, and education. Using these means effectively also meant giving attention to NOW's development. This included learning leadership skills, serving as a catalyst by raising issues, developing positions, generating programs and actions, stimulating communications and support systems, identifying points for leverage and generally moving from consciousness-raising to developing organizations that would "make a difference" in the movement toward indivisible human rights. Occasionally, the activities were exciting, often dangerous for those who risked jobs, reputation and/or family serenity. Activists were ridiculed and portrayed as a lunatic fringe, not at all representative of or sensitive to the "real" needs of American women. More often, the activities were tedious, time-consuming, and energy-draining, costing activists thousands of dollars in telephone calls, contributions, and travel expenses.

Wilma was in the midst of it all. She led and challenged and encouraged others to act with her. She confronted, but she also worked with the people whom she and others insisted must also confront the issues, and sometimes gained colleagues in the EEOC, the Senate, and even to some extent in AT&T. She was persistent – stubborn some would say – and she stayed with an issue until it was resolved. She challenged, but she also sought to share a larger vision with those she challenged. She was always informed and she would not be dismissed on the charge that her statements were only rhetorical. Perhaps above all, she found and expressed exhiliration and gratification in the processes of change.

Actions to change institutional policy, as important as they were to Wilma, to NOW, and to feminism were not sufficient. A feminist approach to social change involved much more – a fundamental philosophy and ethic.

NOTES

1. Heide, Wilma Scott: "Revolution: Tomorrow is NOW!" NOW Conference, February, 1973. Later published in *Vital Speeches of the Day, 1973*. City News Publishing Co., Southold, New York, pp.403-408.
2. Interview with Sally Hacker, Spring, 1978.

3. Freeman, Jo: *The Politics of Women's Liberation: A Case Study of an Emerging Social Movement and Its Relation to the Policy Process.* New York, David McKay Co, 1975.

4. Freeman's book *The Politics of Women's Liberation* includes an excellent discussion of the reasons for the proliferation of women's groups. See especially chapters 2-4. (See note #3).

5. As Wilma points out, it would be accurate to refer to Bell Telephone as "Pa" Bell, not "Ma" Bell, based on who is in charge.

6. *The Wall Street Journal,* Friday, December 11, 1970.

7. Taped interview with David Copus, Fall, 1978.

8. Quoted in Jo Freeman's book, *The Politics of Women's Liberation*, p.189. (See note #3).

9. "Summary." NOW files in Wilma's basement, no date, no author.

10. For further documentation, see for instance Phyllis A. Wallace, *Equal Employment Opportunity and the AT&T Case.* Cambridge, MA, MIT Press, 1976.

11. Reported by Wilma in conversation with me.

12. Press release, NOW, October 25, 1972.

13. Mentioned in a letter from Wilma to Lilley, January 30, 1974.

14. Reported by Wilma and in NOW newsletter.

15. Press release, Statement of William H. Brown, III, Washington, DC, January 18, 1973. Actually a second consent decree was signed in May, 1974, updating provisions and remedying deficiencies in the 1973 one.

16. Tape from Sally Hacker, Fall, 1977.

17. Letter to Wilma from William G. Burns, Vice President and Treasurer, AT&T, August 1, 1977.

18. NOW was also involved with other media. I have already cited the Pittsburgh NOW Chapter's successful action to end stereotyping of want ads. Similarly New York NOW worked to end stereotyping in the *New York Times'* portrayal of women, its failure to report news generated by feminists, and its employment practices. Later the *Times* was subject to a costly suit, which it lost, because of its sex discriminatory employment practices. The *New York Times* slogan is: "All the news that's fit to print." In the early 70's, New York City NOW published several editions of the NOW York Times which it called "All the news that would give the Times the fits."

19. U.S Commission on Civil Rights, *Window Dressing on the Set: Women and Minorities on Television.* U.S. Government Printing Office, August, 1977.

20. Letter to Joan Nicholson from Stockton Helffrick of NAB, October 15, 1973.

21. Letter from Midge Kovacs to Wilma, December 7, 1973.

22. Letter from Wilma to Midge Kovacs, October 30, 1973.

23. Letter from Midge Kovacs to Wilma, November 9, 1973.

24. *New York Times,* January 15, 1973.

25. The ERA lost by one vote in Maine the first time it was before the State Senate but was passed the following year.

26. Quoted in *The Cincinnati Post,* Friday, January 26, 1973.

27. "Some Documented Information about the Equal Rights Amendment (ERA) and Its Opponents: Some Questions to Ask." Unpublished, Wilma's files.

7

BUILDING COMMUNITY

We've had affirmative action programs for white men for
centuries; we just haven't called them that. It's time for us to get
together as women of all races and minority men and educate
ourselves and each other on the interrelationships of racism and
sexism and then educate the rest of society: white men, that *they*
are the minority ... My black and brown sisters and brothers can
no more afford the "feminine mystique" life style than can I. We
all need less of the feminine mystique and more of a joint feminist-
humanist manifesto (or should we call it womanifesto?).

– Wilma Scott Heide[1]

Building Community Among Women

In addition to action for social change, NOW focused on fundamental
philosophic and ethical issues in feminism, issues which individual NOW
members had to think through themselves. Wilma's efforts, through NOW
and in addition to NOW, built the bases of sisterhood and brotherhood to
create the "joint feminist-humanist womanifesto," about which she has
spoken so often. These efforts were to build international community and
community that transcended race, class, sexual preference, and personal
community of friendship and family. Wilma's administration in NOW, with
chapters and members, and within the Board, and her personal leadership
qualities exemplify her ethics in action.

NOW initially was composed primarily of professional, union and business
people, and homemakers. The membership did not include many poor people
or openly lesbian women, nor did it include many whose concerns were
perceived to be focused on minority rights, peace and the environment. Early
NOW, in other words, focused on concrete injustices (particularly in
employment) that other organizations were ignoring and, like any other
effective organization, was composed of those who bore the brunt of the
injustice and/or identified with those who most suffered from it.

But NOW did not and could not remain so narrowly focused. Women's issues cut across all the divisions that ordinarily set people apart. Women are a part of all countries, all classes, all races, all life-styles, all sexual orientations, all religions. Wilma's and NOW's interest in acknowledging this transcendence across political boundaries inevitably emerged consistent with the realities of women's experience.

Building International Community

Since the 1960's many NOW members realized an international feminist movement was imperative. They discussed the idea periodically, and in the fall of 1972 Wilma, Jo Ann Evans Gardner, Patricia Hill Burnett, and Rona Fields began exploring in more detail specific action to develop international connections.

Patricia Hill Burnett became the coordinator of the planning. She was a resident of a fashionable suburb of Detroit, a portrait painter, a runner-up in a Miss America contest, and a feminist committed to a global perspective. She also had the time and means of making contact with women around the world.

Harvard Divinity School and nearby Lesley College in Cambridge, Massachusetts agreed to host a conference. The primary purposes of the conference were to establish communication and begin to build networks, identify common goals and differences, and plan for a major international conference of feminists.

The conference opened on June 1, 1973. More than 300 women from 27 countries convened at Lesley College,[2,p.18] all at their own expense. The majority were from the United States, but there were a number of women from other countries. The countries represented included the Scandinavian countries, the Soviet Union, England, New Zealand and the continent of Europe. There were also women from third world countries – Pakistan, Honduras, Colombia, Egypt, Swaziland, Ecuador, Mexico and Puerto Rico.[2,pp.34-55]

Participants were invited because they were known to the planners. Participants were self-selected, though NOW made significant efforts to facilitate attendance by the poor. Representatives from international women's organizations, churches and universities were included. Poor women, employed women, homemakers were included. High school women and elderly women were included. Women reflecting different life styles and affectional preferences were included.

The conference began on Friday morning with welcoming speeches by Betty Friedan, Wilma, Patricia Hill Burnett, and Elizabeth Duncan Koontz.

> Why is it not only important but absolutely vital that we come
> together to create the feminist-human institutions and behaviors
> our societies and world need to survive as a fully human universe?

asked Wilma in her opening talk.[2,p2] She answered her question by citing examples of sexism world-wide. Her emphasis was on possibilities rather than present realities:

> I trust this conference will unite us to stand together in the sisterhood of all women in egalitarian[3] linkage to the brotherhood of all men to create the fully humane family of nations.[2,p.4]

This was not a "formal" conference with presentation of papers, although papers had been submitted and were available. Instead, meeting in small groups, women explored specific issues of life styles; sex-role stereotyping and the role of education, religion, sports, etc. throughout the world; issues of sexuality and the family; and building a feminist culture. Throughout the weekend, in planned and spontaneous groups, in hours and hours of discussion, the participants worked. Differences and conflicts sometimes overshadowed the areas of common ground and purpose. Class, race, and politics on occasion proved stronger than gender. At times the sheer number of people from the United States engendered suspicion or hostility. There were moments when one could well wonder if the planning conference were to achieve any of its goals.

On Monday, the last day of the conference, the participants met again in plenary session to select a continuing committee to plan an international conference for September 1975 in a country other than the United States. Designing a system to limit the votes of people from the United States, they elected Berit Äs from Norway as Chair. Committee members were: Sawako Takagi from Japan, Gilda Grillo from Brazil, Cicelia Lopez-Negrete from Mexico, Karmela Belinki from Finland, Marietta Stepaniants from the Soviet Union, Maj-Britt Bergstrom-Walan from Sweden, Sheila Prag from Israel, Judy Wenning from the United States, Karin Howard from West Germany, Lilly Boeykins from Belgium, Betty Friedan from the United States, Sue Acheson from New Zealand, Patricia Hill Burnett from the United States, Susan Forge from Hungary, Mary Mdiniso from Swaziland, and Johnnie Tillmon from the United States.

They also discussed location, funding, participants and issues and goals of the conference. A specific site was not selected, but the group agreed the country should be politically neutral, easily accessible, that it should have a strong feminist core of women, and that it should be willing to help support the conference financially. They decided to limit conference attendance to women. The goals that were articulated were those of promoting equality for women in every area of life, developing an international data bank, developing means of crisis intervention, developing an international pool of women experts in all fields and helping women resolve the dilemmas they face. The group agreed that major issues included questions of reproductive control, women's participation in national liberation struggles, sex-role stereotypes, illiteracy, poverty, health care, and ways women can work together in solidarity.

The conference ended on a note of gratitude and at least the beginnings of new understanding. During the final plenary session, many women began to speak spontaneously. Sheila Prag of Israel referred movingly to her "sister from Egypt." She received a standing ovation. A reporter from Geneva, Switzerland acknowledged the occasion:

> I have travelled all over the world as a reporter. I have been to Vietnam and Jerusalem and Syria, and...my Israeli sister has made me cry. [4]

Wilma embraced Prag and noted her courage to express her emotion publicly and commended the Israeli and Egyptian women for finding common ground when national "leaders" had not.

The participants explored the need for an international newsletter to publicize what women and governments around the world were doing or not doing to overcome discrimination. Fran Hosken of Massachusetts, one of the participants, decided to begin one – *Women's International Network News (WIN News)*. Hosken's background was in architecture and urban planning, but much of her energy and interest was directed toward ameliorating and changing the conditions of women throughout the world. She had been instrumental in urging Senator Percy from Illinois to sponsor an Amendment to Foreign Aid legislation to require the involvement of women in planning for and distribution of foreign aid. She had challenged the ways in which tax-exempt foundations were able to perpetuate sexist employment practices, including those who gave to NOW-LDEF. A major focus of *WIN News* was documenting and publicizing the incidence of clitoridectomy and infibulation throughout the world.[5]

Hosken continued to pursue and publicize in *WIN News* information on circumcision and mutilation; she eventually became a consultant to the World Health Organization and organized a worldwide network – The Human Rights/Health Action Network – to abolish the practices and to support women in gaining control over their own bodies. In 1979 she published *The Hosken Report: Genital and Sexual Mutilation of Females.* [6]

Perhaps the most dramatic immediate action outcome of the conference was the first international feminist protest action in support of the three Portuguese women who had become known as "the three Marias." The three women – Maria Isabel Barreno, Maria Teresa Horta, and Maria Velho da Costa – had collaborated on a book of essays, short stories, letters and poetry which chronicled and explored women's lives in Portugal – their isolation, their exploitation, and even their rape and imprisonment by fathers and husbands. The three had been arrested on the charge of "outraging public morals and good customs" by writing and publishing the *New Portuguese Letters.* [7] The trial was scheduled for July 3, 1973.

On June 27 (three weeks after the planning conference) Wilma called a press conference along with Claudia Dreifus, then of *World Magazine*; Sidney Offit, vice president of PEN (an international writer's association); Gilda Grillo and Faith Gillespie, translators of *The Three Marias: New Portuguese*

Letters into English; and Arlie Scott, the primary coordinator for NOW's participation. The group explained the situation to the press, protested the confiscation of the books, the arrest and trial of the authors, and announced plans for protest against the impending trial.

On July 3, the day scheduled for the trial, demonstrations were held before embassies and consulates in France, England, Holland, Belgium, Sweden, and Germany. In the United States protests were held in New York, Washington DC, eastern Massachusetts, Los Angeles, and Houston. Women, men and children marched; they read poetry and excerpts from the book; they wrote letters to the Ambassador from Portugal.

The trial was postponed until October. The reason given was that one of the women was ill with tuberculosis and unfit to stand trial. Eventually, the three women were released, their book published in the United States, and they came to the United States on a lecture tour.

As a result of the conference, Wilma was invited to Sweden at the expense of the Swedish government as a part of its national program for "Opinion Builders." Wilma enthusiastically accepted. Sandy Byrd, a NOW member who worked for Trans World Airlines, made the travel arrangements and decided to accompany Wilma. She felt Wilma needed a travel consultant and a "manager" – as all "important people" have. About the same time, two other friends of Wilma's, Connecticut NOW members, decided to accompany her at their own expense. They were Judy Pickering and Betty Spaulding. Betty Spaulding was coordinating the NOW Task Force on Marriage, Divorce and Family Relations. Judy Pickering, a systems consultant with Univac, had played a major role in gaining ratification of the ERA in Connecticut.

When they landed in Sweden, they were met at the airport by a government representative with flowers, Swedish money, a limousine and driver. Their Swedish interpreter became quite friendly and took Wilma and Sandy home with her for a visit while Betty and Judy were off sight-seeing.

For ten days, they toured the country, met with feminist and labor organizations and government people. Wilma was ceremoniously presented with a key to the city of Stockholm. At the American Embassy, the four led a gathering in singing "I Am Woman." It was enthusiastic, if not very melodious; it did serve to break through some of the formality of the Embassy receptions.

The 1975 conference did not occur. Wilma met with Berit Äs when she visited the United States in 1974. She told Wilma that she was unable to continue chairing the continuing committee. Other commitments and lack of funds made it too difficult. Wilma gathered there were philosophical differences in the committee that would have required a great deal of time and energy to resolve. They were all aware of the forthcoming meeting in Mexico City as a part of International Women's Year (IWY), which would provide the opportunity to discuss issues and accomplish some of their original goals.

In 1975 Wilma flew to Mexico City to attend, unofficially, the International Women's Year Conference planned by the United Nations. There she helped protest, successfully, the decision to hold a follow-up conference in Iran. Wilma had been in correspondence with Iranian women urging her not to be misled by the Shah's "reforms." The conference was later changed to Denmark.

Even though Wilma could not attend, she donated money so that others could attend the first "International Tribunal on Crimes Against Women."[8] Over 2,000 women from over 40 countries attended the Tribunal in Brussels, Belgium, on March 4-8, 1976. They gave testimony, participated in workshops, and proposed a variety of ways of maintaining solidarity and eliminating crimes against women.

Building Sisterhood across Income Lines

NOW addressed poverty in at least three ways – actions to move toward its elimination, actions of sisterhood that transcended class, and development of a philosophical and analytic framework. Actions of economic change were many and generally had to occur by connecting economic injustice with sexism and through implementing policy. One way to address poverty was to provide support services, particularly child care, for women working outside the home. To make child care available meant addressing sexist and classist assumptions about women's roles among policy-makers and among child care professionals.

In 1970, when a White House Conference on Children was announced, Florence Dickler, then coordinator of NOW's task force on child care, brought information about the conference to Wilma's attention. Since no one from NOW had been invited to attend as part of the program, Florence, Wilma and others had first to discover the means by which one was selected as a delegate and then to determine what means to use to become a part of the program. Elizabeth Duncan Koontz was helpful in this regard. Wilma obtained some preliminary papers; she and Carol Burris read and wrote a critique of them. They cited the lack of women in planning, particularly feminists. They deplored – calling it an obscenity – men's deciding matters they knew very little about in any experiential way. They described the sexist value structure that poured money into highways and defense and denied it to programs that could enhance the welfare of women and children, and analyzed the sexist biases in the child care programs themselves.[9,p.306]

At the last minute Carol could not attend the White House Conference with Wilma, ironically for lack of child care for her son, and Wilma went to Washington alone from Pittsburgh. There she helped form and chaired the women's caucus, working out common cause with minority caucuses. She also established ties with the Day Care and Child Development Council of America.

The caucuses brought pressure to bear on the conference planners. In response, one plenary session was set aside to be chaired by the caucuses. It was designed as a consciousness-raising session on the need for good child care to be a higher national commitment. Further, the caucuses brought to the planners a statement on the need for quality day care, which included an end to sexist and racist stereotyping in the care of children.

NOW had a task force on poverty from the beginning; its first coordinator was Dr. Anna Arnold Hedgeman, a Black woman and a social worker. During Wilma's chair of the Board and presidency of NOW, Merrillee Dolan and then Dorothy Haener coordinated the task force on poverty. Both were white women; Dolan came from a poor working class family in the south and Haener was active in the Auto Workers Union.

When Wilma became president of NOW, she worked with and supported the Task Force of Women and Poverty. Merrillee Dolan, a botanist from New Mexico, described herself as "young and inexperienced" at that time, but she knew something of poverty. Her father had died when she was young, and her mother had worked long hours, barely scraping by. Merrillee worked from the time she was thirteen, and at fourteen had a clerking job, working with older women who had families to support on the same amount of money Merrillee was making. When her mother remarried, Merrillee was shocked at what happened. Her stepfather was an alcoholic Air Force man, who grudgingly gave his wife money. Merrillee recalls her mother begging for change to buy a lipstick. As a young woman, Merrillee worked with a Model Cities neighborhood program in Albuquerque, where she saw ethnic groups fighting each other and competing for resources, and she felt that those who were suffering were being left out.

Merrillee knew about poverty first-hand; she knew how women could be thrown into it as well as born or raised in it; she knew also something of the socialization that enforced patterns of economic and psychological dependence. When Betty Friedan asked for a volunteer for the Task Force on Women in Poverty at the Atlanta Conference in 1968, Merrillee volunteered.

As Task Force coordinator, she published a newsletter that sought to raise the consciousness of NOW members, inform them of legislation and actions around the country, and enlist their participation. She kept herself abreast of legislation and testified on legislation affecting mothers with dependent children, Aid for Dependent Children (AFDC). In her testimony, she tried to show Congress that women on welfare are in a "catch-22" situation. The working poor and the welfare poor are to a significant extent the same group, and it is extremely difficult ever to get beyond that subsistence level. The poor, therefore, learn to take advantage of the system for survival and then are blamed for being lazy and "welfare chislers."

Merrillee also wrote a critique of Daniel Moynihan's approach to poverty while he was a chief architect for Nixon's "family assistance" program. Merrillee's paper (unpublished) entitled "Moynihan, Poverty Program and Women: A Female Viewpoint," was a critique documenting the sexism in Moynihan's approach and his assumption that the white, middle-class nuclear family with all its sex-role stereotyping should be the norm for families in this country.

In February 1973, NOW designated that year its action year against poverty. At the national conference, Merrillee succeeded in changing the name of the Task Force from Women *in* Poverty to Women *and* Poverty, since she felt poverty was an issue that potentially affected every woman economically and psychologically dependent on men. She also secured a commitment from NOW to hire someone to work full time in Washington on poverty issues. At the conference, NOW pledged to work to increase the minimum wage to at least $2.50 an hour (it currently was $1.90) and to extend coverage to all workers, particularly domestics. It also pledged to support the Farah and Farmworkers' boycotts.[10] As a part of NOW's pledge to increase and extend the coverage of the minimum wage, Dorothy Haener and Kee Hall, also of the Poverty Task Force, testified before the House Labor subcommittee of the Education and Labor Committee on HR 4757, a bill which supported increasing and extending coverage of the minimum wage. A report from Kee Hall on June 15, 1973, announced that the bill had passed as a result of a major coalition effort, including support from Congresswomen. "So strong was their stand that the issue of coverage of domestics was never even contested on the floor."[11]

In the summer of 1973, Wilma herself testified before the Joint Economic Committee's hearings on "economic problems of women." Characteristically, she turned the topic around and listed example after example of sexism in government agencies which perpetuate the reasons why women have economic problems. She cited sexist language which omits women from the consciousness of the Small Business Administration, funding and programs aimed at men and omitting women, and failures to enforce laws prohibiting sex discrimination. Her point was that women are in effect systematically denied access to what resources are available. Their poverty is significantly maintained through sexism.

Since 1970, NOW had held demonstrations each year on August 26 to commemorate the ratification of 14th amendment of the U.S. constitution guaranteeing women's suffrage and to remind all of us how far we still had to come. In 1970, Betty Armistead from Florida had written Betty Friedan about the idea of a nationwide strike on August 26. Friedan took the idea to the March 1970 NOW conference and it was accepted.

For its 1973 celebration, NOW decided to demonstrate support and solidarity with the Farah and Farmworkers' strikers.[12,p.50] Farah made clothing, mostly pants. Farah workers were non-unionized and most Farah employees were women. Similarly, many of the Farmworkers were women and minority men and also non-unionized.

NOW chapters were urged to find out what stores in their areas were supporting the strikes and which were not. Members then boycotted those who opposed the strikes. The public was informed of what were Farah products and under what names they were sold, and asked to inform Farah and store owners of reasons for the boycott.

In spite of such efforts, however, according to a study of NOW's activities with respect to issues of poverty, only ten percent of the actions NOW took that year addressed poverty.[11] It seemed to many of those most interested in and committed to at least ameliorating conditions of poverty that it was difficult for NOW to maintain the issue of poverty as a priority. In early 1972, Merrillee Dolan wrote a letter to the Executive Committee that expressed some of her frustration:

> It is difficult to belong to an organization which has a rank and file membership which, at a Conference, sees no need for a Workshop on Women in Poverty. Two people (myself and Therese Conant, Pres., Albuquerque Chapter) felt it important. The new President [Wilma] stated she was appalled at this response. Apparently the membership of the Board is not appalled. In fact, one Board Member stated that a guaranteed income was a "poor people's issue" – not a women's issue ... More women need a guaranteed income than an ERA, because a guaranteed income will do a greater good for the greater number of women.[11]

Similarly, in 1973 Aileen Hernandez wrote to Dorothy Haener (the new Poverty Task Force Coordinator) and expressed concern that NOW would not implement its conference resolutions on poverty.[12,p.51] Aileen, Wilma, and the Task Force Coordinators nevertheless kept poverty issues before the Board and NOW membership. When Merrillee was coordinator, she saw as part of her responsibility that of educating the organization. She wrote for a national NOW publication, *Do It Now*, and arranged for meetings between Board members and poor women. When Dorothy Haener succeeded her, she continued Merrillee's work. A woman who had little formal education beyond high school and who worked with United Auto Workers, Dorothy identified with those less affluent and often less educated. She continued to bring poverty issues before NOW, particularly those issues concerning women working outside the home. She worked on analyses of who actually receives welfare and demonstrated that corporations, railroads, highways, etc. receive by far the largest amount of federal money, not the poor. She supported and reinforced NOW's stand in support of a guaranteed annual income, a stand taken in 1970. A union organizer, she also helped raise feminist consciousness among women and men in the unions.

In addition to supporting the Task Force, Wilma worked individually on poverty issues and sexism. She worked with Elizabeth Duncan Koontz, Director of the Women's Bureau, on several occasions, including the Jubilee (50th) conference of the Bureau. Over 800 women attended – women of color, women of all classes, leaders of a wide variety of women's caucuses. Through such activities ground was broken to shift the Bureau's focus away from union-related issues to women-related issues which continued to include union concerns.

In addition to addressing poverty, Wilma and the Task Force sought to open NOW to more active participation within the organization by poor women and to stronger expressions of support of and solidarity with the poor. One action taken in 1973 was to begin reimbursing expenses for officers and National Board members so that people with few financial resources could have a better chance to become leaders. Prior to 1973, NOW reimbursed only those expenses it felt it could. The use of private resources and "piggybacking" on other travel and activities had often made the difference in whether NOW and its programs and meetings happened at all. NOW also adopted a sliding fee scale in 1973 – from zero to ten dollars annually, and encouraged more affluent members to contribute more as "scholarship" money so the organization could meet its financial commitments.

Wilma and the Task Force coordinators sought to strengthen NOW's expression of support and solidarity with the poor by forming ties with other groups working on poverty issues. In 1973, Wilma wrote the National Welfare Rights Organization (NWRO) seeking coalition between the NWRO and NOW. A few instances of cooperative action and demonstrations of mutual support followed.

In a report to the Board on November 4, 1973, Wilma referred to the NWRO as an organization whose orientation was becoming more feminist and as:

> having serious financial difficulties. I recommend that as an indication of our sisterhood and brotherhood we ask NOW members via *Do It Now* to contribute as able to 'Friends of NWRO' ... This could be part of our priority commitment to 'Action on Poverty.'[11]

There should be no strings attached, she argued, since the NWRO knew better than NOW how the money should be used. The Board refused to support Wilma's recommendation primarily because it was fearful of setting a precedent it might not wish to continue.

Other actions of advocacy concerned health care. A policy in Alabama, for instance, permitted the sterilization of young, poor, often minority mentally retarded women. In 1973, two young teenagers had been sterilized. Aged 12 and 14, their mother had given "consent by signing an X on a form she could not read."[13,p.47] Outraged by such practices, Wilma turned to the ACLU. A suit was filed against Alabama. The ACLU, along with the NAACP, the Southern Poverty Law Center, and other organizations, were plaintiffs. As a result, the government began to develop more stringent regulations on sterilization and the meaning of "informed consent."

Another concern was medical experimentation on women. In 1972, Merrillee Dolan called Wilma's attention to information about the research a Dr. Joseph Goldheizer was conducting on poor women in San Antonio,

Texas. A gynecologist, he had been working in a clinic which provided contraceptive services. As women came into the clinic, he gave seventy-six of them placeboes without their knowledge, instead of contraceptives, and also a cream which he told them to use. After four months, ten of the seventy-six had become pregnant.

> When questioned about his procedures, Goldheizer replied, "If you think you can explain a placebo test to women like these, you never met Mrs. Gomez from the West Side."[13,p.45]

Wilma was outraged, as were many others, including: the Third World Women's Caucus; Feminist Women's Health Centers; the Institute of Society, Ethics, and the Life Sciences; and a few physicians. Robert Veach, director of the Institute of Society, Ethics, and the Life Sciences, published a report in which he seriously questioned the relation between Goldheizer and the U.S. Agency for International Development. All the organizations protested, but so far as I know, Goldheizer continued to do this research, funded by *public* monies.

In 1973, Wilma and Dorothy Haener wrote a proposal to NOW's Legal Defense and Education Fund, entitled "Poverty, Thy Name is Woman." The purposes of the proposal were to educate the public and specific agencies about poverty and sexism, and to work toward change. The proposal was not funded. Wilma thought a primary reason for the denial was that the Fund's focus was not on poverty.

There are several reasons why it was difficult to build sisterhood across class lines, difficulties that still exist. NOW was appropriately suspicious of the sexism in many anti-poverty groups. At a May 1979 Board meeting to which he was invited, for instance, the late Dr. George Wiley, then head of the National Welfare Rights Organization, was reported to have said that one of his goals was the restoration of the Black male back into his rightful place as the "head of the house." Such a comment initially did little to generate cooperation between the two organizations; Wiley eventually did change his approach. Many people concerned with poverty and minority issues simply did not identify themselves as feminists nor saw "women's issues" as a high priority.

A factor that influenced NOW's response to poverty issues was the difficulty of perceiving the classism (and racism) among its own membership. It was difficult for many white, middle income members to see that their demands were not yet the demands of all women. Women were discriminated against, women were oppressed. But the discrimination and oppression of a businesswoman was different in significant ways from that of a suburban homemaker and both were different in significant ways from that of a sugar beet field worker or a mother receiving Aid for Dependent Children.

Perhaps the difficulty in addressing poverty issues was reflected in and reinforced by defining the issue as *poverty* rather than *classism* or defining it only as *poverty* and not as *classism* also. To call attention to class would be directly to call attention to middle class women's relative perspective, and at that period in NOW's development the emphasis was on calling attention to the *demands* in the perspective, not on their relativity.

Wilma, the Poverty Task Force, and other individuals continued to press for more concentrated attention to the ways in which those issues had disproportionate and devastating impact on the lives of poor women. Nevertheless, NOW's effort to transcend the differences of class, often a chasm of differences, had barely begun.

Building Sisterhood to Transcend Racism

The story of Wilma's and NOW's work to transcend racism is similar to the work to transcend poverty. Although to equate class and race issues is racist itself, it is also the case that much of the work done to transcend class is integrally related to racism. There were specific efforts to overcome racism and seek solidarity between white women and women and men of color.

Racism, like classism, has been a fact and a curse of American life. It has been and still is a pervasive feature. It is structural, or systemic, expressed in exploitation and in denying some people access to power and to resources this country makes available to others. It is also personal, expressed through our tendency to stereotype in a negatively prejudicial fashion and through sheer ignorance of one group about another. It is to be expected that racism would be present in NOW; at the same time there were efforts to overcome it. The presence of some Black women among its founders and on the first Board, Aileen Hernandez as its second president, Wilma with her background and insights, and the presence of countless members who had been active in civil rights organizations all helped to make NOW relatively more sensitive to racism within its own membership. There was an awareness of some of the differences between minority and white women, and concern to work on issues common to all women in this culture.

As with classism and poverty, racism had to be addressed both within NOW and in the larger society. Following the 1973 conference, the Task Force on Minority Women and Women's Rights sent out a questionnaire to chapters to gather information about the presence of racism within the organization.[14] Sixty-seven chapters responded. Five chapters reported a Task Force on Minority Women and Women's Rights; thirty-one reported coalitions with minority organizations.

Women of color were members of NOW, but most indicated relatively little involvement in the organization. The reasons cited included lack of time and lack of clarity about NOW's purposes. In summary, the Report of the Task Force stated that "all minority respondents and most non-minority respondents felt, witnessed, or experienced (minority respondents) some racism within NOW."[14]

Sometimes the reality of this summary was seen in conflicts that erupted. In Minnesota, for instance, a new chapter was formed in part because of controversy and suspicion around issues of race. A Denver, Colorado chapter had a Task Force on Minority Women and Women's Rights, and was one of the first chapters to adopt the national resolution on minority women and women's rights. But in early 1974, the Task Force withdrew from the Colorado chapter in frustration over conflicts that had emerged.

Many people within NOW continued to work to sensitize the organization and make it responsive to the needs and interests of all women. At the 1973 NOW conference, for instance, a minority caucus was held. Twenty-six women and men explored "the relevance of NOW to Third World Concerns."[15] At that time Aileen Hernandez and Eleanor Spikes became co-chairs of the Task Force on Minority Women and Women's Rights, and through the Task Force sought to address manifestations of racism within the organization. They sought to overcome racism in NOW by seeking the involvement of more women of color for leadership positions, eliminating racist assumptions or statements in organizational literature, and educating members about prejudice and stereotyping.

A somewhat different approach was taken by others. From New York, Elena Alperin wrote Wilma, "I want to bring MY WOMEN, MY LATIN SISTERS into the best Organization for Women in the World."[16] She began setting up committees to accomplish that purpose, met with Latina women, interpreted to white women some of the difficulties Latina women faced in attending chapter meetings, and translated NOW literature into Spanish. In a letter to Aileen Hernandez, Alperin wrote that it:

> is the center of my life to bring women together;
> it does not matter where they are coming from ...
> it does not matter the color of her skin or the
> shape of her body, or anything ...
> Maybe I am a dreamer, but my dreams are a true future ... [17]

Money for Alperin's work came largely from herself initially. But then in a later letter to Aileen, she wrote that her husband was seeking a divorce. "He can't take anymore the person I am 'now'." She was no longer able to pay the expenses of her work by herself and sought money from the Task Force and/or the Board. Unfortunately only a small amount was forthcoming.

Wilma supported and encouraged the Task Force and individual members addressing issues of racism. In addition, Wilma worked with the Board to address racism, as was illustrated by her frustrated efforts to include minority women in the ad campaign. In another instance Aileen had sought from the Board a statement urging that Angela Davis receive a fair trial. Wilma supported this action, and the Board did issue such a statement. Wilma sought Board support for continuing school desegregation policies. The Board, however, decided that school desegregation was not a feminist issue and did not make a statement.

Wilma also supported and even encouraged minority women to form their own organizations. In the summer of 1973, the National Black Feminist Organization was founded in part by women who had been involved in NOW and the women's movement. The founders included Margaret Sloan, an editor of *Ms. Magazine*; Doris Wright, a member of New York NOW; and Eleanor Holmes Norton, a friend of Wilma's, a civil liberties lawyer and a feminist. When Wright talked with Wilma about the idea for a Black Feminist organization, Wilma's response was "swell," and she wrote a letter of sisterhood and welcome to the new organization. The National Black Feminist Organization stated: "Our above ground presence will lend enormous credibility to the current Women's Liberation Movement, which unfortunately is not seen as the serious political and economic revolutionary force that it is."[18]

Wilma continued to seek and establish liaison with other organizations working for racial justice – with caucuses, with minority organizations, and with federal agencies. At the same time a significant amount of her time and energy went into educating those groups about the reality and immediate presence of sexism, and she was not afraid to challenge them.

We have already seen something of the task Wilma and other NOW people performed with the EEOC to increase its understanding of and sensitivity to sexism. In similar fashion, they worked with the U.S. Commission on Civil Rights. Fortunately there were usually feminists, friends, or at least supporters of feminism who worked within the Commission on Civil Rights to whom they could turn. Whitney Adams, who worked with NOW on the AT&T case, worked with the Commission on Civil Rights. Carol Kumersfield was Director of the Women's Rights Division of the Commission on Civil Rights. Leslie Wolf was Deputy Director of the Women's Rights Division. Such women as these worked with the staff responsible for implementing the Commission's jurisdiction over sex discrimination for which NOW had lobbied and provided research and technical assistance to the Commission. They were in close communication with NOW, as well as other feminist organizations, and often served as a liaison between feminist groups and the Commission. During the time they were working with Wilma, the Commission invited someone each year to serve as a visiting scholar-in-residence as a resource for its research and programs. Leslie Wolf urged the Commission to select Wilma specifically to work with the Commission to connect racism and sexism. The Commission, however, refused on the grounds that she did not have a doctorate.

In addition to working with organizations, challenging them, seeking common ground with them, and sharing ideas and values on a personal level, Wilma's primary role in addressing racism, sexism, and the connections between them was through speeches, writing, media interviews, and initiation of projects.

A presentation Wilma gave to the First Black Women's Institute illustrates her approach to the connectedness between racism and sexism. The Institute was sponsored by the National Council of Negro Women (NCNW) and the topic was Hunger. After acknowledging the pluralism of attitudes among

Black women about feminism and sisterhood with white women, Wilma proceeded to ask:

> ...how much racism may be a manifestation of sexism? How much horrendous institutionalized white racist violence has been perpetuated in the bodies and spirits of black people in the name of keeping supposedly inviolate ...the "sanctity" and "purity" of the white woman ...Meantime, the black woman has been fair game for any [white] man ...Sexism and racism are equally anti-human. In all candor, I am convinced that racism will not substantially cease till sexism is eradicated.[19,p.3-4]

She went on to say, "I will not define *for* any other person ...their liberation priorities."[19,p.4] And then she continued:

> Some of you may not yet see me as your sister. I believe, however, that at least as much as the brotherhood of men do we need the sisterhood of all women and together to create the fully integrated human family.[19,p.4]

It was certainly so then and it continued to be a difficult message to hear. In 1975 after her NOW presidency when she was a guest-in-residence at Wellesley College, a group of Black and Hispanic women students asked what feminism could contribute to the Black liberation struggle. Wilma sat down at her desk that evening and made a list of forty-seven contributions by feminists to human rights for all, and presented it in a speech.[20] The list included:

- strengthening the EEOC, including strengthening its legislative mandates and funding.
- working with other civil rights agencies to challenge broadcasters' licenses, educating and pressing the Federal Communications Commission and Broadcasters.
- working with other civil rights agencies for child care.
- supporting and advocating a guaranteed annual income.
- working with other civil rights agencies on affirmative action cases – AT&T, U.S. Steel, General Mills, Sears, etc.
- advocating the right of reproductive choice, opposing the sterilization of poor, young, and often minority women.
- advocating open housing, equal education; opposing Nixon's so-called welfare reform.
- working for more effective implementation and enforcement of various Executive Orders prohibiting discrimination in all included areas.
- working with women in prison.
- supporting more democratic health care policies and self-help movements.
- opposing and exposing sexist and racist policies of United Fund agencies in the U.S.
- generating and supporting more effective work by the Women's Bureau of the U.S. Labor Department.

Wilma concluded with the wry-angry statement, "The news does not yet accurately, fully, or knowledgeably report the contributions of the feminist movement, including minority feminists to the human rights work in this nation." [20] That doesn't mean the work hasn't happened or isn't happening. Those who know her can hear her saying, "and I've hardly even cleared my throat," by which she would mean both that there is more to tell and that there is much, much more to be done.

Often such speeches broke through at least some barriers. People listened and responded positively. They embraced her and on more than one occasion gave her a standing ovation. As early as 1970, speaking at the International Association of Official Human Rights Agencies, she received a standing ovation. Similarly, at an Urban Research Corporation conference in Chicago, Dr. Jeanne Noble of the National Council of Negro Women asked Wilma to clarify what NOW had done for Black women and invited her to join the Council in a press conference. Wilma quickly accepted the invitation.

Building Sisterhood to Transcend Heterosexism

A final area to explore in building sisterhood is that between heterosexual women and lesbian women. Some NOW members did not see heterosexism as relevant; others viewed it as a political albatross, one that would further discredit the movement; and still others shared the cultural ignorance and/or fear of sexuality in general and homosexuality in particular. But like poverty and racism, heterosexism emerged as the feminist issue it has always been.

It was an inevitable conclusion that issues of sexual or affectional preference and related questions facing lesbian women were feminist issues. Clearly, certain other aspects of sexuality were feminist issues. Issues concerning gender and sex-role stereotyping, women's control over our bodies, the interest and need to know about female sexuality on its own terms (not derivative of our knowledge about male sexuality), and the movement toward alternative health care had all been an intrinsic part of the new wave of feminism. Feminists understood both that women have to know about our bodies if we are to avoid patriarchal control over them, and that patterns of understanding, expectations, and control were all rooted in sexist assumptions about men and women. Within that context, two further questions were raised: what were the responsibilities of feminist organizations for lesbian and gay rights, and to what extent were cultural assumptions about and the practice of heterosexual relationships themselves oppressive?

These questions may have been inevitable, but to many they were also frightening. About 1968, as the issue of heterosexism was just being raised in NOW, Wilma discussed it with Gene Boyer, a founding member of NOW and a long-time friend of Wilma's. In conversation with me, Gene observed that once Wilma concluded that it was a feminist matter, she went ahead characteristically with full support.[21] Again, Wilma thought principle must determine policy, not the reverse. Gene added that in her eyes, the support of lesbian and gay rights was one of the two most critical decisions NOW made during the first five years.[22]

Wilma viewed heterosexism as a feminist question for several reasons. First, it was a matter of individual rights. Both as a feminist and as a person long concerned about individual rights, she was sensitive to the question of lesbian and gay rights. In 1969, while working at the American Institute for Research, she had discovered that the Institute had a major national study that included aspects of homosexuality in which the assumption was made that homosexuality was pathological. She had been outraged and had sought to change it – unsuccessfully and with resentment from the project staff.

Heterosexism was a feminist issue also for the reason that as an intrinsic part of other questions about sexuality, it was profoundly related to women's quest for identity and self definition. Heterosexism was a feminist issue because it involved women's relating to women. "It's absurd to say that women should love the agents of oppression and not their own sisters," Wilma stated in response to criticism. Women should be free to love one another, whatever form the expression of that love might take.

In a meeting in New York in 1970, Wilma was told that some lesbian women were soliciting straight women, that the latter were annoyed and yet fearful of being called prejudiced if they protested. At the same time, there were lesbian women who were hurt by the stereotyping and felt afraid to confront the straight women; both came to Wilma and asked if she could find a forum to raise the issues they felt unable to address. Wilma agreed that fears, uncertainties, suspicions and stereotypes, unaddressed, too often interfered with moving toward sisterhood. It was important to clear the air, to create a climate wherein women would have the courage to challenge other women about actions some considered offensive without being perceived as rejecting the other as a person.

Wilma and others, therefore, began pressing the Board to include discussions of sexuality on its agenda. Eventually the executive committee, whose responsibility it was to determine the National Conference Program, agreed to hold a workshop at the 1971 conference. To those who argued that the issue of heterosexism was politically too much of a liability, Wilma responded that they could not allow others outside the movement to determine their agenda and issues. Further, she stated, the very controversialness of it meant that:

> we've struck a nerve and that it's an issue that needs to be faced.
> Yes, there's a risk to it, but so what else is new? We simply have to
> do it and have the courage of our convictions.[23]

The workshop was led by Del Martin and Phyllis Lyons.[24] It drew a large number of participants, and their response was enthusiastic. According to Wilma, Lucy Komisar, who had been vice president for Public Relations and one who had been negative about the idea, said that the workshop turned her around. Workshop participants formulated resolutions that were overwhelmingly passed by the conference. One of the resolutions acknowledged NOW's previous silence on lesbianism, the exploitation and oppression of lesbians and particularly lesbian mothers, the controversial nature of a stand supporting lesbians, and fears about being "labelled lesbian." Nevertheless, they also said:

> We are giving notice that we recognize our sisterhood with all women and that we are fighting for every woman's "sacred right to her own person." As feminists, we can do no less ...[25]

and concluded that each woman has the right "to define and express her own sexuality and to choose her own lifestyle," that "the oppression of lesbians is a legitimate concern of feminism," and that "NOW commits itself to offering legal and moral support in a test case involving custody rights of mothers who are also lesbians."[25]

In a letter to Wilma from Sidney Abbott the following winter, Abbott referred to the "fine resolution adopted last fall in Los Angeles" and thought it was stronger than statements by groups devoted primarily to ending discrimination toward homosexual people.[26]

Before and during the 1971 NOW conference, media people of both sexes predicted that issues about sexuality in general and lesbianism in particular would "split" NOW. At a following press conference, Wilma knew there would be considerable focus on the Sexuality Resolution, which the media called the Lesbian Resolution, and on herself as the newly elected NOW president. She was right. Early in the press conference, as Wilma summarized the many important conference resolutions, she noted that there were lesbian women and gay men in NOW, in the feminist movement, in the news media, in PTA's, in Chambers of Commerce, in government, in churches, and *everywhere* else. The difference was that NOW was being honest and that she saw the NOW resolution as principled action and leadership to "educate ourselves and this nation about the full potential of human sexuality." Then she moved from sexuality politics to the politics and resolutions of other issues NOW had addressed. With the Sexuality Resolution, NOW became the first national organization not focused exclusively on gay rights to openly support lesbian and gay efforts to eliminate discrimination and prejudice.

Some people were upset. A few months later, Wilma received a call from a chapter president in Colorado, informing Wilma that a state legislator who had supported the ERA was going to hold a press conference rescinding her support because of NOW's stand on homosexuality. Wilma checked out the story and then called the legislator collect, as she says:

> for political reasons. This woman had initiated the possible action and I felt she should pay for it. I thought if she accepted a collect call (she did) that acceptance might also signal that she realized how vulnerable she was and also confirm my intuition that she wanted some attention from a "national officer" and acknowledgement for her ERA support.[23]

Wilma and the legislator talked at some length, and Wilma told her that she would send some material about why NOW took the stand it did. Wilma added:

> in justice to yourself, read this material, because from what I understand you're acting from an uninformed or partially informed basis ... Then if you still think it is the right thing to do, go ahead, but in all honesty you should know it will not go unanswered. I don't want you to take that as a threat because it isn't. It's a promise.[23]

The press conference was not held.

Following the workshop at the 1971 conference, a Task Force on Sexuality and Lesbianism was created. Two coordinators were chosen: Jayne Vogan who was not a lesbian but was knowledgeable and sensitive about the issues involved, and Sidney Abbott who was openly lesbian. Their responsibility was to carry out the resolution in all its implications. They monitored and testified about legislation on state and local levels. They led a continuing educational process within NOW itself about the full potential of human sexuality. They led and facilitated coalition-building with other organizations addressing the elimination of oppression of lesbian and gay people. And they worked on understanding and making others aware of connections between sexism and sexual attitudes.

Ad-ministering (to) the Revolution

As president of NOW, Wilma shared considerable major responsibilities and opportunities, some designated to her by NOW By-Laws, others chosen by her. These included organization maintenance and development, chapter development, achieving organizational purposes, developing philosophies and translating them into action programs, and implementing NOW policies as expressed in conference resolutions.

Wilma accepted, deferred to others, initiated, and/or helped initiate speaking engagements and NOW's participation in non-NOW conferences; she participated in generating caucuses and position statements; she pressed for legislation and its enforcement; with task force representatives and others, she met with community, business, political and other groups. In meetings, she was insistent, sometimes embarrassing in the eyes of both those she was with and those who were in conflict with her. But she was not acrimonious, and she did not try to make people feel guilty. She focused consistently on the issue at hand, not on personalities or generalized attacks on people's sexism, classism, racism, and/or ageism.

In the internal workings of NOW and Wilma's participation, there was a similar pattern with some different emphases. Her shared responsibilities for national conferences were many. They added up to ensuring that the conferences ran as smoothly as possible. At both the 1973 and 1974

Wilma Scott Heide during NOW presidency.

conferences she was invited to be the keynote speaker, a NOW tradition. She was responsible for seeing that the business of the conferences was done, although on occasion she turned the actual work of chairing sessions over to someone else as a way of sharing experiences. Some of the time was spent meeting with individuals and groups to hear complaints, responding to appeals to use her influence in one way or another, and greeting friends.

Working with chapters was a deep joy and sometimes a deep frustration for her. The frustrations arose from responding to complaints and mediating conflicts. Members continually wrote or phoned Wilma with grievances, threatening to resign or resigning because NOW had gone too far or not far enough, or because they objected to the means being used. In particular, stands on reproductive rights, sexual preference, and interestingly, the ERA brought such letters. Here are a few excerpts:

> Dear Wilma Scott Heide,
>
> Today I received your plea for help. I'm glad I got it, because I didn't really know what Women's Lib [sic] stood for. Now I do and I don't like it. [27]

Dear Ms. Heide:

I was a recipient of your NOW letter concerning the Equal Rights Amendment.

Let me say that I am in complete sympathy with the Women's Rights Movement and the Equal Rights Amendment. I was writing columns [newspaper] in Chicago on these issues more than 35 years ago.

However, it irks me to no end that NOW does not take very definite stands on all the fringe movements that are trying to latch on to the women's movement – fringes with their own axes to grind and that do not have any legitimate right with the real issues of the women's movement ...[28]

Dear Ms. Heide and the Treasurer:

It is dues time and I am withdrawing my membership after 2 years of belonging here in Cincinnati. I'd like to tell you why I feel maybe I can do better in the League of Women Voters ...[29]

Letters like these reflected real differences of perception of what the movement was about as well as of the appropriate means to achieve its goals. They were answered and served not to change NOW's stands, but to remind Wilma that all must work to interpret the movement so that it could make sense and be acceptable to women everywhere.

In addition, there were tensions inherent in the movement itself which sparked conflict. The chapters, as well as the movement, were composed primarily of women, many of whom had little political experience, who were idealistic and then sometimes disillusioned, who were frightened by the uncharted territory they were moving into, and who sometimes sought in their sisters a nurturing they felt they had not received elsewhere. Such emotions were intense, not always identified, and not always directed toward institutional and cultural change.

A lot of women are looking for a mother, someone to nurture us as we are, an unconditional love, unconditional in feminist terms: we're saying we're angry and we hurt, we insist on some change; we haven't had a language to communicate that, and we haven't had a people who understood. Or if they did, it was too threatening and they couldn't – it's not that our mothers didn't have the capacity to understand, but they were systematically prevented from understanding.[30]

Wilma responded to feelings and conflicts in several ways. She sought to identify the principles involved and to seek agreement on the principle if possible. If agreement on principle was not possible, she sought to mediate the conflict in some other way. At the same time, she encouraged individuals to develop and express their own insights and to have confidence in them. Joan Israel of Detroit NOW spoke of the way Wilma "listened to her seriously."[31]

Jacqui Ceballos of New York NOW recalled that she "gave me faith in myself." [32]

Most letters to Wilma were not negative. Some sought help from her or the organization. In one letter from a woman in Missouri, apparently in response to a newspaper article about NOW, Wilma was commended for her work; then the writer continued:

> Mrs. Heide, Missouri is one of the worst offenders in recognizing the fact that women do have some God given rights ... The Bible states explicitly that man is entitled to pay for his labors. I don't think this means that women are exempt from pay for their labors and should work for nothing more than room and board. This happened to me and I don't think it is right ...
>
> [The state Commission on the Status of Women] are socialite friends who can't stop to see what the working women must put up with ...
>
> Do hope that you will try to introduce some kind of program to help the women here in Missouri ...
>
> Once again, God bless you ... [33]

An ongoing joy for Wilma was personal contact with people. Wilma made herself available to individuals and chapters. When she made speaking engagements, she had the practice of notifying chapters in the area that she would be there, "piggybacking" on the invitation and thus reducing expenses for herself and/or for NOW. Out of such contacts came renewed energy for both Wilma and members, clearer vision and deeper commitment. It was part of that process of synergism, which Theodora Wells named.[34]

Many of the people I interviewed commented specifically on the way in which Wilma and Aileen Hernandez in particular were available for members and respected for their ideas. In 1973, for instance, Mary Lynn Myers, a Board member from South Dakota, reported at a Board meeting that she thought she should resign from the Board. She had recently become director of the state's Human Rights Division, and the chair of the Commission was a "hell-fire and brimstone minister" who learned that she was a "woman's libber." Why he had not realized this before she was hired was difficult to determine since her résumé was sprinkled with references to NOW. Mary Lynn volunteered to resign as coordinator of the Task Force on Compliance since she thought her holding that position and the directorship of the Human Rights Division might be construed as a conflict of interest. But the minister insisted she also resign from the Board. According to Mary Lynn, Wilma and Aileen Hernandez were both especially concerned that the demand violated Mary Lynn's civil liberties and that the implications of the Commission's attitude reflected discrimination on the basis of sex. Wilma and Aileen were influential in getting the Board to refuse to accept her resignation. Wilma also offered to travel to South Dakota and meet with the Commission.

The story of the establishment of NOW in Maine illustrates the way Wilma

Visiting with NOW chapter members, October 1974.

related to local chapters. A large state with a small, largely rural population, Maine had no NOW chapter until 1971 when a couple of women decided to do something about it.[35] One was Ramona Barth, who had been speaking and teaching about feminism around Alna, a small town near the coast, and before that in the Boston area. Ramona wrote Wilma and invited her to come to Maine. The second woman was Eleanor Coffin Robbins, an artist and housemother at a nearby junior college. Eleanor made her house available for Wilma, not sure what she was letting herself in for.

Somewhat to their surprise, Wilma agreed to come and spend a week in Maine. The invitation came at a propitious time. Wilma wanted time for reflection about the NOW presidency and about the possibility of divorce. She also wanted to support feminists in Maine.

On the day she was to arrive, she showed up with a police escort, introduced herself and the officer, and explained that the directions she had been given were wrong. When she turned for help to the police officer, he had simply decided that it was easier to bring her than explain how to get there. Everyone immediately relaxed, and NOW in Maine began on a note of general hilarity.

Wilma spent her mornings at Eleanor's house answering correspondence. Her afternoons and evenings consisted of a variety of activities, involving many different groups of people. She held a TV interview, taking Eleanor with her; she met with the press and confronted the editor with his practice of using sex-segregated want ads. She met with the staff at the YWCA. She spoke with interested people, in Eleanor's words, "shocking people, but to make them think, not just to shock them."

The week culminated with a founding meeting in Portland initiated with a good deal of enthusiasm and some apprehension. Eleanor, Ramona and others "suddenly found ourselves up to our necks in involvement."

In this and other contacts with chapters, Wilma sought to be and was available, making no distinction in her mind between large, politically strong groups and small, more isolated groups. At the same time she sought to involve others in whatever she was doing, so that she could leave with some assurance that they could carry on.

There were many responsibilities and roles that Wilma had in relation to the Board and other officers. Many were the day to day responsibilities of informing and consulting with other Board members, seeking and providing Board consultation. In the process of her contacts with the Board, there were three tasks Wilma deliberately set for herself, and they were ones she felt a good leader should do.

One task was to separate principle from means. Principle, as Wilma used it in this context, was not necessarily a moral principle, although it could be that. Rather, it was the idea, the essence, the *raison d'etre* of whatever was under consideration. She found that often in discussions, people slipped back and forth, unaware, between the principle and ways of executing it. When disagreements arose over the means, or ways of doing something, they were sometimes taken as disagreement over the principle, and such a perception often confused decision-making. For instance, in 1968 some members opposed the ERA because the United Auto Workers did so and the union was providing office space for NOW. Similarly, when a demonstration was proposed that included putting religious veils into a trash can, some opposed the idea because they felt it would alienate some Catholic members. In proposing legislation about education, some felt NOW would lose friends within the schools. In all of these instances, Wilma and other Board members thought that it was important to establish the principle even though the means of implementing it might have some negative consequences. Wilma saw her task to keep the principle, the idea, before the Board, gain consensus on that, and separate that from consideration of how to translate ideas into action.

A second responsibility Wilma set for herself was to broaden the context of discussion. Sometimes this had to be done before a principle could be agreed on. This was the case with respect to the issue of heterosexism, for instance, and to some extent with the issue of poverty. When feminism was narrowly understood as equality for women or justice for women vis-à-vis men, issues such as heterosexism or poverty were seen as not relevant. In contrast, Wilma sought to help others see that the values and assumptions within sexism had shaped attitudes and policy toward virtually every subject involving human beings. It was, in Wilma's view, the responsibility of feminists to understand the connections between sexism and the issue under consideration and also to explore feminist alternatives. Then questions of sexuality became feminist concerns, as did poverty, war and peace and violence, United States international assistance programs and policies, and a host of other subjects. Much of the time, Wilma was particularly successful in these endeavors; it was part of the charismatic quality of her leadership that she stretched people's minds.

A third task she saw particularly incumbent on a leader was to help direct energy away from fighting one another and toward changing society. The tremendous amount of justified anger and energy within the movement sometimes spilled over into confrontation and hostility toward one another. The phenomenon of *trashing* became one expression of this. Trashing was the practice of, in effect, excommunicating a person who was not considered sufficiently feminist or loyal. It was a verbal and public condemnation of that person. Even when the anger stopped short of trashing, it could still pit women against one another with charge and counter-charge flying back and forth.

Sometimes, problems could be avoided by helping people to identify their common ground, sometimes by encouraging members to think through the broader implications of feminism. Sometimes Wilma's approach was to focus attention on feminism as a process as well as an ideology. Sometimes, to use her phrase, "we had to agree to disagree" and get on with the business. Sometimes people agreed to compromise. But as NOW grew rapidly, it attracted people with the idealism of its feminist position, as well as people who were angry and became angrier as their awareness increased. The temptation to trash, to see one's own position as pure and others' as "deviant" remained strong, and on more than one occasion seriously hindered the functioning of the still fledgling organization.

Gene Boyer saw the decision to do direct mailing one of the two most critical decisions NOW made, because the mailings brought in all kinds of people with their own perceptions of what feminism and the movement were about, each with their own priorities. It fell largely upon Wilma's shoulders to hold all of those differences together and get some work done – and to do it at the same time as encouraging members to develop their own ideas and creativity. Sally Hacker observed that:

> again and again in large meetings, where people were having difficulty, Wilma cut through the conceptual level or suggested some practical thing to do at that time. That charactersitic of leadership, coordinatorship, whatever, is one of her most outstanding characteristics.[36]

As conflict surfaced over the range of issues that members wished to address, some feared energy would be deflected away from more narrowly understood women's issues. Again according to Sally:

> Wilma had the ability to strike a liberating, right chord...suggesting that in some areas NOW work with peace groups as well as minority groups to try to make those linkages between feminism

and anti-militarism and to eradicate those structures feeding racism. In other areas, that did not seem such a popular approach...Wilma's wisdom made for much more flexible suggestions: "If it's right in your area, do it. This is a suggestion, not a directive coming down from the top."[36]

But it was not an easy task to gain consensus or even on occasion to "agree to disagree." A particularly bitter and abrasive conflict erupted at the November 1973 Board meeting. At that meeting there were two items on the agenda that proved to have serious and nearly disabling consequences. One concerned a contract for membership services, the other computerization of NOW's membership list.

NOW had contracted with the business firm of Mary Jean Collins and Jim Robson (Collins-Robson Office Programs) in Chicago to process membership services beginning in March, 1970. Collins and Robson had submitted a bid to continue membership services. So had KNOW, Inc. of Pittsburgh. Both bidders were NOW members, and the KNOW bid was lower than the Collins-Robson Programs bid.

Likewise, two bids had been submitted for computerizing data about membership, chapters, finances and fund raising – one by Hartly Data of Illinois and one by Norman Cutri of Pennsylvania, a brother of Eleanor Cutri Smeal, then a NOW Board member. In this case, too, the Pennsylvania firm had the lower bid.

After a three hour discussion, the Executive Committee recommended to the Board that Hartly Data of Illinois receive one contract and that Collins-Robson of Chicago receive the other. Although not the lower bidders, the two firms were chosen because the Committee decided that quality of work, ability to handle the bulk involved, ability to follow-through, and experience outweighed the consideration of cost.

At the Board meeting the next day, the Executive Committee decision was challenged. To resolve the conflict, a committee chaired by Judy Pickering was selected. When the committee reported the next day after an all night session, no compromise had been reached. Finally Judy sought a further two-hour delay, and they again returned to the Board. She announced that an acceptable compromise was found in specifying that Collins-Robson would be engaged for membership services, and that they would subcontract to KNOW some material such as task force literature and membership packets, since the committee felt that this was within the capacity of KNOW to do. The Board vote was 29-1 in favor of the compromise, with two abstaining. Jo Ann Evansgardner, one of the founders of KNOW, was furious. She felt that on the basis of the bid KNOW should have received the whole contract.

The issue was functionally resolved. In Wilma's mind it was "probably the best we could do at the time." But the anger and hurt feelings that were directed at one another remained for a long time, making two camps, as it were, out of the Board, with loyalties going to the "Chicago group" or the

"Pennsylvania group."

In addition to the responsibilities Wilma perceived in her relation to the Board, there were personal dimension of her leadership. Personal qualities that influenced Wilma's leadership were her passion and her sharp, clear reasoning. The amount of energy she poured into NOW and social change flowed from passion, from an intense commitment to her vision and from an integration of self that allowed that energy to flow.

Wilma's passion was expressed both in her speeches and in personal contact with people, and gave an emotional depth to what she said. It invited an emotional, even a physical response as well as an intellectual one. Men seemed to perceive this as much as did women.

> Men will come up to me at conferences and say, "I don't know you well enough to do this, but you'll understand," and just embrace me and say "Thank you for what you did tonight."[23]

Living at that level of emotional depth made it easy for her to be with people. It also, however, helped to distance her from others. Passion meant that Wilma felt deeply, felt the hurts as well as the triumphs, the frustration and bone-aching tiredness as well as fulfillment. But she had to keep many of these feelings to herself, and that task separated her from others.

> We had so much of doubts outside the organization that we didn't need any more. I may have needed to say "I'm discouraged," but I'm not sure the organization or I could have afforded it ...tears are a very honest expression of emotion; the question is can you afford to use it, knowing how it will be used, misused, and interpreted by others.[23]

A consequence of her sense of responsibility not to express every doubt was that she was alone at those times. She had to wrestle with those feelings in her aloneness and was sometimes denied the support for herself that she gave to others. Even people very close to Wilma seldom saw the depths of her feelings. At the Houston conference in 1974, for instance, Ernesta Ballard, an early NOW member from Philadelphia shared a hotel room with another person and Wilma. [37] Ernesta recalled those four hectic days:

> It was an extremely difficult and wearing time – fights, arguments, voting for hours and hours. I tried to be of help – to get her coffee, get her to sleep, be a sounding board ... Most of the time Wilma slept on the sofa; she came in late and insisted we take the beds ...At one time during the meeting when she was attacked and defeated on some measure she was supporting ... she broke down. We went out a side door, and she broke down and wept. It was the only time I've seen her lose control of herself, but she was exhausted.[38]

A further consequence of Wilma's sense of responsibility was that she was perceived as being larger than life. To some extent, her friends separated her from themselves.

> I remember one time talking with Sally Hacker about some things
> that had happened in NOW in the past couple of years, and I
> started to cry, and said I'm so furious about some things and
> concerned about what is going to happen – it really hurt me. Sally
> knew me, but I guess she had never seen this side of me. She
> seemed to be surprised, and being Sally, was very supportive, but I
> think she was feeling "does this person really need this and can I
> give it to her," and yet knowing all the time, of course, I did, and of
> course she could.[23]

Another dimension of Wilma's leadership that contributed both to
bringing her close to members and separating her from them, was that for
many she was a mother-figure. She was exciting, real, competent; for many she
was a living expression of the liberated woman, a woman free from the
trivialization that marked many of their mothers, and yet able to relate with
caring and nurturing. The perception of Wilma as a mother-figure and the
qualities that evoked it brought her into sustained and intimate contact with
many of the women in NOW, sharing many of their personal joys and
struggles. Like her passion it also separated her from them, for women had to
move away from viewing Wilma as a mother and toward viewing her as a
friend and colleague.

Many of the women I interviewed commented on the fearfulness they felt
the first time they disagreed with Wilma. Jo Ann Evans Gardner recalled that
when she was elected to the Board, she initially saw her role as supportive of
and dependent upon Wilma. Jo Ann added that with those perceptions, she
tended to discount alternative points of view rather than listen to them. She
observed that such perceptions also make it difficult for the one on whom you
see yourself as dependent.[39]

In a strong statement, Jean Witter acknowledged that Wilma was an
identity figure for her as well as for many others in the movement.

> If I had to take one thing [dimension of Wilma's leadership] as
> more important than any other, it would be that. That was very
> important; not that many women in this country have that kind of
> strength.[40]

During her years of leadership in NOW, Wilma and the women and men
she worked with brought about fundamental changes in the fabric of this
country's life. A volunteer, largely unseasoned organization, they "took on"
the federal government and big business. They reached out to women all over
the world. They joined hands with women oppressed from sexual attitudes.
At times stumbling, even recalcitrant, they nevertheless sought to be faithful
to the vision that guided them. Wilma was sometimes their gad-fly, sometimes
their mentor and prophet, sometimes their mediator. In the process of

changing society and mobilizing themselves, they also wrought fundamental changes in their own lives and in their families. I doubt that there is a person in this country who was not affected in some way by their presence. They acted and they made an impact. In and through the actions and their consequences, the vision that guided them emerged with increasing clarity.

NOTES

1. Heide, Wilma Scott: "Revolution: Tomorrow is NOW!" NOW Conference, February, 1973. Later published in *Vital Speeches of the Day, 1973.* City News Publishing Co., Southold, NY, pp.403-408.

2. *International Feminist Planning Conference: Proceedings,* edited by Ernesta D. Ballard and Jean Bryne.

3. Wilma has since chosen other adjectives than *egalitarian,* since the term means the *brotherhood* of men.

4. Quoted by Dorothy Austin in "Feminists Part in Peace and Harmony," *Milwaukee Sentinel,* June 5, 1973. Also quoted in *International Feminist Planning Conference,* p. 65 (see note # 2).

5. Clitoridectomy is the removal of the clitoris and infibulation is the sewing together of the labia majora and minora of young girls. The operations are practiced in parts of Africa, in the southern part of the Arab peninsula, and less drastic ones are practiced in Malaysia and in parts of Indonesia.

6. *The Hosken Report* is available from *WIN News,* 187 Grant St., Lexington, MA 02173. In March 1980, *Ms.* published an article on "The International Crime of Genital Mutilation" by Gloria Steinem and Robin Morgan. Fran Hosken issued a press release in which she charged that much of the information in the article was taken from her material without adequate acknowledgement.

7. Barreno, Maria Isabel, Maria Teresa Horta, Maria Velho da Costa: *The Three Marias: New Portuguese Letters,* translated by Helen R. Lane, Doubleday and Company, Garden City, NY, 1975.

8. Russell, Diana E.H. and Nicole Van de Van (Eds.): *The Proceedings of the International Tribunal on Crimes Against Women* Millbrae, Les Femmes, 1976.

9. Hole, Judith and Ellen Levine: *The Rebirth of Feminism.* Quandrangle Books, New York, 1971.

10. The majority of Farah workers were women who were being prevented from organizing. The Farmworkers, under the leadership of Ceasar Chavez, included both women and men struggling to organize agricultural workers.

11. NOW files, Wilma's basement.

12. Mason, Margaret: *Poverty: A Feminist Issue: A Case Study of the National Organization for Women's Policies and Actions on Poverty Issues, 1966-1976.* Senior thesis, Hampshire College, Amherst, MA, 1977.

13. Ruzek, Sheryl Burt: *The Women's Health Movement: Feminist Alternatives to Medical Control.* Praeger, NY, 1978.

14. Report of the Task Force: "Minority Women and Women's Rights," May 1974.

15. "Newsletter to Chapter Presidents, Task Force Coordinators, and National Board Members," from Patsy G. Fulcher, Aileen C. Hernandez, and Eleanor R. Spikes. September, 1973, NOW files, Wilma's basement.

16. Letter, March 26, 1973, in Aileen Hernandez's files.

17. Letter, May 16, 1973, in Aileen Hernandez's files.

18. "Statement of National Black Feminist Organization," no date, Aileen Hernandez's files.

19. Heide, Wilma Scott: "Women's Quest for Equality." Unpublished, April 21, 1972.

20. Heide, Wilma Scott: "Racial Justice and Feminism: Common Cause in the Human Interest." Unpublished, 1975.

21. Telephone conversation, November, 1979.

22. The decision to use direct mail to increase membership was the other critical decision in Gene's opinion. This rapidly increased the membership, and people joined for all kinds of reasons. The result was a continuously expanding program and changing understandings of what were feminist issues.

23. In conversation with me, January, 1977.

24. Martin and Lyons are members of NOW and co-authors of *Lesbian/Woman*, Bantam Books, NY, 1972, as well as many other books, articles and speeches.

25. "Chronological Summary of National Organization for Women Conference Resolutions, Policies and Board Decisions, 1966-1971." In NOW files.

26. Letter from Sidney Abbott to Wilma Scott Heide, February 15, 1972, on file, Wilma's basement. Sidney Abbott is an educator and co-author (with Barbara Love) of *Sappho Was a Right-On Woman: A Liberated View of Lesbianism*. Stein and Day, New York, 1972.

27. Letter from Debra Layne, March 29, 1973, on file, Wilma's basement.

28. Letter from Mary Molek, April 6, 1973, on file, Wilma's basement.

29. Letter from Jane Sandy, April 4, 1973, on file, Wilma's basement.

30. Conversation with Wilma, February, 1977.

31. Interview with Joan Israel, February, 1978.

32. Interview with Jacqui Ceballos, January, 1978.

33. Letter from Mrs. E.J. Rockelman, July 25, 1970, on file, Wilma's basement.

34. Theodora Wells is founder of Wells Associates, a communication and management consulting firm, and the author of *Keeping Your Cool Under Fire: Communicating Non-Defensively*. McGraw-Hill, New York, 1980.

35. Conversation with Eleanor Coffin Robbins, August, 1978.

36. Tape from Sally Hacker, Fall, 1977.

37. Ernesta Ballard recalls the rather inadvertent way she became involved in NOW. Her mother had been a feminist and had written a book on women and music. In 1966, Betty Friedan had called to ask her mother to consider a position on the first Board. Her mother, however, was then in a terminal illness. The daughter volunteered herself: "If there is anyway I can help you, I'll be glad to do it." She was elected to the first Board.

38. Taped interview with Ernesta D. Ballard, 1977.

39. Interview with Jo Ann Evansgardner, September, 1977. In 1980, Jo Ann changed her name from Evans Gardner to Evansgardner. Both names are used in this book.

40. Interview with Jean Witter, September, 1977.

8

IN TRANSITION

The voice and accurate image of woman as a person have been largely absent from discussions and decisions that create and determine our being in common with men. Women must be socialized to speak and act with knowledge and confidence on resources, population, pollution, religion, space exploration, law, health care, education, politics, family forms and styles, finance, existential philosophy – *everything*. Our androcentric society is neither whole nor healthy without the significant participation and leadership of the other half of the population.

– Wilma Scott Heide[1,p.406]

Changing Relationship with NOW

NOW had grown phenomenally in the eight years of its existence. Women and men from all kinds of backgrounds and with all kinds of interests had joined. As it had grown in numbers, so it had changed in structure – from volunteers and a small Board-administered organization to a paid staff, permanent offices, and a large Board that had to leave many of the day-to-day decisions and activities to the staff. As NOW had grown in number and changed in structure, its financial resources had increased with some money available to reimburse Board members for their expenses and funds to conduct an expensive and protracted drive for ratification of the ERA.

The results of this growth were multiple. A tremendous amount of creativity and talent were made available to NOW. But a tremendous amount of anger, frustration, and differences about priorities and means and ends were also created. Some felt the organization was moving too slowly and was not sufficiently radical. Others felt that it was moving much too quickly to champion controversial positions and was in danger of losing "credibility" and thus power for effecting legal and institutional change.

As Wilma's presidency neared an end, the question of NOW's commitment to what Wilma has termed "indivisible human rights" continued to occupy members' time and energy. NOW had worked to overcome racism, classism and homophobia within itself as well as in the larger society. Some actions were taken; some goals were accomplished. But for many, these accomplishments were insufficient, and differences over priorities and activities remained an ongoing part of Board and membership discussion. Aileen Hernandez summarized the positions of those who thought NOW was insufficiently committed to eradicating racism, classism and homophobia by stating that NOW's big push on the ERA and abortion issues "made it respectable, however controversial those stands had been initially."[2]

The question of commitment was accompanied, sometimes in an unarticulated way, by a concern for power. This concern began to be evident with the acrimonious Board meeting in November 1973, which was divided largely along geographical lines – Chicago people and Pennsylvania people. This division persisted to some extent through the next two years. Aileen Hernandez reflects that the presence of one of the national offices in Chicago fostered a perception by some that there was too much concentration of power in Chicago.[2] Similarly, Kathryn Clarenbach speaks of the "fuss between the Pennsylvania and Chicago groups."[3]

Some of these differences and struggles may have been exacerbated by a workshop held for the Board in May 1973, by the Midwest Academy, utilizing Saul Alinsky's approach to organizing and social change. Wilma was in bed with pleurisy and under physician's orders not to attend. The reports she received from some who did attend disturbed her, for the methods being taught seemed predominantly adversarial. Wilma's observation was that such methods were "unhealthy in general and certainly inappropriate for feminists."

Differences and struggles within NOW did not obscure the presence of shared vision and commitment, a presence which was profoundly reflected in the February 1973 conference in Washington. According to many reports of participants, the overall impact of the conference was that of sisterhood and power to change. The differences became especially public during the end of Wilma's presidency and after the election of Karen DeCrow.

As Wilma's presidency drew to a close, she was encouraged by friends to run again. In addition to admiring her, they urged her to continue because they saw no other person with the sophistication and charisma to shepherd the organization in its pluralism and strengthen its effectiveness as an agent of social change. But Wilma decided against seeking the presidency for a third time. She felt strongly that leadership should be shared and that new leaders should be constantly emerging. Her response to her friends was that an organization could not be dependent on personalities and that NOW was strong enough and vital enough to elicit new leaders.

Although not a decisive factor, her decision was also informed by considerations of health. In the Fall of 1969, doctors had diagnosed a brain tumor and urged surgery. After hours of reflection, Wilma decided against surgery. She felt that the risks to her health were severe in either case, and she chose to gamble that the tumor was benign and could be treated by medication. She made the decision alone. The need to protect her privacy, the distance created between her and those close to her in the Movement, and her wish to shield her family from further trauma were all factors in her choice not to share the burden of decision-making with others.

Wilma's decision not to seek re-election was also informed by weariness. She was tired. Although much of her activity was exhilarating and in the company of friends, it was also often frustrating, sometimes frightening, and usually taxing of time, energy and money. Months and years without adequate rest, meals snatched between meetings or late at night, complex negotiations, mediating ambiguous relationships and feelings had drained her resources. The tumor on occasion gave her severe headaches and faint spells. All these things considered, she chose not to seek a third term as president.

With Wilma's decision, the process for electing a new president became competitive for the first time in NOW'S history.[4] More than one candidate seriously sought office, and the competition among them helped to serve as rallying points for the expression of conflicts, both in the Board and in some of the chapters.

Three candidates emerged before the national conference to be held in Houston in May 1974. They were Mary Jean Collins, Karen DeCrow, and Anne Lang. Mary Jean Collins was an early NOW member, president of the Chicago chapter, a state coordinator, and a Board member. She had also been active in other civil rights organizations. Karen DeCrow was also an early NOW member, eastern regional director, and Board member, succeeding Wilma as membership chair. She is a lawyer by profession and the author of *A Young Woman's Guide to Women's Liberation and Sexist Justice.* Anne Lang had been active in the Pittsburgh chapter of NOW. She was on the Board and active in media concerns of NOW.

All three candidates sought Wilma's endorsement. In philosophy, Wilma fundamentally agreed with all three, but she favored Mary Jean Collins and had been encouraging her for some time to think about the presidency. She thought Mary Jean had the administrative and follow-through skills necessary to shepherd an organization from rhetoric through policy formation to action. She also thought that the Chicago woman had mediating skills and that she was able to respect differences and yet find the common ground for action.

Wilma did not actively advocate any of the candidates, however. During the Houston conference itself, she found it necessary to play a role that additionally prohibited her from supporting Mary Jean. The conference became dominated by candidacy politics, and Wilma chose to focus on the success of the conference as a whole, seeing to it that schedules were followed or changed as necessary, that workshops met, that resolutions were discussed and voted upon, and that the ongoing work of the organization continued. Since several other officers were busy campaigning and meeting in caucuses and planning sessions, Wilma felt she had to stay away from partisanship and give her time and energy to the running of the conference and maintaining a trustworthy and fair stance. Only at one time did she modify her position to slip briefly into a caucus of Mary Jean and her colleagues.

The politicking at the conference ran along conventional party lines. There were banners and buttons and platforms; there were speeches and caucuses. On occasion, there were personal attacks and innuendos. Mary Jean's campaign was accused of being "Daley-like." Recalling that time, Kay Clarenbach observed that there were "some unethical things done" and felt that Wilma had "given too much of a free rein" to what was happening.[3] Wilma was furious with the way partisan politics seemed to overcome the conference.

Karen DeCrow was elected president, and Wilma continued her involvement with NOW in three ways. She served on the Board as chair of the Advisory Committee; she remained friend and mentor of members who continued to turn to her for advice and/or support, and she was a participant in many of NOW's activities.

The purpose of the Advisory Committee was to advise NOW on policy and practice, but it had seldom met except as members were together informally or for other meetings. When Aileen was chairing it, for instance, she convened the Committee at a national conference of the organization.

While Wilma was chairing the Advisory Committee, she was also a Guest-in-Residence at Wellesley College in Massachusetts. Since the Committee had few funds to meet expenses, she proposed to Wellesley students that they provide travel expenses for the Committee to meet on campus, and in return the Committee members would hold a series of "feminist forums" for the college. The students responded positively; in the student paper it was described as "a proposal we can't refuse." It worked; the Committee met and held forums for whoever wished to attend.

Through Wilma's continuing official involvement in NOW and her informal network of contact and influence, Wilma observed the persistence of antagonisms and polarizations that had surfaced at Houston. By the December 1974 Board meeting held in New Orleans, the Board was so divided that one part of it named itself the "Majority Caucus," composed of those who had won in Houston.

Again Wilma refused to align herself with any group, either with the "Majority Caucus" or those who opposed it. Sometimes she voted with one and sometimes with the other.[5] Several members thought Wilma hurt herself by not taking sides, causing both sides to mistrust her to some extent. On one occasion, she tried to attend a meeting of the "Majority Caucus," but was told she was aligned with the "other side" and could not be there. Philosophically,

Wilma tended to identify with the "Majority Caucus," which saw itself as the liberal party. But she could not accept what she saw as their non-feminist methods. Also many of the "Majority Caucus" were newer members, and Wilma was unwilling to somehow identify herself as opposed to women she had worked with for seven years. Indeed, she rejected the whole concept of partisan politics and party politics, and of "taking sides." She saw an effort to find common ground as more consistent with a feminist philosophy.

In the spring of 1975, some of the newer Board members who were distressed by what was happening attempted a reconciliation. One of these was a young woman named Wendy Winkler, a Board member from Ohio, who, in Wilma's words, was "devastated" by what was happening. Wendy and others called for a special meeting in Philadelphia. About half of the 38-member Board came. Those who attended were, for the most part, not unilaterally aligned with either group. They did not use organizational funds but came at their own expense, and those who could contributed toward the expenses of those for whom the trip was a financial burden. They did what they could, but what they could do was limited. They discussed the situation and explored ways of ameliorating it.

As the next conference neared, scheduled for Philadelphia in October 1975, Mary Lynn Myers decided to run for the presidency of NOW as a moderate. At that time she was vice president for Finance and had been on the Board since September 1971. She was from South Dakota and had been working there as director of the South Dakota Human Rights Commission.

Mary Lynn called Wilma to see if Wilma thought she was a viable candidate. Wilma encouraged her but expressed concern that if Mary Jean Collins decided to run, she would have a difficult time determining whom to support. Mary Lynn also called Betty Friedan, Gene Boyer, Muriel Fox and others. Some expressed a concern similar to Wilma's; others simply encouraged her to run. Mary Lynn felt she could bring differing factions together and that she was not inevitably already aligned, as was Mary Jean who had been a candidate in Houston and was considering running again.[5]

Both Mary Lynn and Mary Jean did decide to run and Wilma supported neither. Three other members also decided to run. They were Jacqui Ceballos, Shirley Bernard, and Karen DeCrow. On the first ballot, Karen DeCrow and Mary Lynn came in first and second respectively; the others withdrew in Mary Lynn's favor. However, Karen was re-elected.

Wilma came to the conference in Philadelphia after three weeks at a colloquium, as a part of her work toward a doctorate from The Union Graduate School for Experimenting Colleges and Universities. She had been pressed as to whether she was going to complete her PhD, and what she would give up in order to get it. Wilma had replied that she was going to commit herself to the PhD and that she would give up NOW for the time being.

Wilma was distraught by the acrimony and strife at the conference. "The whole conference turned me off. It was a return to old male politics – states and parties ... The American Arbitration Association conducted the election, since no one was able to trust anyone else in NOW." The one hope she perceived was that Ellie Smeal, who was then Board Chair, was making a concerted effort to be fair and seek out some common ground. Finally, Wilma simply left early and went home. She knew that she could not solve NOW's problems alone, and although she was willing to lend support, others had to solve their own problems.

Some people left Philadelphia elated; others left convinced that NOW was destroyed. It had been in many ways a bitter conference, full of anger and accusatory politics, its participants forgetting that they were sisters and brothers of one another and that compared to the larger society they had much more in common with one another than they had difference among one another.

NOW was not destroyed. In the year and a half until the spring 1977 conference at Detroit, the fighting eased, the term "Majority Caucus" almost forgotten, and Ellie Smeal was overwhelmingly elected its fifth president. At Detroit, Wilma and Jo Ann Evansgardner (who had been part of the "Majority Caucus") led a workshop on "trashing and nurturing."

Toni Carabillo describes the struggle as representing "nearly inevitable stages in the process of NOW's organizational and political maturation."[6] Throughout the struggle, Wilma sought a non-partisan stance. Wilma had no quarrel with the substance of the philosophy of the "Majority Caucus." She had been pushing for several years to broaden the range of NOW's concerns and to deepen its commitment to poor women, women of color, lesbian women, and older women. But Wilma objected to some of the means she saw employed by NOW members on occasion. Those means included inuendo and manipulation, demands of total loyalty, and demands of purity – or adversarial politics.

> I was identified more with the non-majority caucus, but not totally, and this made for problems that have to do with friendship. If I agreed with the "Majority Caucus" on one issue, they [the Majority Caucus] thought I would [agree] on all – "Ha! – We can count on Wilma." And if I didn't, the others thought I would agree with them on all. But I don't function that way, and furthermore I don't think it's healthy to function that way. That's the old politics: you scratch my back and I'll scratch yours.[7]

In turn people on both sides felt that Wilma should have taken a clearer stand and/or been more forceful in using her influence for them. Mary Lynn Myers, for instance, stated that she thought that if Wilma had publicly supported her or Mary Jean, one of them might have won the election. Jo Ann Evans Gardner refers to Wilma's non-alignment with the "Majority Caucus" as a "temporary aberration;" since Wilma was philosophically close to the Majority Caucus it seemed illogical that she wouldn't align with the caucus.

The effect of these conflicts was very hard on Wilma, torn between friendship, philosophical agreement with the "majority caucus," and dismay at what was happening:

> ...some people were disappointed in me, some of them understood me, but others didn't and were very insistent, and some of those had been friends of mine. It was very painful.[7]

After her presidency, Wilma had felt release, relief, and concern. But it was not until after the '75 conference in Philadelphia that she realized how tired she was. Until then she had not emotionally stopped; she was still very much involved. After she left Philadelphia, she realized she was "bone weary." Before, she had been getting often no more than two or three hours of sleep a night; now she began to get more rest.

Establishing Other Organizations

Even at her most involved, there remained for Wilma a difference between NOW and her sense of vocation. NOW was one expression of it, but there were others.

Nursing and N-CAP

In the spring of 1974, Wilma briefly turned her attention again to nursing. After consulting with Nurses NOW, she talked with Barbara Schutt, a contributing editor of the *American Journal of Nursing*. Schutt arranged for her to be invited to meet with the Board of Directors of the American Nurses Association (ANA). There she challenged them with a question: What kind of political involvement was the ANA willing to have? She pointed out that any policy it adopted or stand it took, including simply accepting traditional sexist assumptions about women and nursing, was a political decision itself. The Association could not avoid politics; the relevant question was would its politics be sexist or feminist.

The immediate response was minimal. Nevertheless, within several months, the Nurses Coalition for Action and Politics (N-CAP) was formed. Those involved in it later told Wilma that N-CAP was generated by her meeting with the ANA Board, along with pressure from Nurses NOW and other feminists.

National Women's Political Caucus

Wilma was also involved with the founding of the National Women's Political Caucus (NWPC). In July 1970, members of NOW and other organizations, and women active in existing political parties met to address women's participation in electoral and appointive politics. Out of that conference was born the National Women's Political Caucus, and it included both feminists and politically active and ambitious women.

Wilma was a founder but had not intended an active role. She was aware of some ambivalence in the NWPC about their commitment to feminist principles. Although Wilma thought it was important that women run for and be elected to public office, it was also important that they run on feminist principles. When she was asked to run for the first Policy Council, she said "Yes," with the intent of influencing the Caucus to develop a feminist orientation. She was elected to the Policy Council. Some founding members asked her to be a candidate to chair the Caucus because of her experience, because she was trusted, and – Wilma thinks – because others knew she wasn't personally ambitious either in terms of electoral or movement politics. Wilma appreciated the invitation to run for Chair, but declined to be considered. She continued to serve on the Policy Council until 1974 and on its Advisory Board until 1977.

KNOW, Inc.

Another organization Wilma helped establish was a publishing company, KNOW, Inc., which was related to NOW philosophically but not structurally. In 1969, Wilma and 19 other Pittsburgh area feminists and NOW members (including Gerald and Jo Ann Evans Gardner and Anne Pride) began discussing the possibility of buying their own press to distribute the news. Convinced that *freedom of the press belongs to those who own the press,* each person pledged whatever funding they could toward founding a feminist press. No one knew how to operate a press and the group surely could not afford its cost, but as with many movement enterprises, the only relevant issue was that a feminist press was necessary. They would simply have to find ways to finance and operate it.

They set to work and they succeeded. A major contribution to KNOW's financial viability was Phyllis Wetherby, a Pittsburgh resident and feminist. Wilma's primary role was that of support of the press by distributing materials and recommending KNOW, Inc. to others as a resource for publication. They published reprints of many articles and speeches by NOW members and other feminists, including the classic essay "The Tyranny of Structurelessness" by Jo Freeman. They also printed Gabrielle Burton's *I'm Running Away from Home, But I'm Not Allowed to Cross the Street.*

Women's Coalition for the Third Century

The Women's Coalition for the Third Century was founded in protest. Its focus was not political action in the traditional sense so much as philosophical clarification and exploration. The coalition was important because of its effort to provide a theoretical context for feminist action, and Wilma contributed to that effort.

In the early 1970's, the Federal American Revolution Bicentennial Commission, located under John Ehrlichman's domestic responsibilities, began planning for the United States' 1976 Bicentennial celebration. In the spring of 1972, Perdita Huston, coordinator of women's activities for the Bicentennial (a half-time position), made contact with Gene Boyer in NOW, other feminist organizations, and women's groups and organizations, asking them to advise the Commission on women's programs and activities. Gene suggested that Huston make contact with Wilma. Wilma gave Huston other names and went to Washington, DC herself to "advise."

It soon became clear to Wilma, however, that the advice she and many others present could give was not acceptable, and dissatisfaction grew. At a 1972 meeting, several of the women who were advising, including Wilma, formed a coalition and drew up resolutions urging that the Bicentennial Commission put emphasis on the future rather than the past, and on women and racial minorities.[8] At the same time the coalition began working independently of the Commission to reinterpret the meaning and celebration of the Bicentennial.[9]

Finally, the members of the coalition walked out of the advisory group. They continued to meet and they kept in touch with Huston. They named themselves the Women's Coalition for the Third Century, and they saw their purpose to be a humanizing and maturing influence on the Third Century of this country's life.

The Coalition drafted a statement of its philosophy – a statement of interdependence:

> We are interdependent with the good earth, with all people, and with divine reality... We affirm our common humanity and we respect one another's uniqueness. We accept our responsibility to share the visions, hopes, and needs of one another and pledge ourselves to protect each other's freedom...

> In declaring our interdependence with the earth we affirm our reliance on it, our mutual responsibility for it and the rights of all persons to the fruits thereof...

> In declaring our interdependence with Divine Reality we recognize the possibilities of a sacred mystery within and around us...

> We women and men and children make this Declaration living in the midst of a world in which women are subservient and oppressed, men are repressed and brutalized, and children are violated and alienated. In making this Declaration we seek a new order and covenant ourselves to a fully interdependent society...[10]

Under each declaration, specific statements of intent are included. Under the declaration of interdependence with one another the specific statements reflect commitment to the well being of each person, not simply the satisfaction of basic needs. Equally, there are statements about each one's responsibility for leadership in every area of life. Under the declaration of interdependence with the earth are statements stressing responsible use of the earth's resources and sharing those with all people. This section also includes the statement:

> We shall enjoy and cherish the sacredness and privacy of our bodies and shall bring into the world children who are wanted.

Under the Declaration of Interdependence with divine reality are statements of commitment to support each other's pursuit of truth, to reject exclusive claims, to be open to "revelations that extend beyond the boundaries of our current understanding and wisdom."

Along side of the Declaration of Interdependence is a Declaration of Imperatives, which Wilma insisted on including. Although agreeing with the philosophy of the document, she was afraid that it would enable people to move to a supposedly humanist position without addressing the needs and resources of women. The Declaration of Imperatives is to be seen as a prerequisite of the Declaration of Interdependence, not an application of it. The "we" in the Declaration of Imperatives, therefore, refers to women, while the "we" in the Declaration of Interdependence refers to women, men and children. The Declaration of Imperatives includes:

> We will not be taxed without representation.
> We will not be bound by the authority of legal systems in which we participate only minimally in the making and administration of the laws ...
> We will not be the only ones responsible for child care ...
> We reject educational systems that distort our reality.
> We will not accept philosophies and theologies that deny our experience ...
> We will not be the principal source of morality for this nation ...
> We will share the leadership of society and its government ...

The Declaration of Interdependence and Imperatives articulates a feminist philosophy for living harmoniously and justly with all reality. As such, it reflects something of the maturing and broadening of the second wave of feminism. Without losing sight of specific women's issues, it strongly and boldly announces that *all* issues are women's issues, and seeks to describe the principles by which those issues are to be met and resolved.

The overarching principle is interdependence, a principle that combines equality with uniqueness, mutual dependence with autonomy, and respect with care. It is interdependence *with all that is*. Human rights, women's rights are located in a universal context of relatedness. Interdependence reflects a major shift in understanding of specific issues – a shift away from an emphasis on *rights* to an emphasis on *relationality*. Equally, interdependence is a shift from a view of reality that stresses individualism, groups in conflict and competition with one another, to one that sees reality as a whole and thoroughly, intrinsically connected. At the same time, interdependence retains the basic norm of equality. A genuinely non-hierarchical ordering of reality is present in the Declaration.

The Declaration authorizes on-going attention to specific issues women face. At the same time, it prohibits parochialism; it demands attention to all issues as women's issues:

> ...we seek a new order and covenant ourselves to a fully interdependent society ...

On September 10 and 11, 1973, the Coalition held an organizational meeting. Representatives of twelve feminist and women's organizations and Linda Grant De Pauw as consultant historian signed the document and became members of the new Coalition. They were:

Priscilla B. Ransohoff – Federally Employed Women (FEW)
Marion L. Carr – Leadership Conference of Women Religious (LCWR)
Sister Ann Getlen – National Coalition of American Nuns (NCAN)
Wilma Scott Heide – National Organization for Women (NOW)
Colleen S. Alexander – National Women's Political Caucus (NWPC)
Jean L. King – Professional Women's Caucus (PWC)
Marjorie Heller Adler – United Presbyterian Church, USA (UPCUSA)
Patricia Budd Kepler – Women's Coalition for the Third Century (WC3C)
Mary Blocher Smeltzer – Women's Equity Action League (WEAL)
Naomi Marcus – Women's International League for Peace and Freedom (WILPF)
Lynn Cox Scheffey – Interstate Association of the Commissions on the Status of Women (ACSU)
Debbie Langal – Interstate Association of Women Students (IAWS)
Linda Grant De Pauw – Consultant Historian

The membership signing took place in Philadelphia at Congress Hall, next to Independence Hall. Wilma and Patricia Budd Kepler, an ordained Presbyterian minister, were elected co-chairs. The membership signing was followed by an outdoor rally at a nearby mall. Except for a few local papers, the event was ignored by other news media locally and nationally, although they had been informed of the event. Excited by possibilities of relating philosophy and action, the Coalition began planning for an alternative Bicentennial celebration. It sponsored a symposium on women in the colonial era, held in Philadelphia during the celebration of 1976. It also hung a copy of the Declaration at the Women's Center in Philadelphia and there several hundred women, men and children signed it.

The Coalition explored ways of re-enacting the alternative protest celebration of 1876. In 1876, Elizabeth Cady Stanton, Susan B. Anthony, Matilda Joslyn Gage and others wrote a Declaration of Rights for presentation at the Centennial observation.

> We thought it would be fitting for us to read our Declaration of Rights immediately after that of the Fathers ... as an impeachment of them and their male descendants for their injustice and oppression. [11,p.310]

Refused permission, six of the women decided to attend the Centennial ceremony and after the reading of the Declaration of Independence, they rose, made their way to the platform and presented their Declaration of Rights to the presiding officer. They then scattered copies to the audience as they left, while General Hawley, "beaten in his audacious denial to women ...shouted 'Order, order!'" [11,p.313]

The women proceeded outside, and Anthony read the Declaration aloud, including the impeachment of the United States government. They then went to the Unitarian Church, and for five hours a large crowd heard speeches and sang songs in celebration of women's independence.

As part of the re-enactment, Wilma pressed for interrupting the official proceedings, but she was unable to gain agreement for doing so. Instead, on July 4, 1976, members of the Coalition gathered in the same Unitarian Church to thank their foremothers and to share the only document from women in the 1976 Bicentennial – the Declaration of Interdependence.

On October 3, 1977, the Coalition presented the Declaration to the United States in a ceremony at the Smithsonian Institution. Kepler presented a five-foot high version of the 1976 Declaration of Imperatives and Interdependence, signed by many on July 4, 1976 at the Philadelphia Women's Bicentennial Center. It is now hanging in the Smithsonian beside the 1876 Declaration of Sentiments.[12]

Following that event, although the coalition continued to meet sporadically for another year, little was done. Exhausted by her years with NOW and determined to finish other projects she had postponed during those years, Wilma decided she could not make the commitment needed to develop the Coalition further. Other members were reluctant to assume major leadership responsibilities. The Coalition still exists – it has not been formally ended, and Wilma and Pat Kepler occasionally represent it at other conferences and meetings.

In Transition

The years from 1974 to 1980 were years of transition for Wilma. She continued action on many of the issues she had been involved with in NOW, but there was a growing disengagement from investing a major amount of time and energy to NOW. She began to explore other ways of carrying out her vocation, moving away from the past and toward a different future.

Women's Conferences

Wilma was involved in two major government-sponsored conferences held during this period. The first was the International Women's Year Conference in Mexico City in 1975, sponsored by the United Nations. The second was the National Women's Conference in Houston in 1977, legislated by the United States Congress.

The Mexico City conference had two major meeting areas – one for governmental representatives and one for everyone else. Wilma flew to Mexico City with other NOW members, including Anne Hazlewood Brady from New York, Joyce Mitchell from Vermont, and Pat Kepler from Massachusetts. Wilma represented NOW at the non-government site, the Tribune, where thousands of people gathered each day for speeches, workshops, and hundreds of international artistic and cultural events. The conference proceeded in spite of conflicts that erupted and in spite of efforts of governmental personnel to control women representatives. The Plan of Action, the official statement under discussion, was distributed to participants at the Tribune. Pat Kepler, Jacqui Ceballos, Wilma and others helped to organize women from all over the world to study the Plan and make recommendations to the governmental representatives.

As Wilma and her colleagues at Mexico City discussed implementing the Plan of Action, they decided it called for a national conference in this country to be preceded by state conferences. Accordingly, upon returning home, they talked with many people, particularly people in Washington about the idea. Bella Abzug, who had also been at the Mexico conference, Margaret Heckler, and others sponsored legislation authorizing Congress to appropriate money for state conferences and a national conference.

At each state conference, workshops were held on the many issues facing women around the world. Out of the workshops came resolutions to be taken to Houston where the national conference was planned. At the state conferences, delegates were elected to attend the national conference. Delegates were to reflect the women's population of the state. Diversity of age, income, racial and ethnic backgrounds, and sexual preference were to be considered. Wilma was elected as a delegate from Massachusetts, receiving the largest number of votes of any delegate though she was a write-in candidate.

The Women's Movement no longer belonged to a minority of women and men. By 1977, it had become a part of the lives of a huge majority of women in this country. Women who previously had been hostile or indifferent to the movement were beginning to participate. Similarly, women who were still wary or little informed of some aspects of the movement were beginning to organize – or be organized by men – to register opposing voices or to try to defeat feminist positions. The state-wide conferences became the context and the occasion for the expressions of new interests and oppositions. Thousands of women turned out for many of them. Lesbian women organized, women opposed to freedom of choice with respect to abortion organized, minority women caucused – sometimes together across racial-ethnic lines. Resolutions were passed in spite of vigorous attempts to defeat them by more conservative groups.

In some states, non-representative groups succeeded in being elected to the Houston conference. In Mississippi, for instance, an all-white, middle-class delegation, including a couple of men, was elected. Nevertheless, most of the states observed, at least to some extent, the rules of demographic representation, as well as the intents of the Houston conference, which were to:

- recognize the contributions of women to the development of our country;
- assess the progress ... by both the private and public sectors in promoting equality ...
- assess the role of women in economic, social, cultural, and political development;

- assess the participation of women in efforts aimed at the development of friendly relations and cooperation among nations and to the strengthening of world peace;
- identify the barriers that prevent women from participating fully and equally in all aspects of national life ...
- establish a timetable for the achievement of the objectives ...
- establish a committee ...to provide for the convening of the second National Women's Conference ... [13,p.10]

The Houston conference, like Mexico City, had two settings: one for the delegates, official observers, and those general observers fortunate enough to get seats; the other a place for exhibits, performances, and speeches. Wilma spent her days with the delegates voting on resolutions in the National Plan for Action. Perhaps the most moving event of that long weekend occurred when women of different minority backgrounds caucused together. Hispanic, Black, Native American, Chicana, and Asian-American women met and together worked out new resolutions to substitute for those in the proposed National Plan with which they took issue. A representative from each group then read a part of the new resolutions. After the new resolutions were read, there was some discussion and a vote was taken. The proposed new resolutions passed overwhelmingly. Pandemonium broke loose. People danced and cried and hugged and kissed one another. Black women, brown women, and white women knew for a time the reality of sisterhood. Afterwards, women of color who were movement feminists told Wilma they were confident the resolutions would pass; others not previously involved in the movement had not been so confident. Those who had been doubtful told Wilma they realized they had been led to believe what most of the mass media said or implied about the women's movement.

Although Wilma played a relatively small role in the Conference proceedings, she did prepare and distribute a couple of position papers on the conference issues and international development. But for the most part, she remained with the Massachusetts delegation, aside from greeting and talking with old friends. She felt others with less experience needed the opportunities the Conference afforded.

The Houston conference is significant because it reflected something of the growth of the movement, which Wilma had shaped in major ways. The Houston conference was also significant to Wilma because it deeply reaffirmed her decision to move away from a major leadership role in the movement. The struggles around the issues were almost a replay of the struggles five to ten years earlier, and it was time for others to address them. Many issues that at one time were difficult for NOW to establish firmly, that seemed too radical or not feminist issues, were now taken for granted by a large cross section of American women. Lesbian rights, freedom of choice, financial security, adequate and free child care, security for older women, adequate education, and many, many more concerns were voted on and supported. As Wilma stated, "It was gratifying to see thousands cheer what a few of us were criticized for even mentioning just a decade or less ago."[14]

Equal Rights Amendment

Wilma continued to work intensely for the ERA, but again her actions reflected seeking a new approach. In July 1976, Wilma was invited to present workshops for the Nursing Education Chautauqua in Vail, Colorado. She and Judy Pickering decided to drive out and back in a motor home and make the trip an occasion for gathering support for the ERA. They chose the name LOGO-MOBILE, from the Greek word for *word* or *speech* and the English word *mobile*. A large sign "ERA LOGO-MOBILE" was attached to the top front of their rented Winnebago. On the back was:

RATIFY THE EQUAL RIGHTS AMENDMENT
IT'S THE AMERICAN WAY

On the left was:

FEMINIST FEATURES PRESENTS
WILMA SCOTT HEIDE AND COMPANY[15]
NON-SEXIST SONGS, SPEECHES, DRAMA AND HUMOR
COME AS YOU ARE
DISCOVER WHAT YOU CAN BECOME

And on the right was:

SIGN THE DECLARATION OF INTERDEPENDENCE AND
IMPERATIVES
SPONSORED BY
THE WOMEN'S COALITION FOR THE THIRD CENTURY

Wherever they stopped, they attached copies of the Declaration to the side for people to read and sign. Many did.

They decided to portray Elizabeth Cady Stanton and Susan B. Anthony as if they had returned to earth, from a feminist heaven, but decided the term "feminist heaven" was redundant. Wilma was Stanton and Judy was Anthony, and when they performed they dressed in 19th century attire, gathered by Judy's mother Yvette Pickering. As the two indefatigable foremothers had toured the country speaking about a century before, so Wilma and Judy were doing it now.

They performed in the ratified states of Connecticut, Pennsylvania, Ohio, Iowa, Nebraska and Texas; and in the unratified states of Illinois, Oklahoma, Missouri, and Indiana; and in Colorado where there was a move to rescind ratification. Wilma comments:

> Whether coincidental or cause and effect, Indiana was the only
> state to ratify the ERA in 1977 and Colorado did not rescind its
> ratification ... [16,p.34]

Wilma and Judy had originally intended to keep up conversation with truckers through a CB radio. Since the Teamsters Union supported the ERA, they thought they could do some consciousness raising with individual truckers and enlist their help in lobbying. Their radio, however, never worked, so they were limited to conversations in cafes and service stations. Wilma summarized their efforts:

> Two of the truckers may never support the ERA; all the others were or became supporters, and we would like to believe the promise of most of them to do some lobbying of their legislators. [16,pp.35-36]

Occasionally, mechanics refused to service them, and once they were nearly forced off the road. Generally, however, responses to their camper were positive.

In still another way Wilma continued to work for ratification of the ERA and the extension of time for ratification. In 1978, Fran Kolb, coordinator of NOW's economic boycott, asked Wilma to help move two nursing conventions out of unratified states. One was a conference of the American Nurses' Association scheduled for Georgia in 1980; the other was the International Council of Nurses scheduled for Missouri in 1981. Wilma agreed, and working with others sympathetic to the boycott, succeeded. The result was that the ANA became the largest organization to that date to honor the boycott. Missouri, one the host states boycotted by ANA, sued NOW and later ANA, charging that the boycott violated anti-trust laws. Missouri lost both suits.

Education

In part because she wanted to and in part because it seemed to open other options for her, Wilma decided to finish a doctoral program through the Union Graduate School. Wilma had enrolled at the Union Graduate School (UGS) of the Union for Experimenting Colleges and Universities in 1975 partly at the invitation of its then president, Sam Baskin. Students chose their area of work and their doctoral committee, with the approval of the School. Wilma decided to focus on feminist theory and its implications for public policy. The Committee members she chose were: Rita Arditti, Jessie Bernard, Sally Hacker, Rhetaugh Graves Dumas, and Barbara Sterrett.

Rita Arditti is a core faculty member of the Union, a biological scientist, and a co-founder of a feminist bookstore, New Words, Inc. in Cambridge, Massachusetts. She is a co-editor and contributor of several books, including *Science and Liberation* (Boston, South End Press).

The second faculty person, Jessie Bernard, asked to be on Wilma's committee, much to Wilma's delight. An internationally known sociologist, professor at Pennsylvania State University, writer, consultant and activist, she first met Wilma at a New York Academy of Sciences conference. One issue addressed at the conference was feminism and fertility. According to Bernard,

> Some of us suggested that some feminists be brought in. He [Jerry Combs of the population division of the Institute for Mental

Health] did and much to his surprise, they practically took over. It was such a revolutionary experience for him and the very proper academy people, and I'm sure they were never the same again. Margaret Mead was chairing one of the sessions, and she was scolding them [the feminists] for being obstreperous, but I thought they were great. Wilma was there and quite a lot of the very avant garde women – Dello Jolio, Roxanne Dunbar, Jo Ann Evans Gardner ... Wilma was exciting, she was stimulating, she was dynamic; in her very quiet way, she was exploding bombs all over the place.[17]

Wilma and Jessie Bernard were immediately attracted to each other. The sociologist summarized her appreciation and respect for Wilma by simply stating: "I think she is one of the most creative women I know and a very courageous woman." Similarly, Wilma said of Jessie Bernard: "a caring sociologist, brilliant scholar, cherished friend and a national treasure."

The third faculty person was Sally Hacker. Wilma selected Sally because of her credentials as a sociologist, and because of her ethics. As Wilma says, "Sally lives her values."

Rhetaugh Graves Dumas and Barbara Sterrett were both peer members of the committee. Both are graduates of UGS. Dumas had done her work on Black women and is a registered nurse. Sterrett is a poet and activist. Patricia J. Marion, UGS Core Faculty, was chosen to be a third reader outside of committee involvement with the thesis.

Wilma finished the work for her doctoral degree with a thesis entitled: "Feminism for the Health of It: A Covenant with Truth." It was six long essays on scholarship, health care, President Carter's proposed "welfare" reform, higher education, media in the human interest, and international affairs.[18]

Wilma's doctoral work suggested to her the possibility of selecting academia as a place for significant institutional change. She began seeking employment there. After a brief stint at Goddard in its Adult Degree Program, Wilma accepted a position at Sangamon State University in Springfield, Illinois. Sangamon State is the Public Affairs University of the Illinois University system. Its curriculum is for upper level and graduate students. Wilma's position there was professor of Women's Studies and Innovative and Experimental Studies, and Director of Women's Studies. Her responsibilities included teaching one course each semester, coordinating the Women's Studies program, and integrating the resources of people of color and feminists in Women's Studies and the larger institution.

This last responsibility was for Wilma the most exciting and fruitful possibility for structural change. It gave her the opportunity to introduce less hierarchical ways of locating power and authority, consensus styles of decision-making, inclusive and feminist criteria for program evaluation and for committee selection.

She immersed herself in the university in characteristic fashion – on the one hand seeking to broaden and deepen people's understanding of Women's Studies and feminism and, on the other, bringing those perspectives to bear on every aspect of institutional life. She sought to broaden the university's understanding of affirmative action to include education as well as employment and to deepen the university's support for Women's Studies by increasing its budget. With others from Women's Studies, she collaborated on a series of feminist 5-minute commentaries on peace and conflict resolution, economics, violence, men's participation in feminism, poverty, and inclusive language. The local Public Broadcasting System (PBS) affiliate broadcast the series and since then the commentaries have been played on other stations throughout the country. Wilma later edited the series into a book called *Feminist Forum*.[19]

Wilma continued to press for other fundamental changes. Each spring the university sponsored a week-long Intersession that addressed an area of public policy from an interdisciplinary perspective. The first year Wilma was there, she succeeded in incorporating feminist perspectives into the theme of the spring Intersession – The Energy Decade: Food, Environment, and Resources. The second year, a Women's Studies Committee assumed major responsibility to hold a conference on the Struggle for Peaceful Conflict Resolution.

Wilma also became a member of the program evaluation committee, which examined each program of the university every five years. She consistently challenged the qualities of programs if they did not significantly reflect both feminist perspectives and those of Third World and minority peoples. The result was often stormy. Some colleagues protested that Wilma's concerns denied academic freedom. Wilma responded that it was not freedom but accurate and responsible scholarship that was at issue.

Wilma sought appointment to the Public Affairs Council, a major policy-making body, whose members held administrative responsibilities within the University. Wilma was denied because she did not hold the required upper level administrative post. Wilma protested that she had more experience in public affairs than any of those already on the Council, and that the structural qualification perpetuated discrimination. In this, however, she was strenuously opposed by the Vice President of Academic Affairs.

After two and a half years at Sangamon, Wilma resigned. Health problems continued to plague her, and she wished to return east to explore alternative medical help. She felt increasing pressure at Sangamon to confine herself to teaching, and decided that a more efficient use of her resources was to work as a consultant. In addition she found the location unsettling; the violent thunder storms and tornadoes unnerved her and the isolation of Springfield from major transportation routes continued to frustrate her. In the Spring of 1982, she left Sangamon although many encouraged her to remain. She moved to

Norristown, outside of Philadelphia, where a good friend, Annette Wall, found her a place to live. She continued to speak and serve nationally as a consultant on institutional change.

Peacemaking

The clearest new direction for Wilma emerged in peacemaking. In the winter of 1977-78, Wilma accepted an invitation to enroll in a ten-week course on arbitration sponsored by the American Arbitration Association. What she found there convinced her that much of what women traditionally have learned to do is what people like arbitrators are now (sometimes) practicing without realizing that this has always been "women's work." In her book, *Toward a New Psychology of Women*, Jean Baker Miller writes that psychiatrists and counselors have been doing "women's work." Wilma would add and "those involved in settling disputes." The experience in the arbitration course served as a catalyst in focusing her attention on conflict resolution.

The following year, in the late fall of 1979, Wilma was asked to be a resource for an embryonic organization of women who became Feminist Women for Peace, SOS (Sisters Organized for Survival). She also became part of the National Women's Leadership Planning Group for the Commission on Proposals for the National Academy of Peace and Conflict Resolution.

In June 1983, Wilma travelled to Finland for a two-week invitational meeting on peace with Scandinavian and Soviet women. Initiated by the Scandinavian women, the conference provided an international opportunity to explore feminist values as a resource and conditions for peace, and analyze masculinist values as a cause of violence. Wilma was particularly excited with the opportunity it afforded for the Soviet participants to be a part of that exploration because it served to redefine what feminism was about. A follow-up conference was held the following year in Leningrad. Wilma was unable to attend but heard from participants that the exploration of feminism as a resource and conditions of peace continued. Still other follow-up conferences were scheduled for Norway in 1985 and the United States in 1986.

In the summer of 1983, Wilma also participated in the Seneca Women's Peace Encampment. Her continuing involvement in peace issues, and particularly her experience at Seneca, convinced her of a growing, powerful groundswell of active feminist commitment to peacemaking, a movement that in effect gives her space to explore still further what her role should be. She has been considering establishing a study-action center to explore feminist approaches to peacemaking, for instance, and many of her friends have been urging her to move in that direction.

NOTES

1. Heide, Wilma Scott: "Feminism: the *Sine Qua Non* for a Just Society." *Vital Speeches of the Day*, Vol. XXXVIII, #13, April 15, 1972, pp.403-9.
2. Aileen Hernandez in telephone conversation with me, March 1980.
3. Kathryn Clarenbach in telephone conversation with me, April 1980.
4. The only exception to the previously non-competitive elections was in 1973, when Jacqui Ceballos was nominated by Irene Diamond as a tribute to Jacqui. Both, however, also supported Wilma.
5. In taped interview with Mary Lynn Myers, Summer 1977.
6. Carabillo, Toni: "Perspective – For the National Advisory Committee and Leadership." Vol. 1, #1, 1976 (Hernandez's files).
7. Conversation with Wilma, Spring 1978.
8. Three years later, in July 1975, Patricia Schroeder, Congressperson from Colorado, stated that 2.5% of the Bicentennial funds were committed to women's programs; and those included such projects as "archaeological excavation of Andrew Jackson's home, sponsored by the Ladies Heritage Association, a plaque sponsored by a state DAR, landscapings, flower plantings, and musical history programs sponsored by the Junior League." (Patricia Schroeder, *Statement* to the American Revolution Bicentennial Board, July 22, 1975, Wilma's files). Wilma had suggested to feminists in Colorado that they persuade Congressperson Schroeder to investigate the ARB Association's funding by sex and program orientations.
9. Other coalition members, in addition to Wilma, included Patricia Budd Kepler (minister), Sister Margaret Ellen Traxler, Sister M. Concilia Moran, Jean King (Attorney), Dr. Edith Tebo (scientist), Nancy Gager (historian), Linda Grant De Pauw (historian).
10. "Declaration of Interdependence." The full text is in Appendix A.
11. Stanton, Elizabeth Cady: *Eighty Years and More: Reminiscences 1815-1895*. Schocken, New York, 1971.
12. The Declaration of Sentiments is a declaration of women's rights written by Matilda Joslyn Gage and Elizabeth Cady Stanton for the Centennial, July 4, 1876.
13. National Commission on the Observance of International Women's Year: *The Spirit of Houston*. U.S. Government Printing Office, Washington, DC, 1978. The Commission to organize the State and National Conferences had both the authority and obligation under the enabling legislation to see that delegates were demographically representative of women by the appointive process.
14. Unfortunately, little recognition was given to those pioneers, and this absence was a serious weakness of the Houston Conference.
15. Wilma would have chosen to have both names prominently displayed.
16. Heide, Wilma Scott: *Program Summary*. Unpublished Paper for the Union Graduate School, Union for Experimenting Colleges and Universities, 1978.
17. Interview with Dr. Jessie Bernard, October, 1977.
18. Wilma's dissertation, revised and updated, is now published: *Feminism for the Health of It*. Margaretdaughters, Inc., P.O. Box 70, Buffalo, NY 14222, 1985.
19. Persons interested in obtaining the tapes should call or write their local Public Broadcasting System station for further information. The book *Feminist Forum* is available from Sangamon State University, Springfield, IL 62708.

9

ETHICS IN THE HUMAN INTEREST

> ...we seek a new order and covenant ourselves to a fully interde-
> pendent society. We live in a world in which love has yielded to
> war, art to science, religion to materialism, and sexuality to vio-
> lence. We are committed to the discovery of a humanity which
> lays claim to the fullness of life.
>
>   – Women's Coalition for the Third Century[1]

What is Ethics?

The word 'ethics' can be used in two distinct ways. It can be used to refer to a disciplined investigation and body of knowledge. In this sense the term is like 'physics' or 'sociology'. The subject matter of ethics is morality and discussions about morality. 'Morality' is a term that includes decision-making and the criteria for determining good decisions, traits of personhood or character, an ethos, rules, values, ideals, principles.

'Ethics' also can be used to mean a particular system, or body, or pattern of morality. I use the phrase 'Wilma's ethics' in this second sense. Wilma has a pattern of beliefs and values and principles in light of which she seeks to act and to be. As the author of this book, I am "doing ethics" in the first sense as I organize, explicate and analyze Wilma's ethics in the second sense. In order to avoid confusion about these two meanings, in this chapter when I use the first meaning, I will use the phrase *ethical inquiry* and reserve the term *ethics* for the second meaning.

Ethical inquiry has traditionally concerned itself with actions and traits of personhood, doing and being. When traits of personhood are being explored, a central question to ask is: "what traits or dispositions or qualities of a person are valued and/or are valuable?" Traditionally, those which have been deemed to be valued or valuable have been called 'virtues' or 'excellences'. The word 'virtue' unfortunately is rooted in the Latin *vir* – man, although it has tended to be used today to describe chaste women. The word 'virtuoso' suggests more accurately the connection with excellence. The virtuoso violinist is an artist who has such a command of an instrument that s/he can play it excellently – with great skill, precision and effortlessness.

Much of the classical Greek ethical inquiry was concerned with excellence – with the good person. Medieval Christian ethical inquiry continued this tradition. When St. Augustine said, "Love God and do what you will," he had a tradition of thought about personal excellence behind him. The lover of God, the self with its disposition to love finely honed, will act appropriately, rightly.

In more recent times, inquiry into considerations of right action has tended to pre-empt concern with excellence. "What ought I to do?" has been a much more central question. When addressing this question, ethical inquiry has examined the intentions and consequences, principles and rules of action, ends and means. It no longer seems sufficient to answer the question "What ought I to do?" with the injunction to love God or be just, as Augustine or Plato might have answered. Being-well does not seem automatically to lead to doing well. Many questions of right action are enormously complex at the level of specific choices. How should we eradicate poverty? How should we respond to the energy shortage? Should we maintain nuclear parity? The answers to such questions depend not only on ethical inquiry but also on economic, sociological, and political inquiry; and even then we are likely to disagree about what is the right answer.

Today, inquiry into both excellence and action is complicated further by a fundamental challenge to the ethics of such inquiry. The challenge is that the inquiry itself is elitist and largely self-serving; it is unethical. Ethical inquiry has been done by primarily white, affluent men and has generally had the effect, if not the intention, of preserving their position in society and legitimating only their perspectives.

Feminist ethics is a central part of the challenge to ethical inquiry. Feminist ethics includes both a critique of the elitism of much of traditional ethics and ethical inquiry, and explorations into alternative patterns.

Feminism: An Ethic

For Wilma, feminism is an ethic; to speak of a feminist ethic is redundant. Feminism is a profound values revolution, ie, transformation in our understandings and formulations of personal excellence, of action, and of the criteria for action. One major source and resource of this values revolution is a subtle combination of women's experience and feminist vision and experience.

Women's experience refers to the variegated ways women have fashioned a living out of our own lives in a society which has assigned us a subordinate position. It includes responses to the dominant culture; that is, we have found ways of living with and/or in the presence of men in and out of the home. It includes relating to our own rhythms, life developments, fears, hopes and confusions. Although we have lived and will continue to live among men, we have our separate existence – a separate culture, as if it were a sexual apartheid. Some of women's experience is shaped by physical changes and rhythms; much of it is shaped by the roles and responsibilities assigned and/or chosen by us. It is shaped by certain freedoms and certain constraints on us as women. It is shaped by the survival techniques we have learned or been taught, which may enable us to survive but may also keep us imprisoned. It is shaped by the resources and strengths we have discovered in order to live with beauty and dignity and grace in the midst of trivialization, oppression, poverty and pathos.

The ethic of feminism is rooted also in feminist vision and experience. Feminist vision and experience name as resources for ethics: the longing and imagining of wholeness, of freedom; the cry for justice; and the desperate struggle against violation and violence. Feminism is intrinsically a *political* ethic, generated out of action for change.

The two components, traditional women's experience and experience of political action, are in critical dialogue with each other. The combination is what Wilma calls a gynandrous ethic: an affirmation of the "feminine" in both sexes as they are related to those values is necessary for effective social change.

Humaneness/In the Human Interest

Women's experience and feminist vision are starting points for ethics. Another starting point is what Wilma calls *humaneness*, or *the human interest*, and it too is in continuous dialogue with women's experience and feminist vision.

"The human as an entity is relatively in its infancy," she states.[2] Societies have operated for centuries on principles of class, sex, and race privilege and hierarchy, but not on genuine concern for the humane. Even in the United States, the eras of "the common man" (sic) – such as Jacksonian democracy – and of individualism served the well-being of selected groups, primarily white males of western European heritage.

The principle of *humaneness/in the human interest* puts human need and human possibility at the center, as the only justifiable reason for the existence or structuring of institutional and interpersonal relationships. In light of the principle of *humaneness/in the human interest* all other reasons are subject to questioning and testing, whether they be reasons of natural law, God's will, or the greatest good for the greatest number; whether they be reasons of defense pacts, profits, maintenance of power, or stereotyping about groups. Wilma asks again and again: Do any of those really serve the well-being of the human being in society or the world?

The principle of *humaneness/human interest* puts human need and human possibility at the center. Both are important – meeting human needs and appreciating human possibility. Together they suggest a way of understanding the concept of human well-being. *Humaneness/in the human interest*, means respect, and respect suggests distance – ie, those making policy decisions should not predetermine what another's well-being is and seek to impose that on that person or group. *Respect* means listening to and conversing with that person or group and determining policy together.

Similarly, *well-being* means the intrinsic combination of meeting needs and appreciating possibility. It means creating space for people to grow, explore, emerge, become, take responsibility for one's own well-being and that of others.

> What is human is very precious, it is to be cherished, it is to be nurtured. "In the human interest" means a divine appreciation of virtually unlimited possibilities.[2]

The normativeness of human well-being includes both individual well-being and the common good, or corporate well-being. Individual and social well-being need not be opposed; neither should be sacrificed for the other. They come into conflict because we have either ignored the principle of *humaneness/in the human interest* in policy formation or have confused this principle with a "do your own thing" ethic. Any society can and should have constraints on individual action, but unfortunately it is much easier to continue to add constraints than to eliminate the reasons for destructive behavior. It is easier to multiply regulations around those who receive welfare checks than it is to eliminate poverty. But the elimination of poverty is much more *humane/in the human interest* than increased regulation.

Wilma's point is to remove all the layers of conventional "wisdom" about individuals and societies until we get down to the fundamental question – is it *humane/in the human interest?* Will it help make us happy – at home with ourselves, our neighbors, and the universe? In the imagery created by Anne Hazlewood Brady:

> We moved fifty brass screws
> stripped canvas to skeleton canoe
> and laid the gunnels down
> like long thin modern s's.
> We scraped away the painted years
> green, white, and battle grey
> until we got down eventually
> to brass tacks and two women
> rebuilding from raw wood
> a slim-skinned, silent boat
> that puts upon the waters
> nothing but its weight.[3,p.20]

What then, is the content of *humaneness/in the human interest?* The principle is abstract, as principles are. The principle remains abstract in part because the human as an entity is still relatively in its infancy; we do not yet know what we might become if we took it seriously. However, because we do know something about humaneness – and women in particular do – humane rather than cruel, humane rather than unyielding, humane rather than destructive, humane rather than manipulative, the principle can be made more specific. Humaneness points to consideration for others and oneself, generosity or graciousness toward others and oneself, nurturing toward others and oneself, honesty toward others and oneself, and aliveness to the senses of others and oneself. Women in particular know this principle because of our life experiences, not because of our sex; thus men can learn it also.

Because we have so little experience of living our public lives humanely, the idea is breath-taking. What experience we have comes primarily from the private, interpersonal sphere, and that has not been considered a valid example for humaneness in public life. We do not know, but we can dream and ask the right questions. For instance, what would an educational system be like if it facilitated, encouraged and rewarded competence and nurturing? What would our mass media be like without contests against opposing players, stories of violence and conquest, quiz shows with thousands of dollars and prizes for the winner, "comedies" that demeaned the human beings portrayed in them? What would our economic system be like if there were no poverty, no alienation of workers from their labor, if repetitive tasks "too petty for the human spirit" were either eliminated or shared by all? We can fantasize answers to questions like these, but we cannot fully plan them because we do not yet know.

Wilma tends to turn away from abstract discussions of justice and equality, and works on the tasks at hand, hoping that as new opportunities emerge and are created, the experience will provide more insight and fuller commitment. One does not simply wait to see what happens. The connection between the future and the present lies neither with a blue-print of the future nor with the hope that something will occur, but with planting the seeds or building the foundation – beginning with what we do and what we know, and being alert to discover more.

An example of action in the human interest demonstrates how the action can begin to shape a different future. If I am convinced that organic farming is superior for political, environmental and health reasons, how do I begin to create change? I do not know all that needs to be known about organic farming to feed the world; no one else does either. But if I am committed to the principle, then I do what I can, begin to move in circles where organic farming is discussed and explored, support research, reward those who do it, and perhaps even make a few discoveries myself. As I move, I may find ways to combine some aspects of "inorganic" farming that might increase yield but still remain ecologically sustainable. I become part of a process, one that in its own way is revelatory, and in so doing I become increasingly sensitive, open to more insight, open to revelation.

A humane society is one that, among other things, is willing to risk the first steps toward human well being.

We seek the transcending humaneness that sanctions valuable traits of caring, daring, competence, nurturance, interdependence in individuals and institutions.[4]

To make humaneness an overarching paradigm is to turn to the practical questions of means and ends – of first and second steps. We get to a more humane future by taking what we already know of humaneness and seeking to internalize it and act on its principles. We get to a more humane future by becoming more humane now and acting in more humane ways. In short, the means shape the ends.

Analysis of Sexism

From the starting point of *humaneness/in the human interest* an analysis of the status quo of sexism is possible. In the United States, we are the inheritors of many strands of traditions of morality, containing both consistencies and inconsistencies. We have assumptions and expectations about personal excellence and we have been bequeathed principles and rules to guide our actions. What has until recently tended to be ignored is that the traditional ethic has been largely the ethic of a minority of men in relative positions of power, prestige, and responsibility for the public realm.

Not only has the traditional ethic been normal; it has also been assumed to be normative and natural. It has been accepted and viewed as acceptable; and it has been considered "the way things are." Sexism, therefore, is an ethic. Descriptively speaking, sexism is an ethic that has been equated variously with human nature, humanism, western thought, and/or the Judeo-Christian traditions.

For those who are feminists such an ethic is not only limited and incomplete, it is also prejudiced, unnatural and oppressive. It is wrong. It is built on and reinforces exploitation and castes; it denies human wholeness; it perpetuates violence; and humanity is denied the resources of over half the human race. By holding that there are different excellences and criteria for excellence appropriate to different groups on the one hand, and that those of affluent, straight, white males are finally normative on the other, the ethic puts everyone else into a double-bind. Women are expected to be and do in certain ways, but if they wish to share the privileges and responsibilities of men they must be and do in other ways. The same kind of dual, contradictory set of expectations are true for other out-groups. If one falls into two or more of those out-groups, the double-bind multiplies quickly.

Sexism denies human wholeness. By dividing excellences and criteria for excellence along sexual lines, both women and men have been denied essential parts of their humanity. Stereotypically, men have been denied, in the United States at least, some of their emotions; and women have been denied certain uses of their rationality. This denial has also been reflected in theories about the separation of body and mind, a separation that has a long philosophical history. In the United States, the separation has meant ironically, for men, a denial of themselves as sexual beings, precisely because of the connectedness between sexuality and the emotional life. Psychoanalyst Jean Baker Miller writes of this separation:

> Learning to master passion and weakness became a major task of growing up as a man. But sexuality, precisely because of its insistence and its intense pleasure, can become an area of threat, something that undermines carefully developed controls.[5,p.23]

Sexism and violence are intrinsically linked and the connections are many.[6] Violence is related to sex-role stereotyping; it seems to be a consequence of such stereotyping. The ethos expects of men more than it does of women, both to defend themselves at the risk or with the intent to harm *or* kill others and to exploit others in order to "get ahead."

As a child, for a boy to be called a "sissy" is much more devastating than for a girl to be called a "tomboy." To refuse to fight, to mediate, to be willing to be defenseless are suspect, signs of "giving in," of "going soft," of "not being able to take it." Not only are boys and men expected to defend themselves; they are also more often than women expected to maintain an adversarial stance toward others. They are to be "on guard," they are to "beat" the other out of the business deal or promotion, they are to win. Nearly every institution reflects this pattern of expectations. The legal institution is but one example. Anne Strick says of the law:

> It is a method of dispute settlement that requires all persons who go to law to settle differences to behave as enemies ... Out of that battle, adversary "rationale" maintains that the truth will be revealed ... [Yet] each side must present *not* all it knows, but only its own "best case;" must assail the opposition; must attack and counterattack, "discover" and avoid discovery.[7,p.19]

This adversarial mode is deeply embedded in our thinking. Even when people protest the wrongs of American society, they tend to think adversarially. They are *against* as much as or more than they are *for.* Or they pose issues in a rights vs rights framework. It becomes women's rights vs Black rights, for instance (and in that formulation Black often means Black males), a right to one's body vs an embryo's right to life, the rights of parents vs the rights of children. A conflictual and an adversarial relationship is assumed. Wilma has counselled law schools, the legal profession, and others to move away from this adversarial phrasing to alternatives: such as "in the interests of Smith and Jones," rather than "Smith vs Jones," to identify any common ground and then acknowledge disagreements, adjudicating wrongs, and facilitating dispute resolutions in ways that will discover, not hide truths.

A second connection between sexism and violence is found in the pattern of hierarchy. Violence against subordinates has been taken for granted in the United States and around the world. Violence becomes a means of social control of subordinates. Women and children are beaten and sexually abused.

Further, as capitalism is added to stereotyping and hierarchy, other forms of violence appear. Women and children constitute a great majority of poor in this country and elsewhere.

> Of the 24.3 million poor people in the U.S., 19.6 million are women and children. In 1976, twice as many women age 16 and over than men lived below the poverty level ... One third of single female parent families were in the poverty group, including 891,000 single female parent families where the mother worked and earned less than the poverty level.[8]

In 1976 it was proposed that to meet the Defense budget, the government should eliminate supplementary food for the poor and for pregnant women, cut free school lunch programs and milk for children and remove low income workers (mostly women) from food stamp eligibility.[9]

Violence against the earth is equally justified by the ethic of sexism. Men continue to conquer nature (which is usually called "she"), even though the conquerors themselves cannot live without clean air and water and food. Not only have the consequences of environmental contamination been disastrous for much of the natural world and for those who have conquered, they have also embroiled human beings in continual social conflict – in competition for resources, in exploitation and conquest of people living in naturally rich areas of the earth, and in impoverished existence. In a terrible and savage twist of irony, violence against men themselves is generated and sanctioned – total annihilation, not once and forever, but several times. The United States and Russia have the destructive power to kill each person twenty times over and to destroy all life on the face of the earth for thousands of years – all in the name of "security" and "peace."

A third connection between sexism and violence is found in the legacy of dualism. In the past 30 years many have pointed to a loss of intimacy which is connected both with sex-role stereotyping and the legacy of a dualism between body and soul, nature and spirit. Rollo May and J. Glenn Gray have described this loss, but without relating it to sexism.[10] Rosemary Ruether, among others, has provided this missing dimension, and I have sought to redefine and reclaim intimacy as an excellence of being, essential to living humanely with all that is.[11]

Where intimacy is lacking, alienation and suspicion are more likely to be present. Intimacy is a correlate of friendship and nurturance. Where a sexist ethos prevails, status, and/or wealth become some of the surrogates for closeness and at-homeness. Thus a sexist ethos perpetuates a double bind; in alienation from one's body and emotional expression, one seeks substitutes, but the substitutes one seeks further increase the lack of intimacy and the pervasiveness of competition and conflict.

Words themselves reflect the connections between sexism and violence. The word 'peace', for instance, is associated with a dove or a woman with a laurel wreath around her head. 'Peace' is a soft word; it suggests peacefulness –

calmness, harmony, rest. Robert McCan, testifying on the need for a peace academy in the United States, described peace as:

> the positive face of humanity, the harmonious balancing of all forces, the at-homeness with ourselves and with our world, with our conception of the ultimate.[12,pp.37-38]

In contrast, war is associated with a hawk, a predator, or with Mars, the god of war. War is a hard word: loud and strident. There is aggression and destruction, the clenched fist, the defiant posture. War suggests what is called heroism and cowardice. Peace suggests saintliness. Peace is a feminine word; war is a masculine one. David Halverstam once described President Johnson as being:

> haunted by the idea that he would be judged as being insufficiently manly for the job...He wanted the respect of men who were tough, real men, and they would turn out to be the hawks...Hearing that one member of his Administration was becoming a dove on Vietnam Johnson said, "Hell, he has to squat to piss." [13,p.17]

Initially one of Carter's appeals may have been that he did not portray this kind of "macho" image to a country weary of the lawless and destructive consequences of sexism, although it was not so named. However, as crisis after crisis confronted Carter, he too began responding in an increasingly "get tough" mode.

The connection between violence and what has come to be called "the masculine mystique" has been documented over and over again. Whether it is the history of the west or of organized crime, whether it is the street gangs of the ghetto or fights in bars, whether it is James Bond or Ernest Hemingway, whether it is among the Ku Klux Klan or revolutionaries, violence and masculinity and male supremacy or longing for male supremacy are intrinsically intertwined companions. The twisted way in which that connection informs attitudes toward war is best summarized in the following quotation from Ernest Hemingway:

> There are worse things than war; and all of them come with defeat.
> The more you hate war, the more you know that once you are forced into it, for whatever reason it may be, you have to win it.[14]

Sexism denies humanity the resources of over half the population. Women have resources that have emerged from our responsibilities and roles. The skills of mediating and nurturing, and the administrative skills of learning how to survive with dignity and compassion, could all be applied to enhancing the common good. Jean Baker Miller writes:

> ...the characteristics most highly developed in women and perhaps most essential to human beings are *the* very characteristics that are specifically dysfunctional for success in the world as it is.

That is obviously no accident. They may, however, be the important ones for making the world different.[5,p.124]

Or as Wilma puts it,

> ...Human justice and a humane society are impossible without feminism. *Whatever* the political-economic system, androcentricity and justice are mutually exclusive.
>
> No *significant* change in the future is possible without women's human rights and liberation from centuries of blatant and subtle bondage. Only those women and men free enough from stereotyped notions of "femininity" and "masculinity" to be secure about our common humanity are as yet liberated enough to move with the level of self-confidence to create an androgynous [she would now say gynandrous] society and world. Women will demand it. Men will eventually welcome it. Our children deserve it. No woman should ever have to stand alone or be criticized for advocating and creating our own, our mothers', our sisters', our daughters' personhood. It's a matter of human justice. [15,p.409]

Philosophical Bases of Feminist Ethics

A person's ethic is set into a framework of perceptions and beliefs – those fundamental means of relating oneself to all that is. We hold certain beliefs about reality. Those beliefs arise out of what we have assimilated, our own experience as individuals and as members of certain groups, and our vision of the future. Our beliefs inform our perceptions. We tend to see, to attend to those aspects of reality that cohere with what we believe. At the same time, perceptions inform beliefs. We see, we understand in a new way, and that perception becomes a means of revelation, a disclosure of the nature of reality of which we were not formerly cognizant.

For feminists, much of the time there is a conflict between what we have been taught to believe and our experience and vision of the future. This discrepancy and the sheer compelling quality of the experience and vision make us see, or enable us to see the world quite differently from many.

Perceiving and believing have both cognitive and affective dimensions. The *self* perceives and believes, not the head or the heart alone. Perceptions and beliefs on the one hand, and ethics on the other, should move dynamically toward a general congruence. One's values should be, and are to a lesser or greater degree, consistent with how one fundamentally sees the world. Such consistency is at times a struggle and can be felt in the sense of being untrue to oneself. As Wilma describes the consistency, "Finally it's a matter of integrity."

The beliefs that underlie Wilma's ethics are much less articulated than the ethic itself. Nevertheless, there are several convictions that are essential and central – freedom, humaneness, and the divine.

Freedom

The freedom on which Wilma's ethic is based is not simply freedom of choice but rather ontological freedom. An intrinsic dimension of human nature is freedom – change, becoming, dynamism. Nature is fluid, open, unfixed. We do not *have* to be and act as we do; we can be and act differently. As a culture, as a species we can be different; we can re-create ourselves and our world.

Wilma's conviction about freedom is perhaps best expressed most often in her statements about sex-roles and human nature. In earlier formulations she stated that *"only* being a human incubator, an ovum donor, or a wet nurse excludes all men and *only* being a sperm donor excludes all women."[16,p.69] More recently, she has dropped the exclusion of men from breast feeding, since there is both experiential and scientific evidence that some men have learned and can learn to breast feed. Her point is that only the obvious reproductive functions are sex-specific. All other behaviors are learned and can be unlearned and changed. Indeed, they should be changed in the direction of making them available to other women and men; they should be part of the "human repertoire."

Wilma's conviction about the ontological base of human freedom also finds expression in other statements. When she speaks of "men learning to be brave enough to care about the quality and equality of our common life" and "women learning to care enough to be brave," or when she says that "the power of love must exceed the love of power," she is implying that human nature can change in fundamental ways.

More concretely, we do not have to have wars and rumors of wars; there is nothing inherent in human nature that dictates the eternal reality of violence. If human beings were not basically more mutually cooperative than not, humanity would not have survived. Acts of cooperation in the millions and millions have not been considered dynamic and exciting and have not been celebrated, but they exist. "It is normal but not natural," Wilma says of this violent reality and of a host of others. We do not have to have poverty and injustice. Overcoming these conditions is "do-able," although, to be sure, it may take a long time and requires the consciousness and commitment to humane alternatives in private and public policies.

This conviction about freedom enables Wilma to redefine realism. Often, "realism" suggests a shrewd sophistication, as opposed to "naive idealism," and a lowering of expectations about what can be accomplished. For Wilma, what some call "realistic" too often becomes a matter of short-changing the possibilities of human nature, and Wilma is suspicious when others try to tell her to be realistic. "Being realistic," for Wilma, is a matter of "knowing the pervasiveness, the depths of sexism" so one is not easily, or at all, disillusioned by the strength and stubbornness of the forces one is seeking to eliminate. Given her conviction about freedom, Wilma recognizes the freedom that people have to construct oppressive structures; it is also our freedom from which we accept the responsibility to change such structures.

Humaneness

There are obvious limits to freedom beyond which we cannot go – limits of oxygen, food, water, and air – although many continue to ignore them. There is also another limit, the limit of *humaneness* itself. The concept of *human nature* includes *freedom*; but it also includes *humaneness*. Human nature is both possibility and norm. If we create ourselves and the world in certain ways, beyond a point we lose our humanity in the process. Anatomically, we may still look like human beings, but we will cease to *be* human beings.

The word 'human' fits with Wilma's fundamental criterion of humaneness. To be human can be *to be humane*. There is a structure in us, one that must be nurtured, valued, developed – our capacity to be humane. In a backhanded way, sexism acknowledges this capacity and has assigned it to women to express for the whole of culture. As women are degraded and de-valued, humaneness itself is devalued and seldom gets a hearing.

What we as a human race should be about then, is change in the direction of increased humaneness. Such change is possible. It is the task of change agents to be constantly pushing in that direction and necessarily making the connections between lack of humaneness and sexism, and between humaneness and feminism. The two, in each case, are the warp and woof of the human condition and human promise, not the totality.

For Wilma, the capacity for change in the direction of increased humane-ness means transformation in the way we think, talk and act. It is incumbent on change agents to abandon adversarial thinking and behaviors, and replace them with language and behaviors of promise and hope. Other people, whose values, positions, and ideas are in fundamental conflict with that of feminism are not "enemies" or objects to be overcome or defeated but are "not yet feminists," – those whose humanity or understanding, at least on a given occasion, has not been fully stirred or given a chance to flower. They are not targets but beneficiaries of one's action; they are given an opportunity to exercise humane concern and decency.

In the eyes of some, Wilma sometimes seems inconsistent. She can be extremely tough, "coming on too strong;" yet she can be extraordinarily generous in her estimate of others. There may indeed be inconsistency on occasion, since she, like others, is changing. But what is often seen as inconsistency is instead action consistent with her beliefs about human nature. The depths of sexism are profound, the possibilities of humane change are yet more profound and more fundamental. She is willing, therefore, to be tough, to risk alienating friends and supporters because of their capacity for increased awareness and because of the desperate, crying need to eliminate sexism, including the sexism in oneself and friends and supporters. On other occasions, however, she can be patient and gentle for essentially the same reasons, because all of us are human beings and caught in the web of sexism. Although she can be very pragmatic and realistic, in the popular sense of that word, her pragmatism and realism stem not only from political reasons (ie, gathering support to achieve certain objectives), but also from fundamental convictions about human nature. What seems inconsistent when interpreted in a conventionally political framework is not inconsistent when understood from the philosophical framework of ontologic freedom of all humans to be humane.

The Divine

Freedom and humaneness are central to Wilma's understanding of human nature philosophically. Another concept that is equally significant is the connectedness between what is called *the human* and what is called *the divine*. Wilma describes herself as an agnostic about belief in God. By this she means that the definitions and descriptions of God available to her from her childhood and from sexist theology have been found wanting. She is suspicious of the formulations, and she is skeptical of the credentials of the formulators.

At the same time, feminism and humaneness (which is intrinsically feminist) are an expression of the divine. It is spiritual, but it is more than spiritual. The divine is in touch with and an expression of an empowering creativity, of which we all partake.

Feminism is not simply the women's movement perceived as another secular, social movement, a movement that seeks social justice for women and the end of sexist values, behaviors, and institutions. Rather, in the movement for social justice is an empowering and an emergence of new personal identity. As laws are being changed, so people are being reborn and transformed. There is a religious depth, or dimension to the movement. But that dimension does not point to a religion in competition with other religions, either matriarchal or patriarchal. Rather it is an essential part of the transformation prerequisite to the revitalization of any religion.

The connection between feminism and spirituality lies in Wilma's ethics – it is an ethical spirituality and ethical-spiritual-secularity. Contact with life-giving power is always in the direction of more inclusive humaneness – within the individual, among all people, and within institutions. An ethical spirituality is nothing less than the missing and utterly vital link to the process of making those acting as "enemies" into friends, not necessarily always individually but certainly in terms of ethos.

Personal Excellence

One can be excellent in different ways. One can be an excellent pianist or gymnast or typist, honing talents to a fine edge of dexterity and command. One can be excellent in any of those ways that involve individual skills and aptitudes. Ethicists have also held that one can be excellent as a person.

Ethical inquiry addresses questions like: What is the excellence of personhood, or of being? If the excellence of a typist is typing well, ie, doing something well, what is it that a person *does* to achieve excellence as a person? The answers to that question have varied. For Aristotle, excellence lay in the development of those qualities that attended the good life for the Greek male citizen of the state. In medieval Christian, western thought, excellence lay in a redefinition of those qualities of the "good life" to include those which brought one close to God, the "supernatural" virtues of faith, hope and love. In contemporary philosophy, little attention has been paid to excellence except among a few religiously-informed moral philosophers. [17]

Both in her writing and acting, Wilma reflects a theory of personal excellence. Personal excellence is an important part of her ethics and is reflected in two ways. First, Wilma believes that we must re-value and bring into the public realm those values which have traditionally been made peripheral to the larger society. One way to do this is to internalize the values, to make them a part of our lives – men's and women's – so that the policies we make will be shaped by humane values. Internalizing values is a part of the process of becoming excellent.

Second, personal ethics arise out of the character of feminism as an ethic itself. Two of the classic claims of feminism are that "the personal is political" and that "the process is part of the product." Both of these ideas point us toward a theory of personal excellence. An ethic of personal excellence enables us to bring those personal resources of excellence to the political realm in the attitudes and sensitivities of the actors. A person who is just in one area of life is just in another, if justice is authentically a part of her/his being. Similarly a person who is nurturing in one area is also nurturing in another area, whether that be family life or at an international conference table. Personal excellence guarantees that the ends are going to be as we wish them to be. If we seek a nurturant society, our means to those ends must be nurturant. If nurturance is a part of the excellence of the actors, the means will include that dimension and so will the ends.

In the clearly understandable passion and commitment to a more just and humane society, it is tempting to take shortcuts. The use of violence is often, perhaps usually, such a shortcut. Operating on hierarchical and manipulative concepts of power is another, as is using deceit or half-truths. What Wilma calls "diplomacy by guile" is still another. Particularly, in the press of events and crises, we justify actions we later regret, as rules and principles slip our minds. But as we incarnate those principles and values in personal excellence, we consistently bring them with us into the time of decision.

Feminism as an ethic points to the opportunity and necessity of an understanding of personal excellence. But as we appreciate its appropriateness, we must redefine it. Excellence for radicals – ie, for those seeking to challenge and transform the very roots of oppression – is not the excellence of the male citizen of Greece or of the medieval Catholic. It is the excellence of those who dare to be humane in an inhumane world, who dare to be friends in a hostile world, and who dare to be open and nurturing in an alienated and antagonistic world.

What is such an excellence? Wilma addressed it experientially but not theoretically until 1975-1978 when she wrote her doctoral thesis for Union Graduate School.[18] Her focus was on a gynandrous theory, which is not only a positive valuation of "feminine" characteristics, but a new unity. Gynandry combines "positive dimensions of feminine and masculine phenomena in a more advanced phenomenon."[18,p.18] For instance, women traditionally have learned to have affective strengths and men cognitive ones. If women and men were to express and value both equally and fully, responding to the world out of both, not just responding cognitively sometimes and affectively at other times, what would our response be? What would it be like? What name could we give to it? Wilma suggests *discerning*, which blends cognitive and affective dimensions into a new unity.

Another example of personal excellence is Wilma's combining 'nurturing' and 'governing' (or being in charge), into ad-ministering, or ministering to. The English language does not yet have a word for that combination; Wilma had to resort to a play on words to point to genuinely humane administration. Still another more obvious example is the combination of independence and dependence. Feminist have for a long time sought an alternative to those two concepts, and the generally accepted name for that alternative is interdependence, though women need considerably more relative independence as a prerequisite.

What Wilma is experimenting with is both similar to and different from what others have been doing or are beginning to do. Notably, Jean Baker Miller and Anne Wilson Schaef have written and/or spoken along related lines. In her book, *Toward a New Psychology of Women*, Miller's thesis is that women have many strengths that have traditionally been considered weakness and indeed have sometimes become handicaps, when evaluated by androcentric norms.[5] But they are strengths for building a more humane world. Schaef, another psychoanalyst, describes or maps in papers and speeches what she calls the *female system* and the *male system*. For instance, she states that men tend to know how to make decisions quickly, whereas women tend to consider and ponder a wide variety of data and decide more slowly. In contemporary jargon, women "process" and men choose. Another example Schaef uses concerns time. In the male system, and indeed the white male system, time is seen to be what the clock measures; in the female system, the clock is irrelevant to time. Time is circular, rhythmical, procedural. In commenting on the two approaches to time, she observes:

> Neither of these ways of dealing with time is right ... Some ways are more functional in some situations and some in others, but where we have a system that says that one is the way the world is and the other is either sick, bad, crazy, or stupid we don't get that input.[19]

Both Miller and Schaef are exploring in detail how women, when they are being women, operate in the world, at least in our culture, and probably to some extent throughout the world. Wilma imaginatively envisions a world in which the way women operate is fully understood and valued. In such a world we will not simply on some occasions use clock time, to use Schaef's example, and on other occasions be cyclical. Rather, because our resources will be more diverse, our responses will also be different; a new kind of human being will emerge – a humane being.

Three excellences that Wilma returns to again and again are interdependence, nurturance and courage. Interdependence is a new combination, nurturance has been called a feminine excellence, and courage has been called a masculine excellence. A brief examination of each concept can help to understand some of the implications for ethical theory in Wilma's approach.

Interdependence

Interdependence combines the strengths of being dependent with those of independence. It acknowledges that we are not self-sufficient but rather intrinsically relational. It acknowledges that we can and should be vulnerable both in the sense of "able to be hurt" and in the sense of "responsive to, willingness to be affected by others." It also acknowledges that each one is a unique self and should be responsible for the care and development of the self and for the consequences of the actions the self takes.

An interdependent self then, can and does celebrate its relatedness; it acknowledges its need for and enjoyment of community. It is not threatened by awareness of needs and longings and commitments. It appreciates the ecological character of human nature.

Nor is the interdependent self threatened or limited by aloneness. It is or can be complete – a self in itself. Its identity transcends as well as includes relational identities, whether they be familial, economic, religious, class, political, sexual, or any other. Indeed, because the self is independent as well as dependent, it can risk intimacy with others and at the same time allow others to grow and change.

Nurturance

For Wilma, nurturance is a vital excellence but also a relative one. She sometimes describes it as a *bona fide occupational qualification* for leadership. The excellence of nurturance is a continuing readiness to provide conditions for others to grow. Specifically, nurturance is growth toward humaneness, the overarching norm. Among the conditions required for nurturance is openness to alternatives so that one need not be dragged kicking and screaming into the future. Nurturance is enabling oneself and others to find points of attractiveness about the future and move toward it willingly. Nurturance also includes making available the resources of growth – including self-confidence and knowledge of the available choices. In

Wilma's words, it is "supporting the ideas of others as much as possible, certainly supporting the people, and generally working with each other to build on strengths." Nurturance includes providing sheer physical resources of food, clothing, fresh air. The nurturing person seeks more than minimal survival resources. S/he seeks "significant soil," the rich, composted soil, that which genuinely encourages others as well as the self to grow.

A nurturing self perceives her/his relation to the world, as does the interdependent self, in a non-hierarchical fashion. The universe does not exist for the individual; valuing of the universe is not primarily utilitarian. Nor does s/he perceive it in primarily adversarial terms. If one's stance is nurturing toward others one is in conflict with, then justice *and* reconciliation are the primary considerations, not revenge or victory.

A part of the pathos of many women's experience is that we have been expected to give but not to receive, turning a New Testament insight about the importance of giving into a legalism about *only* giving. The disposition of nurturance can and should also be directed at oneself just as toward others; the self is viewed as a being working on growth toward humaneness. The self need not be excluded, indeed must be included.

Courage

One of the vital excellences is courage. Courage has been considered a traditional "masculine" virtue in the sense that it has been expected of men. Women have been courageous nevertheless – consider for example: pioneer women, Vietnamese women, slave women, women facing terminal illness in themselves or in those they love. When Wilma thinks of courage, however, she is thinking of the disposition to stand up for what is just, to go after justice in the public realm, to risk reputation, security, and perhaps even one's life. It is the courage to "demonstrate our values." It is the willingness to challenge the giants, the authorities, the "powerful" – the Senate, the EEOC, AT&T, the broadcast media.

In this context, courage is the ability not to be torn by doubt, paralyzed by timidity or fear of retaliation, ridicule, or hostility. It is the ability to act, to shape the future closer to the heart's desire. Courage is our foremothers who handcuffed themselves together, who refused to be force-fed, who refused to be deterred.

Courage includes a willingness to risk, resoluteness, determination, steadfastness. It does not mean what passes for courage outwardly – the clenched fist, the rock-like jaw, or throwing of rocks, the shouting of obscenities and taunts. Courage can be very quiet; it can indeed be gracious but it is not to be stopped.

Courage is not blind or fanatical. A courageous person can and does listen to discussion and argument about means and ends and consequences. It simply is that willingness to do, consistent with feminist values, what needs to be done.

Criteria for Action

Personal excellence and criteria for action are correlative concepts. Considerations of personal excellence guide moral development; criteria for action guide the choices of ends and means as we seek social change. There are two kinds of criteria that are significant in this part of Wilma's ethics. Both are normative in that both point to ways people *should* bring about change as well as descriptive of the way Wilma tries to do it. One set of criteria concerns procedure or style, how we should go about change. The second concerns the choices we make.

Procedural principles

Wilma's procedural principles are obligations on the revolutionary. They are obligations because they are independent of, in addition to, considerations of ends and means. One of the principles, as Wilma sometimes puts it, is that we should live our values; that we should demonstrate behaviorally what we are about. We need to live our values because we profess commitment to them, not because being nurturant and being honest will necessarily bring about a better society. That is not to deny the importance of the values for change, but that is not *why* we live them; we live our values because we think they are intrinsically important, regardless of calculations of consequence. Wilma's principles for decision do point us to the ends we hope to achieve – including sisterhood, new kinds of brotherhood, justice, nurturance, freedom of choice. We make choices on the basis of the possibility that these choices rather than others will contribute toward a friendlier, more just, more nurturant, and more graceful world. In order to ensure the goal, of course, the choices we make must have some fairly overt connection with the procedural principles. The emphasis is on the means as much as on the ends. With Wilma, we always come back to the present, the time of action: what are we doing, and how are we doing it?

Wilma's procedural principles include:
- broadening the interpretation of the situation for which decision and/or action is called;
- using humor;
- ensuring that women are among the major actors in a situation;
- living (or demonstrating) our values;
- and confronting a situation in a non-adversarial way.

Broadening the context: As Wilma saw a major responsibility on her within NOW to broaden the context of discussion, she also saw that same responsibility even more necessary outside of NOW. One can see this obligation most clearly in her written testimonies and speeches. For instance, in written testimony submitted to the Joint Economic Committee on the "economic problems of women" in the summer of 1973, she began not with problems of women, but with ways in which the Labor Department had or had not enforced civil rights laws and executive orders. [20] She concluded:

Most men are demonstrably unable, without the equal partnership of women at every level of public life to fully conceptualize, let alone solve, our deepest problems of sexism, racism, poverty, and violence. Indeed the very absence of women may *be the problem* itself.[20,p.5]

Similarly, in testimony delivered to the Senate Judiciary Committee, November 9, 1971, on the nominations of William H. Rehnquist and Lewis F. Powell, Jr. for the Supreme Court, she began with a description of sexism and then proceeded to an elaboration of how the criteria for qualification and the nominees' behavior were sexist and should disqualify them. She cited the language, the president's emphasis on the need for a "strict constructionist interpretation" of the Constitution (which according to Wilma meant bad news for women, since women were and are not in it), Rehnquist's equivocation on the ERA, and his position on alimony as reflecting ignorance of the real status of women. With respect to Powell, her charge was directed more to his not doing anything for women when he had multiple opportunities, rather than specific detrimental stands.

Many of her speeches were similar to her testimonies. Speaking to the National Easter Seal Society about volunteerism in 1973, for instance, she acknowledged that she too was a volunteer and then presented NOW's position on volunteerism, which was that:

> We oppose service volunteering that gives band-aid or symptomatic treatment to problems that may require serious analysis and radical societal, institutional change ...Society's various victims deserve valuing *enough* to stop shortchanging them by pretending their needs can be met by volunteers locally and individually, however compassionate we know most volunteers to be. [21,p.1]

She elaborated on ways in which volunteerism often reinforces sexist, racist, and classist values by perpetuating donor/donee relations, depressing funding of needed services, supporting sexist institutions (eg, the United Way and the Jaycees), and denying to victims real access to society's resources. [21,p.2-5;22]

> Compassion entrapment blunts pressure to more equitably distribute wealth and power and perpetuates the more negative anti-humane aspects of capitalism. [21,p.4]

Finally, she asked the Society to join feminists and others to "volunteer" to press for changing these realities.

Wilma's shifting the context or redefining the situation certainly was unpleasant for many, more so when they saw themselves as the experts. Her insistence on changing the rules must have been quite provocative. She refused to treat her audiences as adversaries but rather, in her terms, as "not-yet-feminists." A part of this attitude was expressed in the appeal to their good will and her willingness to transcend the differences, to work together, and to provide a new definition of what needs to be worked on.

Use of Humor: A further and significant means Wilma used for moving beyond a narrowly defined context was humor and wit. "Sometimes," she once said to me, "you can laugh people into changing." Sometimes the humor was a result of pointing out absurdity and illogic. In speaking of mythologies about human nature, she commented in the Easter Seal speech that one myth was that women were morally superior to men, and responded with "Poppycock! If people believed that, women would be forced to be our priests, ministers, rabbis, and leaders of all our social institutions."

Other statements, phrases, and words which humorously drive her points home included such now classic ones as:

I refuse to be called a housewife for the simple reason that I did not marry a house.

If you are filling out a form that asks for sex (after that became illegal), here are some answers you might put: What did you have in mind? Sometimes. I gave at home.

Being a secretary is not a secondary sex characteristic of all women, as is our ability to be diplomatic; that's why we're so often Secretary of State and Ambassadors to other countries.

In addition to humor there were turns of phrases that made the point and have become memorable:

She includes he, and woman includes man, unlike the reverse in both cases.

The generic use of womankind (which you note, includes mankind)...

S/he is risen!

The power of love must replace the love of power.

Much of Wilma's power lay in her capacity to combine emotional and factual material into speeches laced with such word-play. Her words thus evoked responses on both cognitive and affective levels. Together with enabling the audience to laugh at the absurdities of positions and assumptions they might have defended five minutes earlier, many of her speeches had tremendous power and were part of the holding together and nurturing that so often we have found Wilma doing.

Women as Principle Actors: A third procedural principle is that women should be among the principle actors. Women must become actors because they have brains and hearts and have insights and perspectives to contribute. This voice could help humanize decisions. Further, those who are being affected by policy should as a matter of right have some say in formulating it. The poor should be a significant part of any decisions about legislation and programs and policies affecting their lives, as should minorities, as should women. They are the ones who most intimately and immediately have to live with the consequences of the decisions; they know the pain and humiliation attendant on much legislation about them in a way most legislators and policy makers (not poor, white and male) cannot begin to understand. When half a society or world is denied a significant role in decision-making, the results can only be less than what they should be.

Women should become actors for still another reason. So long as they are acted on or acted about, an oppressive and stereotypical pattern is reinforced. Only when women begin to take responsibility for the direction of their own lives – and of the society as a whole – can that pattern be effectively broken and re-oriented. Women's experience of power begins to break that pattern. Wilma's own struggle to take control of her life, the rise of NOW, and the emergence of countless individual women and other organizations reflect the validity of this principle. Liberation and humanization depend not only on certain policy changes but also on the process itself of women in leadership.

Living Our Values: A fourth principle is that we must live our values. Wilma refers to this principle as a behavioral demonstration. To live one's values means that one does act, and that there is at least an approaching integration between convictions and behavior. It is direct action with integrity. We cannot continue to postpone speaking and doing in ways consistent with what we value. A behavioral demonstration is injecting into the world feminist values and insisting that those values have a hearing, be recognized as valid, and be centrally integrated in all issues that relate to or include human beings.

A behavioral demonstration also provides an opportunity for others to live their values. It brings out into the open what the values of people are and can be. If after a significant period of time a promised action is not forthcoming, the behavior of activists must change so that new responses are possible and a less equivocal opportunity is given to embody the values to which one is committed. A behavioral demonstration forces the issue. Wilma's decision to have the poster removed at the Labor Department and her decision to challenge the Senate sub-committee responsible for the ERA are but two of the more dramatic instances of behavioral demonstrations.

It is thus that often Wilma's actions were directed at apparent friends of feminist values. This may well disconcert or even "temporarily alienate" them, but Wilma believes that if they are indeed friends, they will remain so. If they withdraw their previous support, it is also important to know that.

But challenging others to live their values is more involved than learning whom to trust. Without increased and real commitment to feminist values, whatever goals gained are precarious at best; laws can be repealed or ignored, affirmative action programs can be only tokenly followed, and interest can shift to some other cause. While it is true that pressing for legal and policy change is vitally important and such changes can begin to influence behavioral changes, it is equally true that change of ethos and behaviors must accompany legal and policy changes if the latter are to endure.

A behavioral demonstration is just that; it enables oneself and one's friends or not-yet-friends to demonstrate behaviorally what their loyalties and values really are. In so far as there is positive response, it helps make those values a part of our public life and give affirmation and courage to others to act on their convictions with strength and confidence.

A behavioral demonstration is a link between action and personal excellence. As individuals publicly act on their values, it is likely that they will find it easier to do so again. The actions lead to discovery of something about the self that is satisfying – one discovers one can act with integrity without the world collapsing; and as one discovers that, one becomes less vulnerable to pressure to "play it safe."

The discovery is true not only for those within political and other structures responding to challenge from change agents; it is true for the agents themselves. At the time of interrupting the Senate hearing to insist on action on the ERA, there were only a couple of women who had ever done anything like that in their lives. It was an "unlady-like" action. But in taking it – with knees trembling and hands sweating – they demonstrated their values, gained in self-confidence and the awareness that their own lives can make a difference, helped to eliminate stereotyping about what it means to be a woman, and contributed further to the causes of justice. As Wilma puts it, "They'll never be the same."

Non-adversarial Confrontation: A behavioral demonstration, for Wilma, implies a non-adversarial confrontation. Non-adversarial confrontation is a procedural principle that involves confrontation on the issues, but it is not against someone or some group. It is not an attack or a vituperative or hate-filled action. It is a demonstration of one's values, which for Wilma are intrinsically humane. Whatever anger may be part of motivation (and anger is often present and appropriate), the focus of the act is on the issue at stake.

Wilma reminds her friends and opponents of this again and again, often by changing the language used to interpret what is happening. Those whom one is confronting are the "beneficiaries," not the targets or enemy. One is promising certain kinds of action, not threatening. Jo Ann Evansgardner tells a story about being so angry with someone that in mentioning it to Wilma she said, "I'm so mad I could go for the jugular." And Wilma immediately translated, "You could give him a transfusion?"

Wilma's actions reflect a commitment to a growthful outcome for all. She appeals to shared values between her and her hearers and seeks to inspire them as well as challenge them. In speaking to the National Easter Seal

Society, Wilma commended their concern for crippled children and then related that concern to national and global issues. In doing so, she sought to share a vision of the future, when crippled children would not be objects of compassion and peripheral to the daily lives of most people, but accepted as intrinsically valuable and as significant members of society, entitled to the same rights and responsibilities as other citizens.

This inspiring quality of her speeches is not only in content; it is also in style. Wilma builds with a repetition of phrases and ideas that is biblical in style. In "Feminism: The *Sine Qua Non* for a Just Society," her recital of the changes that women and men are seeking and creating began with constitutional and legal, then moved to education, politics, child care, mass media, population choices and the environment, assumptions and expectations about women and men, politics and economics.[15] In each area there is a factual example of the way women are under-valued, a refusal to countenance an ethos that encourages such a devaluing, and the offering of an alternative. As she turns to each one, there is building momentum. Her speeches build and build, rolling like waves, not to a climax but to an invitation to share a calling. She consistently assumes shared values at the level of ends and vision. She appeals to her hearers' good will to re-evaluate their means in order to work for the ends and realize the vision they have in common. The following is characteristic:

> To date, we have presumably taught men to be brave and women to care. NOW, men must be brave *enough* to care about the quality and equality of our common life and learn how sexism cripples us all from developing our full human potential. NOW, to my sisters on this panel, in this audience and elsewhere: we must care *enough* to bravely assert that our place and our authentic voice must be everywhere from advocacy for and with crippled children and adults to the universe of a profound behavioral revolution known as feminism. Sooner or later, everyone must know and accept these realities if we value our survival and full humanity. So why not NOW? And as you do, please know that I extend to you my hands, my head, my heart and my love.[21,p.6]

After such a speech, some in the audience would be very angry at what was perceived as an attack on their own loyalties and activities; others would burst into tearful and thunderous applause, rising to their feet and bringing many more somewhat reluctant ones with them.

Principles for Decision-making

The above criteria for action are principles of right action. They are obligatory on a feminist activist. They establish the ground rules for playing the game. They do not tell me what decision to make, but they tell me to *act*, not to be afraid to act, and to act in ways which, while not denying differences, seek common ground and assume common humanity.

The procedural principles set a context in which other considerations can function. The other considerations include the principles for decision-making. Together, they reflect a gynandrous ethic. Four of the most important principles for decision-making for Wilma are justice, nurturance, sisterhood or brotherhood, and freedom of choice.

Justice: Justice moves one in the direction of equality. To do justice is to work to make human resources and opportunities more equal than they are now. Realistically, a goal of absolute equality is impossible and probably undesirable. People simply will not be equal in health, income, temperament, or preparation for life provided them by parents. But one can move toward equality of health by creating nurturant environments, policies and inter-relationships so that health care and nutritious food and healthy habitats can be the minimum norm. One can move toward equality of income by adherence to the simple rule, "equal pay for equal work" and/or work of comparable value, and by redistributing economic resources that at least narrow the gap between rich and poor. One does not seek equality of temperament, but one can reduce the reasons for anxiety and frustration and increase the opportunities for personal satisfaction in work and play. One cannot and should not seek equality of discipline and love, but one can move toward creating an ethos where gynandrous expectations and values exist.

The principle of justice moves us toward equality of common resources and of opportunity. It also includes a compensatory dimension that helps to create equality of resource and opportunity. It is affirmative action, action that is both remedial and transforming. Remedial action takes the form of Women's Studies, for instance, of goals and timetables for hiring women and minorities, or receiving back pay. For Wilma, such action does more than integrate the dispossessed into the system. As women and men who share feminist values become part of those gaining access to the system, the system will be increasingly transformed. Compensatory justice is both a matter of including people and of including new values.

Nurture: The principle of nurture is one which is similar to the excellence of nurturance. As a principle, it helps to determine ends and integrate ends and means. It demands that we work toward a world in which people are nurtured, cared for and enjoyed, and that we do so by caring for the concrete people around us with whom we are in contact and sometimes in conflict.

Sisterhood and Brotherhood: A third principle is that of sisterhood and new kinds of brotherhood. Sisterhood, like the other principles of decision-making, is more of a goal and hope than a total present reality, so it calls us to act to realize that goal. We are called upon to challenge anything that divides women from one another – race, class, political conviction, religion, or sexual preference. For Wilma the issue is homophobia or heterosexual privilege, rather than homosexuality; it is capitalism and socialism when made into an ideology that divides; it is population concerns that ignore the relevancies of sexism to population pressures; it is environmental concerns that fail to acknowledge patriarchy as a source of rape and pollution of our environment.

The principle of sisterhood was one of the overarching concerns that led others and Wilma to work on the international feminist planning conference in a manner that acknowledged and attempted to transcend factors of race, class, and sexual preference. In Wilma's view, the principle of sisterhood enables us to acknowledge both our commitment to other women and the relativity of our own insights. It does not deny differences of interest and need among individual women or among groups, nor does it deny the legacy of centuries of classism, racism, and sexual privilege that continue to distort our perceptions and/or engender suspicion and hostility. Sisterhood calls us to honor diversity and correct our own myopia. The principle of sisterhood functions to enlarge the context within which a particular group's decision is to be made, to seek real understanding about what divides us, and to re-examine our own priorities to include or allow space for the priorities of other women.

Freedom of Choice: Freedom of choice is an extremely important principle both intrinsically and because feminist insights are still very much in process. Full personhood and the common good demand choice, and demand equal possibilities of choice among the many groups of society. But such freedom of choice is also important because we don't know enough about an "only" right option. Freedom of choice implies that population *choice* is preferable to population control; making available *real* choices to women about abortions is more humane than continuing the financially biased system we have now. It is also more humane than a prohibition of abortion, either qualified or absolute. There is simply no way to resolve the question of whether or not, or to what extent embryonic or fetal life is human. When people differ on fundamental issues and on matters of conscience, the wiser choice is to provide space for all.

Freedom of choice is a principle that informs other areas of decision as well and pushes Wilma to work pluralistically. Although she is personally opposed to contemporary military systems and the very idea of preparations for violence, she is in favor of enabling women to be at every level of military life, if that reality exists. The option to participate is not Wilma's decision but the individual's choice. This is true as a matter of principle, but it is also a continuing conviction of Wilma's that as the cast of characters changes so will the script, particularly as the new cast brings increasingly feminist scripts to bear on the institution, ultimately eliminating military institutions and militarism itself. Feminist "scripts" may be prerequisites to that happy day.

Action for Wilma, therefore, is principled. It is principled both deontologically and teleologically. It is pragmatic in refusing to be ideologically pure and/or making either-or choices, eg, to work within the system or outside it. Wilma welcomes any source and resource for social change – government officials, "contacts," people on the right and people on the left, professional people and lay people, poor people and middle income people. She and others on occasion take to the streets; on other occasions she speaks at conferences and Congressional hearings.

Wilma is pragmatic in taking seriously where people are. Realism, she has said, is being willing to start where people are; there is no possibility of any of us starting anywhere else. She is pragmatic about choosing both reformist and transformative goals. Desegregating want-ads could be construed as reformist; indeed NOW's originally stated purposes could be so construed. Actions like these seek to open up American society to fuller participation by women and different participation by both sexes. In this respect, the ERA is also reformist. Reforms may be necessary interim steps to and foundations for more radical changes. In Wilma's contacts with women in all areas of American society, there are emerging transformations of the ways they go about their work, transformations that will change fundamentally our ethos, our policies, and the ways we earn and spend our money.

Wilma is pragmatic about using specific means. Her primary criteria are effectiveness and feminist process: what will gain a hearing, what will make the differences? The criteria do not include anything destructive and/or violent. In some instances a rational, factual approach is effective, as was her speech to the Pittsburgh Human Relations Commissioners. In other instances, a factual approach does not seem effective, and something more drastic is called for. An interruption and/or intervention may be necessary or an economic boycott or a law suit that demonstrates some of the consequences of a given policy or action. This kind of action occurs only after other actions have been tried and ostensibly responsible people are non-responsive, or if there is not time to try others.

Wilma's ethic is *process* – process that is rooted in a vision and general goal of a more humane society – an ongoing, life-long vocation to making that vision brighter and clearer, a matter of reality. The process has many specific policy goals, under the two general rubrics of affirmative action and bringing feminist perspectives to bear on decision-making. Because of her ethic's character as process as well as because of the specific values that inform it, it is also an ethic which is determined neither primarily by one goal or purpose nor by right action, but it is one in which the emphases are on the means-shaping-the-ends. It is an ethic in which ends and means are so integrally related that the means are a part of the ends and the ends are contained in the means.

Feminist Perspectives

Wilma's ethic is particularly illustrated in three areas – economics, health care, and her personal life.

Economics

Wilma's approach to addressing economics is first to broaden the context of discussion and illumine the role of sexism. In testifying on HR 9030, the Carter administration's proposal for reforming the welfare system and process, she said:

> ...the ways most people, and indeed HR 9030, characterize poverty and the poor in this country inhibit understanding of the problem, let alone the finding of solutions.[23]

Wilma pointed out that government analysis is confused and contradictory, and that the confusion and contradictory character of the analysis is rooted in sexist assumptions and biases. For instance, HR 9030 assumed that a young-to-middle-aged male will be the principal wage-earner, an assumption that is neither just nor accurate, since by far the majority of poor in this country are women, children and the elderly. At the same time the bill assumed that it is appropriate to give billions of dollars of public money to primarily white middle-class or rich business people (usually men) but not to the poor males it had mistakenly identified as the primary recipients of "welfare." Public money aid goes to ailing railroads, public highways, shipbuilders, oil producers, agribusiness. Wilma stated: "This is public welfare, literally, in the sense of faring well; it just hasn't been called *welfare*."

The discrepancy in distribution of public funds is explained by the ethos that prevails. Those activities engaged in mostly by affluent white males are more valued than those engaged in by subordinates, whether male or female. It does not seem to matter that the activities of the dominants are vastly more destructive of resources and of human health and life than the activities of subordinates. Even from the unsupportable perspective of sheer greed, it would make sense to provide the poor with sufficient income so that they can become a part of the needless patterns of consumption, or at least survive and continue to fuel the activities of dominants. Subordinates are devalued by the dominants and the paradigm for their subordination is sexism.

With this kind of unexamined, unconscious sexism, legislators cannot effectively grapple with the real issues posed by poverty. Wilma proposes new legislation that would employ the poor to participate in framing and implementing economic laws and practices. The ideas sound preposterous, absurd, simplistic to some. Minority folks are not qualified, it is alleged. There is deep-seated fear among the affluent that even a relative loss of power of control means disaster for them. Many women, dependent on the status quo, share that fear. In Wilma's view, society apparently prefers to hold on to chains of inequity and inhumaneness, and with them patterns of domination and subordination – of sex, and/or race, of class, and of age.

Wilma's proposal is not a romanticization of the poor. It is rooted in·the very clear perception that those who benefit the most from the status quo cannot perceive the depths of injustice in the system and/or find realistic remedies for the injustice. Their socialization, their miseducation, many business practices, their religion, politics, and consciousness collaborate in making them unfit for the responsibility to right the injustice. There is no guarantee that the poor and other relatively powerless groups in this society will eliminate poverty since it is rooted in oppressive hierarchies and values and not simply in unequal acquisition of money. But clearly powerless groups have some awareness of what they need and who needs it. The poor know that children must be fed and cared for; the poor know that life is dehumanized by continuous invasions of privacy; the poor know that it is unfair to be singled out and condemned for wanting what other Americans take for granted as their birthright – the right to survival.

Wilma's proposal is that of initiating a process. She does not suggest that the powerless "take over" the running of the economy, or the government. She does suggest the beginnings of a shift in the power relations, of instituting the poor into positions of paid advice, decision-making and administration, not to the exclusion of others, but *with* others. The United States could easily create "think tanks" of the dispossessed to work out proposals and legislation; competent poor could be chosen to work with Congress; the President's Cabinet could include them, with no more than a majority of one of either sex (ie, at least half women) in the cabinet or any other public body.

In contrast to many people who are concerned about and committed to fundamental economic and political social change, Wilma does not easily identify herself with a particular ideology. She is willing to call herself, on occasion, a "socialist feminist," but it is the noun "feminist" that has much more weight than the adjective "socialist." Although she believes feminism is implicitly socialist in many ways, she does not think that replacing capitalist patriarchy with socialist patriarchy has made that significant a difference so far in human history. Women are still dependent on the largesse of men; and feminist perspectives, policies and imperatives remain secondary or less.

Health Care

By virtue of both experience and education, Wilma has been a long-time advocate of change in the area of health care. Like other institutions and practices, health care has been androcentric. A hierarchical pattern of power and authority has typically existed within the institution, with the more powerful generally being men. The concept of "allied health professions," which are usually occupied by women (allied to men), reinforces the reality of an androcentric pattern. "Allied" is a euphemism for "peripheral" and "secondary" to physicians.

The health care system is sexist in the control it gives men over women's bodies, particularly women's reproductive organs. Typical of sexist thinking, approaches to health care compartmentalize the patient into uterus or bones or heart and treats what is amiss in an atomistic fashion.

A feminist approach to health care seeks not only to open options for more women to become physicians and men to become nurses but also to re-evaluate the nurse-physician relationship and redefine the roles of each. In

Wilma's view, health care is primarily an interrelational phenomenon that may be augmented by medicine and technologies. She proposes that since only about ten percent of the quality of a society's health is influenced by medical care (by physicians), to allow health care – its definitions, power and control – to be determined mostly by physicians is itself pathological.

> Nurses, increasingly influenced by feminist consciousness, are not only rejecting the oppressive "handmaiden" role but are assertively redefining the nurse as the humanist who can best guide the total care of the whole patient. In this changed context, physicians are recognized as highly trained technicians prepared for instrumental roles but not as gods.[18,p.10]

As these roles are re-defined and valued, the relationship can become more collegial in power and authority, and recognition given the nurse's role as the critical and primary providers of care. Clearly, leadership of health care needs to be mostly done by women, who are over 75% of health care providers.

In addition to and along with working for change within traditional institutions of health care, Wilma has encouraged and supported the growth of self-help approaches for examining our bodies, and the development of methods for controlling our bodies. The values of self-help are both the control by women over their own bodies and the self-confidence such activities help generate.

Wilma has called for a gynandrous approach to health care, one that emphasizes the strengths of a self-help approach and also acknowledges the value of technical resources. A gynandrous approach emphasizes the need for fundamental change, not simply setting up alternatives to existing institutions. Self-help is primary for this approach because it "demystifies and deprofiteers the experience and therapeutically empowers the consumer and eschews hierarchies of control and power over them."[24] Wilma wishes to avoid the perpetuation of inadequate public funding for alternative approaches. Self-help should be supported as a part of strong political organizing to monitor, influence, and participate in national health policy. This is happening, to some extent, through the National Women's Health Network, of which Wilma is a member. "The radical critique of existing health care conception and systems by feminists is crucial as is assuring that public funding goes to feminist self-help, to wholistic health care, simply because they are in the public interest, will lower costs, and are healthier models than the medical model."[24]

Personal Life

A similar approach is seen in Wilma's attitude toward her own life. Commitment to the vision of humaneness and living her values led her to turn her back on most of the traditional means of achievement and security until she ceased to fit into most prevailing institutional patterns.

She left Sangamon State, frustrated by the confines of a relatively open academic structure. She supports herself by lecturing and careful investing of her income in enterprises that meet in significant measure her standards of responsibility and justice. At the same time, she generously gives, lends, and barters money and possessions to those in need. She calls it "recycling." She usually takes the initiative, offering a sum of money, for instance, long before the potential recipient thinks to ask for it. If the response to her offer is hesitation or demurral, she counters with the query, "Would you offer it to me if our roles were reversed?" That usually settles the matter.

She lives alone, choosing not to remarry or enter into another intimate relationship, but her friendships are precious to her, transcending the often very real differences of life style and commitments. She accepts some of the responsibility for the well-being of her family of origin although in many respects she feels very distant from them. She loves her daughters deeply and seeks as well as she knows to support them, not to impose on them, to call them to account on occasion, and to be available to them.

She enters into the care of her own health as a colleague rather than a patient or client. She refused surgery for the tumor and ignored the demands of her body if other concerns took priority. She sought alternative forms of healing. One of her reasons for returning to the Philadelphia area was to try acupuncture for the tumor.

Perhaps her decisions around the tumor reflect as well as any some of the ways the dimensions of her ethics shaped her personal life, blending as they do a realism about life and courage that is in the human interest. Wilma's perception of the Women's Movement in 1968 and of her role in NOW led her to conclude that knowledge and, even more, publicity about the tumor could jeopardize both. Inside and outside the movement, people looked to her as a strong, competent, challenging teacher, mother and advocate. Knowledge about the tumor could undermine NOW's positions with real or imaginary questions of the health of its leadership; it could also be a further strain on the steadfastness of its members; and it could be a source of, for Wilma, over-solicitous concern from friends and family, and efforts to restrain her own actions.

She chose silence and risked times of isolation when she needed to be held. But having decided on silence, she did not follow the stereotypically masculinist stance that everything was all right. She did not deny the presence of pain and anxiety. In loyalty to her vision and what was to become a gynandric understanding of courage, she works *with* her body. She refuses to accept more than she knows she can do, conserving her energy whenever possible, and allowing her own body to deepen her commitment to humaneness by reminding her daily that life is too short for pettiness and pique and revenge, and honing ever more sharply her ability to grasp the heart, the principle, of the matter.

An ethic rooted in humaneness/the human interest is a rich, multi-sided ethic. It seeks structural challenge and change and experiments with alternative possibilities. It reflects personal excellence and policy reformulation. It affirms an intrinsic relation between means and ends. It values dimensions of what has been called "feminine" and "masculine" and transforms those into "feminist." It is pragmatic and principled, realistic and visionary, courageous and caring.

It is an ethic that arose out of and then shaped the daily, tough, complex decisions Wilma and other feminist women and men were making in the 60's and 70's. Simultaneously with the development of this ethic and since, other perspectives and insights into feminist ethics have emerged.

NOTES

1. "A Declaration of Interdependence." See Appendix A.
2. Conversation with Wilma, April 1979.
3. Brady, Anne Hazlewood: "Bonded," *Unwritten Testament.* Camden Herald Publishing Co., Camden, 1972.
4. Heide, Wilma Scott: "Feminism Means that *SHE* is Risen to Redefine and Reassign Power for Life." University of Idaho Outlawry of War Foundation, April 2-4, 1973. Available from KNOW, Inc., P.O. Box 86031, Pittsburgh, PA 15221.
5. Miller, Jean Baker: *Toward a New Psychology of Women.* Beacon Press, Boston, 1976.
6. For an extended discussion of some of the connections between sexism and violence, see Eleanor Haney and Wilma Scott Heide, "Testimony: HR 8356 to Establish a National Peace Academy Commission." Hearings for the Subcommittee for International Operations of the Committee on International Relations. 95th Congress, 2nd Session, January 24-25, 1978, U.S. Government Printing Office, pp.241- 265.
7. Strick, Anne: "What's Wrong with the Adversary System: Paranoia, Hatred and Suspicion." *Washington Monthly*, January, 1977, pp.19-28.
8. *Proposed National Plan of Action,* National Women's Conference, Houston, Texas, November 18-21, 1977.
9. Steffins, Dorothy: "Women and Economics: Our Nation and the Profit System." Address, May 15, 1976. Women's International League for Peace and Freedom, 1213 Race St., Philadelphia, PA 19107.
10. See for instance J. Glenn Gray, *The Warriors,* Harper Torchbook, New York, 1967, pp.232-240.
11. See Rosemary Ruether, *New Woman/New Earth,* Seabury Press, New York, 1975; and Eleanor Haney, "Turning Toward Peace," lecture delivered May 14, 1981, Moorhead State University, Moorhead, Minnesota.

12. McCann, Robert: *Hearing Before the Subcommittee on Education of the Committee on Labor and Public Welfare.* U.S. Senate, May 13, 1976, pp.37-8.

13. Quoted in "Psycho-Sexual Roots of Our Ecological Crisis," unpublished paper by Elizabeth Dodson Gray, 1978.

14. Komisar, Lucy: "Violence and the Masculine Mystique," *Washington Monthly,* July, 1970, pp.39-48.

15. Heide, Wilma Scott: "Feminism: The *Sine Qua Non* for a Just Society." *Vital Speeches of the Day,* Vol. XXXVIII, #13, April 15, 1972, pp.403-9.

16. Heide, Wilma Scott: "A Feminist-Humanist's Concept of Employment Including Public Service." In *Public Service Employment: An Analysis of Its History, Problems and Prospects.* Alan Gartner, Russell Nixon and Frank Riessman (Eds.), Praeger Publishers, New York, 1973, pp.69-74.

17. I think, for instance, of Joseph Pieper: *Prudence.* Pantheon, New York, 1959.

18. Heide, Wilma Scott: *Feminism for the Health of It.* Doctoral Dissertation, Union for Experimenting Colleges and Universities, 1978. See also *Feminism for The Health of It* , 1985. Margaretdaughters, Inc., P.O. Box 70, Buffalo, NY, 14222.

19. Schaef, Anne Wilson: "It's Not Necessary to Deny Another's Reality in Order to Affirm Your Own: The Systematization of Dualism in the White Male Structure." Address given to the First National Conference on Human Relations in Education, June 20, 1978, Minneapolis, MN.

20. Heide, Wilma Scott: Typed statement, June 1973, Congressional Joint Economic Committee chaired by Congresswoman Martha Griffiths. Available from U.S Government Printing Office, Superintendent of Documents, Washington, DC 20403, 1973.

21. Heide, Wilma Scott: "A Feminist Perspective on Volunteering for a Healthy Society." Unpublished paper, 1973, Wilma's basement.

22. At the time of this speech, many more United Way funds went to male organizations and activities than to female ones. The Jaycees either excluded women or put them in the auxiliary Jaycettes; yet, they received federal money for voluntary work on poverty issues.

23. Heide, Wilma Scott: "Testimony on H.R. 9030 'Welfare Reform'." Welfare Reform Subcommittee of the House Committees on Agriculture, on Education and Labor, on Ways and Means, November, 1977. Part II, Supt. of Documents, U.S. Government Printing Office, Washington, DC 20402.

24. Heide, Wilma Scott: "Feminism: Making a Difference in Our Health." In *The Woman Patient.* Malkah T. Hotman and Carol C. Nadelson (Eds.), Plenum Press, 227 W. 17th St., New York, NY 10011, 1978, pp.9-20.

10

A FEMINIST LEGACY

No greater gift, no more sacred trust and no more gratifying ideals than those of feminism and its real values could I offer and share with you ...[This is my vision] of the potential for women, for men, for children, and for all of our institutions and society itself. Without vision, people perish, and we do want to celebrate life.

– Wilma Scott Heide[1,p.4]

Major Insights

For Wilma, the phrase 'feminist ethics' is redundant. Feminist ethics is not one kind of normative ethics, nor is it primarily an area or areas of ethical inquiry. Rather, to be moral is to be feminist; similarly, to be feminist is to be moral. The moral life today is a life committed to feminism.

One reason that moral life and feminism are integral is that the universe of women's lives is an essential component of ethical analysis and action. The understanding of injustice is incomplete, inadequate, and inaccurate without an understanding of sexism. An analysis in terms of race and class primarily or only, although critical and imperative, will not allow one to grasp the roots and fundamental paradigms of oppression and violence. Equally, decisions of policy and program will be finally ineffective without radical changes for and by women. Legislative failure to ratify the ERA is a grievous sign of a diseased body politic; it is a reminder of the precariousness of all other human and civil rights legislation in this country.

Traditional ethics, like all other reflection, has typically assumed that the subject is male. Whether theology, ethics, aesthetics, or epistemology, concepts, categories and concerns have reflected men's perspectives and interests. To put feminism in the center of the stage of morality is to bring women into the center as subject, as agent, as actor. Wilma's definition of feminism does not eliminate men from being actors also; it simply intrinsically includes women as independent and essential actors, for it is our story, our heritage, our visions that must be told and heard.

Women's experiences – our stories, heritage, and visions – are an essential source for the content and development of normative ethics. Our experiences challenge other sources for ethics – religious traditions or a natural law tradition, or some other understanding of "good." Our experiences serve as a source for determining what values and principles should be primary and how they should be understood.

The conviction that the moral life is a feminist one is sometimes difficult for others to understand, both feminists and non-feminists (Wilma would say "not-yet feminists"). Many would agree that women's concerns are properly an object of moral inquiry but not necessarily a source of ethical theory or essential for securing social justice and personal well-being. Wilma, however, insists that women must become actors in our own interest and for the welfare of the world and that our experiences are essential to developing normative ethical theory. In the absence of women as actors and knowledge of women's experience, involvement in moral action and reflection, however serious, are inadequate and misguided.

Another major emphasis in Wilma's thought is vision and the future. Her understanding of the content of feminism is rooted in a portion of what has traditionally been called feminine, but it is also rooted in an imaginatively selective appropriation of what is valuable in that which has been called feminine and in that which has been called masculine. The determination of what is valuable is based on her vision of what humanity can become. Her overarching concept to identify that vision is humaneness. Humaneness includes reconciliation between women and men, a reconciliation that arises out of redefinitions and redistributions of power and authority. It includes justice, a redefining and sharing of power and resources. It includes friendship, relations of respect and interdependence.

This emphasis on the future has shaped Wilma's own intellectual and practical actions. She is relatively less interested in an understanding of the past or in finding resources in the past, although she is meticulously careful in "doing her homework;" she gathers all relevant data about the past and present of given issues. Her focus remains on imagining and creating the future.

Wilma's emphasis on the future and vision does not lead to romantic or vague goals. Since the future is to be created, since its outlines are still largely a matter of the longing of the heart and the knowledge of intuition, actions can be very practical. Her immediate goals are not the eradication of sexism, in general – it is the reduction or elimination of sexism at AT&T or in the World Future Society. Action is concrete, building brick by brick, without a blueprint but sustained by vision.

Wilma's emphasis is on the *what* but equally on the *who*. Over and over one hears the refrain in her speeches, her letters, her acting: feminists, and particularly feminist women, should be making decisions. No more than a majority of one of either sex should be on any public board, commission, cabinet, task force, decision-making body, and such bodies should be demographically representative by race and income as well. In speaking before the Commission on Population Growth and the American Future, she challenged the concept of population control, not because she is opposed to limiting population growth but because it is hierarchical – a decision made by a few for many. When decisions are made by some on behalf of others, these decisions should be guided by the principles that enable all of us to help shape our own future. In place of population control, there should be self-control, and self control becomes viable when there are options to choose among. Wilma advocates making options available so that people can control their own destinies, and together shape a common future.

Wilma's focus on the *what* and the *who* is guided by her commitment to excellence. Excellence compels Wilma, and excellence is what she demands of others. Excellence means both the best that one has to offer, as well as specific qualities of courage, compassion, integrity, and passionate commitment to justice. When a friend in exasperation challenged Wilma with "sometimes I think you want perfection from us," Wilma's reply was "no, not perfection, but excellence."

Peacemaking

In recent years Wilma has moved more and more into the area of peace. She is still an ardent champion of the ratification of the Equal Rights Amendment and other legal, social, and education gains for women, but her heart is with peacemaking and a more just world order.

This commitment was expressed in the establishment of the Women's Coalition for the Third Century, a dream to establish a feminist institute for peace, and her work on establishing the Boston-based organization Feminist Women For Peace. Gratified by some connections being made between feminism and peace (including the Seneca Women's Encampment for a Future of Peace and Justice), Wilma has focused increasingly on international peace contacts and gatherings.

Wilma does not see her commitment to peace as being in competition with or an abandonment of her commitment to feminism. Rather, it is an extension and application of her insights and values into an area perhaps most blatantly reflective of patriarchal values and practices and desperately in need of feminist analysis, vision, and action. Some significant themes in her approach to peace are clear, including the role of anger in peacemaking, an understanding of violence, the place of the imagination, and an insistence on feminists as decision-makers.

Violence, according to Wilma, is to be restrained and overcome, if not eliminated. A primary means of restraining violence is by acknowledging and cherishing your own anger. Anger is an appropriate response to violence; we should be outraged. Such anger is not negative and need not be paralyzing. Anger can become a correlate of caring; it can be generative and constructive. Then it becomes a part of a driving passion that sustains one through disappointments and is not diminished by successes.

Realism, according to Wilma, is awareness of the depth of oppression; idealism is awareness of continuously emergent possibilities. Success is not merely the achieving of specific goals but the processes of challenge, growth and change themselves.

In this context, anger is related to a non-adversarial stance. Those who unknowingly or unthinkingly identify with oppressive structures and policies are at least potentially capable of more humane attitudes and actions. They are sharers of a common destiny.

Another response to violence is self-defense. When groups or individuals intrude into space necessary for one's own power and action, when they seek to rob the self of power, they must face the consequences of their actions. Resistance is a necessary part of the ongoing process of constraining and creating space for oneself and others.

Self-defense may take many forms. Fight may be one; determining policy and legal change may be another. What is true on an individual or local level may also be true on a larger one. The choice of means is imaginatively pragmatic, with the emphasis on *imaginatively* as much as it is on *pragmatic*, since the process itself is part of the product. In an article for Ms., Wilma enumerated a number of ways in which we have not exhausted our imagination although we may have exhausted some conventional non-violent means. We have not, for instance, yet seriously explored massive civil disobedience in refusing to pay taxes; we have not collectively refused to engage in sex with those who identify with and practice oppressive policies; we have not begun policing the streets ourselves; we have not interrupted television programming until demands are met.[2]

Wilma's view of peacemaking extends to and often redefines a wide range of issues of daily life, including seemingly diverse issues as abortion and military spending. Values of nurturance, anger, and a non-adversarial stance lead to action, but not necessarily to pacifism as the appropriate action. They lead to connecting personal and political issues of violence and to considerations of the development of power that renders violence unnecessary or at least very rare. A nurturing society neither spends most of its money and skills on weapons, nor legislates a pacifist stance on the part of some of its people. It affirms that moral selfhood is rooted in freedom, substantive freedom over one's life, including bodily existence. It affirms that those subject to the effects of policy should have a significant voice in the determination of policy.

In the determination of policy, women should be major actors. In the case of abortion, women must have the right and responsibility to determine policy. In the case of military spending, women should help significantly to shape policy. Further, these two areas are connected: a nurturing society makes life-affirming options available to people. Such options include day-care, medical care, sufficient economic security to care for children, security from enforced pregnancy, and the security of a future. A nurturing society will spend its money on providing those options within the nation and will share in providing those options throughout the world, not on more and more weapons. In the absence of such a society, feminists will continue to claim power and refuse to be forced to be the bearers of non-violence for the rest of society.

Further, for Wilma, the claim that fetal life has a right to live that is in conflict with the mother's is hypocritical and misogynist. In a nurturing society, all life is to be cherished – including those who are now poor, elderly, and oppressed. In a country that callously continues to deny most of its citizens access to basic resources, the enforced valuing of biological, fetal life is simply another, particularly brutal example of the devaluing of women.

Toward the Future

This book has focused on Wilma and those related to her, her actions, and her emerging ethic. Since Wilma began acting, speaking, and writing as a feminist, other major directions in feminist ethics have emerged, including ethical reflection by feminists of color, lesbian feminist reflection, feminist liberation ethics, and nature-goddess feminist spirituality and ethics. The resources in Wilma's ethic can be viewed in dialogue with the others for the continuing development of feminist ethics.

The emergence of diverse feminist perspectives has deepened, sharpened, and expanded our understanding of feminist ethics. Our understanding of systemic, structural injustice, oppression and violence is much clearer. The prevailing structure is a structure that includes roles, values, hierarchies of power and value, exploitation, stereotyping, and sustained inequities. Feminist perspectives have revealed structures that interlock and power relations that are global; structures that pit marginal people against each other and continue to exploit in the name of development and national security and the American – or Christian – way. Our understanding of the pervasiveness and recalcitrance of racism, sexism, classism, heterosexism, imperialism, and militarism is profoundly more sophisticated and complex than it was. That advance has been made possible through the continuing emergence of feminist perspectives and tools for analysis in addition to those available to Wilma.

A major direction that is not incorporated in Wilma's approach is that of goddess-nature-feminism. Represented by writers such as Starhawk and the editors of *Womanspirit*, this approach celebrates the female body in relation to the rhythms of the seasons and the goddess symbolism of the cycles of birth and death and rebirth. It also brings together New Age and Native American themes and resources with its nature-feminism.

The writings of liberation feminists and Socialist feminists bring a Marxist perspective and a focus on capitalism as well as sexism that also is distinctive and not typical of Wilma's approach. Her analyses of capitalism tend to be located within the context of sexism rather than an independent area of investigation.

Feminist ethics has developed in different directions. Feminism has deepened both its analysis and its vision. It has become a richly woven tapestry of women's lives, visions and understandings, and actions. Wilma's ethic contributes to the future weaving of that tapestry in several significant ways.

One contribution of Wilma's ethic is her twin emphasis on values and women. It is feminist values that must become normative in public and private life. As she puts is, "Both the cast of characters and the script must be changed." Women must become actors, and the values that guide choices must be feminist. Rights are not enough; structural change is not enough. Equality of opportunity is not enough. Equal distribution of resources is not enough. Unless the values of respect, shared power, courage, nurturance – the values of humaneness and openness to friendship – are also institutionalized, any legal, economic or political institutional change is incomplete and not sufficiently radical. Unless women do in fact become decision-makers, unless there is that concrete reality of a shift in power, the values mask continuing oppression. The same can be said of other oppressed groups. Wilma's insistence is that women – of all ages, colors, classes and sexual identity – must be included in that real shift of power.

Another contribution of Wilma's ethic is her refusal to equate female, feminine and feminist, or male, masculine and masculinist. Female is not equal to feminine, nor is either equal to feminist. The same is true for male, masculine and masculinist. Wilma's valuing of each of the terms is different. 'Female' and 'male' are biological terms. The terms 'feminine' and 'masculine' have dimensions that are valuable and dimensions that are destructive. The term 'feminist' is inclusive of humane and just values, while 'masculinist' refer to misogynist, destructive and unjust ones.

When the distinctions between 'female', 'feminine' and 'feminist' are blurred, the result is confusion, and it can be suggested or implied that to be female is good and to be male is bad. This kind of dualism is wholly contrary to Wilma's ethic. Distinguishing these concepts enables Wilma to ask a fundamental and critical question: By what criteria are characteristics of "feminine" and "masculine" assessed as good? Her answer is: the criterion of humaneness – in the human interest.

Another contribution of Wilma's ethic is her willingness to engage in specific and sustained actions. Feminism is a risky, continuous, tedious, unpopular, tremendously rewarding action after action after action. It is not primarily a theory but a commitment, a way of life. It is a vocation. That call may take one into wholly new, uncharted ways; it may make one risk family, health, even life, even though it bestows family, health and life. It is concrete, and it is sustained action.

Related to all other contributions is the spiritual grounding of her ethic. Wilma seldom invokes the goddess; in fact, she thinks of "goddess" primarily as a derivative term and prefers not to use it; she equally seldom invokes god. But her ethic is rooted in a deeply covenantal basis – it is deeply interpersonal and faithful. Wilma's fidelity is not primarily to an ideology but to values, individuals, to groups, both to those who are with her and to those who may be opposed to her. It is a commitment to others as unique beings, to bring to them the best she has to offer, and to challenge them to the best that is in them – to humaneness, to feminist insights and values. Wilma's is a spirituality that is based on respect and at the same time offers, elicits, and demands political action and individual transformation. It is an ethical spirituality that offers and challenges us all to excellence.

Such a spirituality can acknowledge the experience of connection, harmony, balance, at-homeness in the world, but it also and equally can acknowledge alienation, dread, the experience of the abyss. While harmony and peace are fundamental, they are also often elusive, visionary, and accompanied by an experience of the abyss. The experience of the abyss calls us to the awareness that all is not right, not only with us as individuals, but with the way our lives have been arranged. It is not so much an experience of the malaise of a self isolated from the world; it is the call of a vision of what can and ought to be – what I sometimes name the cry of the human heart. In effect, it is also the plumb line that measures how askew the world is.

Wilma's feminist religious experience includes an experience of both at-homeness and nothingness, not in a paradoxical or even dialectical fashion, but as light pierces depths of water or as springs continuously mingle with and renew a lake. A spiritual quest or growth or journey includes a finding of and integrating oneself, and living on the boundary – in the rich and sometimes very painful matrix between vision and actuality.

What I have written is a beginning. Much of this book will be elaborated on, refined, and changed as other perspectives and insights emerge. But Wilma's legacy is unmistakable – to choose the future we want for ourselves, our children, and the planet, and go after it with our heart, mind, soul and body. As she said once, "I don't want or expect perfection, but I want and expect excellence. Humanity literally yearns for what feminism portends."

NOTES

1. Heide, Wilma Scott: "Feminism for Healthy Social Work." *Smith College School for Social Work Journal.* Northampton, MA, Winter, 1976, pp.1-4.
2. Heide, Wilma Scott: "Why Don't We ...?" *Ms.* June, 1976, pp. 88-9.

Wilma, speaking at the National Vigil for the ERA, State House, Springfield, Illnois, June 13, 1979.

EPILOGUE

Wilma died on May 8, 1985. She was returning to Norristown from a visit with her daughters Terry and Tami and friends in Boston and Connecticut. After turning off the Pennsylvania Turnpike, she stopped at a clinic and described pains in her chest and difficulty breathing. She was taken to a hospital. There she died.

The hospital called her daughters. Terry and Tami asked Patricia Budd Kepler, an ordained Presbyterian minister, to arrange a service. Wilma's body was cremated, and a small service of commemoration and celebration was held in the Chapel of Reconciliation at the University of Pennsylvania in Philadelphia. Those present were: members of Philadelphia and Pennsylvania chapters of NOW; Wilma's brother Harold and his wife Pat, Wilma's sister Ginny and her husband Henry Poiser, Wilma's former husband Gene and his wife Betty Tipton, her daughters Tami and Terry, Peggy Chinn and Charlene Eldridge Wheeler of Margaretdaughters, Annette Wall, Pat Kepler, Debbie Leighton, myself, and long-time friend Gary Akovenko.

Later, in Portland, Maine, at a gathering of the Feminist Spiritual Community, which Wilma attended when visiting friends in Maine and of which I am a member, we held a service of remembering, celebrating and covenanting (one of Wilma's favorite words). It seems appropriate to close this chapter of the feminist movement with a selection from that service:

Dear Wilma,

You are one of the most courageous people we have known – not because you were not afraid but because you *had* to live your values of caring deeply, passionately. You knew the truth that we are still struggling to learn – that silence and inaction will never save us.

You asked others to come with you, and sometimes that journey was too frightening, for we saw our weaknesses and thought we had too many other responsibilities.

And you were always willing to come with us.

Now we must say good-bye to you and to the presence of such courage and challenge and support.

You are one of the most generous people we have known. You gave time and energy to individual people and to all who are oppressed. You were willing to explain and explain and explain. You always responded to requests, to pleas, to fears, to challenges. You shared your home, your money, yourself. You continued to work with those you described as "not yet friends."

Finally, you gave your life.

Now, we must say good-bye to you and to the presence of your unconditional fidelity.

You are one of the most radical people we have known. Your actions are grounded in a vision of humaneness, and in light of that vision, people's inhumanity stands unmasked.

But you never simply opposed, never simply contended, never simply challenged; you also affirmed, you also called us to alternatives that are more humane, more loving, more just, more powerful.

At the very heart of your vision are women loving, joyful, strong, vulnerable, refusing to play by the old rules, creating our own.

Now we must say good-bye to you and to the transformation your life has brought.

You leave us before the promises are fulfilled for you or for us.

You leave us deeply tired and very much alone, idolized and misunderstood, hated and feared as well as loved and celebrated and needed – still deeply needed.

You leave us before the vision is real, at a time when the vision seems further away than ever.

But still we must say good-bye.

You leave us and return.

Your dying says to us that we can and must continue; the mantle is passed to us to speak, to be brave, to hold one another's hands. We inherit the vision.

We also inherit the spirit. You are with us, pushing, challenging, enabling. You are here with us now. You are here with each one of us.

One of your favorite words was *covenant* – a covenant with truth. You were willing to make a covenant with us. We now promise you:

    – that we will tell your story and share your vision;

    – that we will live our values personally and politically;

    – that we will stand firm against cruelty, violence, injustice;

    – that we will work with all who struggle to live more fully, more powerfully, more humanely.

And then I saw a new heaven and a new earth. The old has passed away; behold the new has come.

S/HE IS RISEN – TO REDEFINE AND REASSIGN POWER FOR LIFE!

DECLARATION OF INTERDEPENDENCE

Preamble

Two hundred years ago the United States of America was born of the courage and strength of women and men who while searching for liberty, gold or adventure, endured to lay the foundation of our nation with their lives.

Believing in a people's right to govern themselves, they drafted a Declaration, initiated a revolution and established this republic. Some who struggled for freedom were not fully free themselves: youth, native Americans, blacks, women of all races, and the unpropertied.

Each of us emerges out of the past with a different story to tell. We inherit a nation which has broken through to a technological age with all the dangers and promises that holds. Responsibility rests on us. We are committed to the Constitution of the United States, amended by the Equal Rights Amendment, and the evolving democracy it protects. We believe in the right of all people to self-government.

History teaches us that both unlimited power and powerlessness breed corruption; that where all human beings are not valued, humanity is violated; that where differences divide us, they limit and distort us; that independence is an illusion and unlimited freedom is tyranny, plunging whole societies and people into chaos and bondage. Human survival requires interdependence.

We have been called to new consciousness by impending crises that threaten to overwhelm us if we obediently serve institutions that do not serve us.

We will no longer endure the corruption of power which risks the world's future by ignoring the rights and well-being of persons and communities. The imperative of the present is to integrate the struggle for greater humanization. To be more fully human is to share life, to respond to the dignity of ourselves and others, to be committed to the growth of one another, to develop and vitalize human community. It is necessary then to risk, to be in conflict, to suffer, to love and to celebrate.

Declaration

We therefore make this declaration. We are interdependent with the good earth, with all people, and with divine reality.

In declaring our interdependence with all peoples, we recognize geographic communities of persons and their interdependence with one another. We affirm our common humanity and we respect one another's uniqueness. We accept our responsibility to share the visions, hopes and needs of one another and pledge ourselves to protect each other's freedom.

We shall be dedicated to the empowerment of all people and to the expression of each person's creativity.

We shall commit ourselves to a world in which food, shelter, clothing and health care are the rights of all people.

We shall seek protection for people in need of care in our society, and work to provide support systems for those responsible for their care and nurture.

We shall create a climate for the creative development of each persons' human potential, and for the utilization and enjoyment of all human resources for the good of all people.

We shall respect the dignity and privacy of expressions of individual personality and living relationships.

We shall be committed to lifelong learning with access to education for all persons and for the responsible uses of communication media.

We shall be committed to all people's responsibility for public institutions of government, law, education, business, and religion, and to the concept that those institutions be responsive to the direction of the people.

We shall value and share use of free access to all public information and shall protect and value individual privacy.

In declaring our interdependence with the earth we affirm our reliance on it, our mutual responsibility for it and the rights of all persons to the fruits thereof.

We shall enjoy, protect, restore and improve the world that we inherit.

We shall produce the world's resources and share them among all peoples.

We shall enjoy and cherish the sacredness and privacy of our bodies and shall bring into the world children who are wanted.

We shall use and control technology for the survival and protection of nature and all people.

In declaring our interdependence with Divine Reality we recognize the possibilities of a sacred mystery within and around us.

We shall honor and protect people's right to gather as they choose in religious communities.

We shall support each other in pursuit of truths which emerge from our diverse experiences and histories, rejecting those exclusive claims to truth which deny the sacred existence of others.

We shall be open to revelations that extend beyond the boundaries of our current understanding and wisdom.

We shall recognize the divine within ourselves and in one another.

We women and men and children make this Declaration living in the midst of a world in which women are subservient and oppressed, men are repressed and brutalized, and children are violated and alienated. In making this declaration we seek a new order and covenant ourselves to a fully interdependent society. We live in a world in which love has yielded to war, art to science, religion to materialism, and sexuality to violence. We are committed to the discovery of a humanity which lays claim to the fullness of life.

We disclaim any right to privilege in order to honor the full dignity and development of all and take up responsibility for instituting freedom.

We long for light to shine on our darkness and life on the shadow of death, and for our feet to be guided in the way of peace. We shall live with grace and struggle with courage through the transitional years that lie ahead.

The Women's Coalition for the Third Century offers this Declaration of Interdependence to the people of the United States for response. In so doing we declare our intent to be architects of our Third Century. The future belongs to those who can dream with courage and creativity, plan with intelligence and wisdom, and act with power and compassion for the liberation of humanity. We invite others to join us in this declaration.

Declaration of Imperatives

We are aware of humanity's suffering, for as women we have been in bondage to unjust systems. Now we will define ourselves and find release from the values, images, myths, and practices that for centuries defined us.

We will no longer be governed by institutions that do not seek, respect, and include our leadership.

We will not be taxed without representation.

We will not be bound by the authority of legal systems in which we participate only minimally in the making and administration of the laws.

We will not be exploited in the labor force.

We will not be the only ones responsible for child care, homemaking and community building.

We reject educational systems that distort our reality.

We will not accept philosophies and theologies that deny our experience.

We will not abide prophets of the future who ignore our struggle.

We will not be reduced to sex symbols nor have our sexuality determined by others.

We will not be the principal source of morality for this nation. We insist that our contributions to conscience be incorporated into the public as well as the private sector. And we will not be destroyed by unethical and immoral leadership. We will not be divided by the distinctions that have traditionally alienated us from one another.

We will share the leadership of society and its government. We will demand respect for work inside and outside the home. We will share in the labor force and treasure leisure. We demand education that maximizes human potential. We will share in raising families. We will develop philosophies and theologies. We will enjoy our sexuality. We will create the future and act with strength in the fulfillment of these imperatives.

The Women of the Coalition for a Third Century make this Declaration to make certain our rights are not once again denied and our value and values ignored. Our concern for interdependence requires of each full partnership with all in the search for a human order.

Reprinted by permission of Patricia Budd Kepler, President of the Women's Coalition for the Third Century and author of the first draft of the Declaration. The Declaration was revised and adopted by member groups of the Coalition and over 200 women who met in Boston in 1975.

APPENDIX B

BIBLIOGRAPHY OF WORKS BY
WILMA SCOTT HEIDE

Dissertation

Feminism for the Health of It: A Covenant with Truth. University Microfilms International, 300 North Zeeb Rd., Ann Arbor, MI 48106, 1978.

Book

Feminism for the Health of It. Margaretdaughters, Inc., P.O. Box 70, Buffalo, NY 14222, 1985.

Published Chapters in Books

"Women's Liberation Means Putting Sex in Its Place," in *Women In the Work Forces, Confrontation with Change,* Mildred E. Katzell and William C. Byham (eds.). Behavioral Publications, 2852 Broadway, Morningside Heights, New York, NY 10025, 1972.

"A Feminist Humanist's Concept of Employment," in *Public Service Employment, An Analysis of its History, Problems, and Prospects,* Alan Gartner, Russell Nixon and Frank Riessman (eds.). Praeger Publishers, 383 Madison Ave., New York, NY 10017, 1973.

"Feminism, RX for Health Nursing," in *American Nurses' Association Clinical Sessions.* Appleton-Century-Crofts, New York, 1975.

"Introduction," in *Hospitals, Paternalism and the Role of the Nurse,* by Jo Ann Ashley. Teachers College Press, New York, 1976.

"Feminism for a Sporting Future," in *Women and Sport: From Myth to Reality,* Carole Oglesby (ed.). Lea and Febiger, 600 S. Washington Square, Philadelphia, PA 19106, 1978.

"The Quest for Our Humanity via Higher Education," in *Learning Tomorrows, Commentaries on the Future of Education,* Peter H. Wagschal (ed.). Praeger Publishers, 383 Madison Ave., New York, NY 10017, 1979.

"Feminism: Making a Difference in Our Health," in *The Woman Patient, Vol. I,* Malkah Notman and Carol Nadelson (eds.). Plenum Press, 277 West 17th St., New York, NY 10011, 1979.

"Feminist Activism in Nursing and Health Care," in *Socialization, Sexism and Stereotyping,* Janet Muff (ed.). C.V. Mosby Co., 11830 Westline Industrial Drive, St. Louis, MO 63141, 1981.

Published Articles and Essays

"Poverty is Expensive." 12-part series in *Valley Daily News, New Kensington Daily Dispatch,* New Kensington, PA, and other area newpapers, Apr. 1965.

"Cultural and Psychological Impediments; Are Mental Health Practitioners Contributing to the Problems?" and "Some Egalitarian Alternatives to Androcentric Science." *The Impact of Fertility Limitaions on Women's Life, Career and Personality,* Esther Milner (ed.). Annals of the New York Adademy of Sciences, Vol.175, Oct. 1970.

"What's Wrong with a Male-Dominated Society?" *Impact of Science on Society*, a publication of the United Nations Educational, Scientific and Cultural Organization, Vol. XXI, No.1, Jan.-Mar. 1971. (note: WSH preferred title of: "Why the World Needs Women's Liberation;" editor chose the title used.)

"Women's Liberation Means Putting Nurses and Nursing in Its Place." *Imprint* a publication of the National Student Nurses Association, Vol.18, No.3, May/June, 1971, pp.4,5,16.

"Sexism is Dangerous to your (Spiritual) Health." *Church and Society* Boards of Christian Education of the United Presbyterian Church, Sept/Oct. 1972, pp.5-8.

"Employment and Humanpower." *Women Speaking.* The Wick, Roundwood Ave. Hutton, Brentwood, Essex, England, Oct. 1972, pp. 4-5.

"The New Feminism and the Health Profession," *Sociological Abstracts*, 1972; Society for the Study of Social Problems, Aug. 1972.

"Nursing and Women's Liberation – A Parallel." *American Journal of Nursing*, May, 1973, pp.824-826.

"Feminism: A Necessity for Humanist Politics." *Political Reform: The Forensic Quarterly*, National Ofice of the Committee on Discussion and Debate, Prince Lucian Campbell Hall, University of Oregon, Eugene, OR 97403, Nov., 1974, pp.501-508.

"Feminism and the 'Fallen Woman.'" *Criminal Justice and Behavior.* Vol.1, No.4, Dec. 1974, pp. 369-373.

"The Genetic Manipulation of Woman." *Women Speaking*, The Wick, Roundwood Ave., Hutton Brentwood, Essex, England, Jul.-Sept., 1974, pp. 4-6.

"The Language of Sexism." *The Sunday Times* in Hartford, CT, Sept. 1974; *The Connecticut Sunday Times*, and *Wellesley News*, Oct. 25, 1974.

"Mechanism for Change Viewed in a Political Context." *No Longer Young: The Older Woman in America, Occasional Papers in Gerontology.* The Institute of Gerontology, No. 11, 1975, pp.65-73.

"No Room for 'Sexist Politics' in Education." *University Bulletin*, University of Massachusetts at Amherst, Feb., 1975.

"Why Don't We? A Womanifesto for Change." *MS.* June, 1976, pp.88-89.

"Scholarship/Action in the Human Interest." *Signs: Journal of Women in Cultura and Society.* Vol.5, No.1, Autumn, 1979.

"Nurturance and Peace: Some Feminist Connections." *Peacework*, Newsletter of New England American Friends Service Committee, 2161 Massachusetts Ave., Cambridge, MA 02140, Spring, 1980.

"The Struggle for Peaceful Conflict Resolution." *Feminist Forum.* Commentaries from Members and Friends of Women's Studies Committee, Sangamon State University, June 1982, pp.16-17.

"Child Care – Who Cares." *Feminist Forum,* Commentaries from Members and Friends of Women's Studies Committee, Sangamon State University, Springfield, IL 62708, June 1982, pp.7-8.

Published Testimony

Testimony given as member of Pennsylvania Human Relations Commission at Hearings before the Subcommittee on Labor of the Committee on Labor and Public Welfare, United States Senate, First Session on S. 2453, To Further Promote Equal Employment Opportunities for American Workers, 1969.

Testimony given as Chairwoman of the Board, National Organization for Women, Inc., at hearings before the Subcomittee on Labor of the Committee on Labor and Public Welfare, United States Senate, Ninety-First Congress, Second Session on HR 10948 and HR 17596, 1970.

Testimony given as Chairwoman of the Board, National Organization for Women, Inc., at hearings before the Subcommittee on Constitutional Amendments of the Committee on the Judiciary, United State Senate, Ninety-First Congress, Second Session on S.J. Re. 61, "To Amend the Constitution So As to Provide Equal Rights for Men and Women," 1970.

"Women's Liberation – Pregnant and Overdue." Testimony at Public Hearings of the Commission on Population Growth and the American Future at the White House Conference on Children, Washington, DC, December 16, 1970, pp.17-20.

Testimony as President of the National Organization for Women, Inc., on "Criteria for Justice and Justices." U.S. Supreme Court, Senate Judiciary Committee, *Congressional Record,* Nov. 1971.

"A Feminist Manifesto" HR 11167, Employment and Manpower (sic) Act of 1972, Hearing Record.

"Sexism is Dangerous to Your Health," Statement given at the Cardiology Conference, Hartford, CT, Sept. 1973.

Written statement from NOW, "Economic Problems of Women." Hearing before the Joint Economic Committee, Congress of the United States 93rd Congress, First Session, Part 3, Superintendent of Documents, U.S. Government Printing Office, 1973, pp. 559-563.

Written testimony for NOW, the National Organization for Women, Inc., Submitted as President of NOW to the Congress of the United States Joint Economic Committee, Hearings on Economic Problems of Women, Summer, 1974.

Testimony given with Eleanor Humes Haney at the Hearings before the Subcommittee on International Operations of the Committee on International Relations, House of Representatives, 95th Congress, Second Session, on the proposed National Peace Academy, 1978.

"Proposed Communications Act of 1978, HR 13015: A Travesty of Justice." New England Field Hearings, *Record of Hearings,* Boston, MA, Aug. 1978.

Testimony for the Record and Inclusion in the Final Commission Report to the President and Congress from the United States Commission on Proposals for the National Academy of Peace and Conflict Resolution, July, 1980.

Testimony on S. 1889 in the Senate of the United States to Establish the United States Academy of Peace and for other Purposes, Record of Hearings of Senate Subcommittee of Education, Arts and Humanities, Spring, 1982.

Reviews

Review of *Time of Transition* by Heather L. Ross and Isabel V. Sawhill. Published in *Social Policy*, Jan/Feb 1977.

Review of *Toward a New Psychology of Women* by Jean Baker Miller. Published in *Social Policy*, May/June 1977.

Review of *Woman's Worth: Sexual Economics and the World of Women.* by Lisa Leghorn and Katherine Parker. Published in *Issues in Radical Therapy.*

Speeches as Articles

"Some Feminist Alternatives to Androcentric Science." American Psychological Association, Washington, DC. Theme: "Psychology and the Problems of Society," Symposium: "What Can the Behavioral Sciences Do to Modify the World So that Women Who Want to Participate Meaningfully Are Not Regarded As and Are Not, In Fact, Deviant?" Published by KNOW, Inc., P.O. Box 86031, Pittsburgh, PA 15221, 1969.

"The Reality and Challenge of the Double Standard in Mental Health Society." Speech presented at Chatham College, Pittsburgh, PA, symposium on Mental Health, Dec. 1969. Published by KNOW, Inc., P.O. Box 86031, Pittsburgh, PA 15221.

"Employment Practices and Utilization of Women's Talents." Speech delivered at 35th meeting of the Industrial Health Foundation, Inc., *Transaction Bulletin* No. 44, 1970, pp. 54-60.

"Women's Rights, An Educational Imperative," Institute on Women in Higher Education, June 1971, University of Pittsburgh, PA. Published by KNOW, Inc., P.O. Box 86031, Pittsburgh, PA 15221.

"Feminism, the Profound Behavioral Revolution," at conference, Rhode Island Women's Day. Available from Rhode Island Advisory Commission on Status of Women, Providence, RI, Oct. 17, 1971.

"Feminism, The Sine Qua Non for Humanistic Institution of Health," at Symposium on "How Valuable is Human Health" at American Association for the Advancement of Science, Dec. 1971. Available from *Society for Health and Human Values*, Witherspoon Building, Philadelphia, PA 19107.

"The Feminist Cause *Is* the Common Cause." Presentation at the American College Personnel Association, Chicago, IL. Published by KNOW, Inc., P.O. Box 86031, Pittsburgh, PA 15221, Mar. 1972.

"Equal Rights Amendment" under 'Women and the Law' in *Women's Role in Contemporary Society,* Report of the New York City Commission on Human Rights Hearings, Sept. 21-25, 1970, Avon Books, New York, 1972.

"Child Care and Feminism," address delivered to Board of Directors, Day Care and Child Development Council of American, Inc., published in *Voice for Children,* Vol. 5 No. 4, Apr. 1972.

"Feminism: The Sine Qua Non for a Just Society." International Conference on Law and Justice, University of Nebraska, Mar. 1972. *Vital Speeches of the Day,* Vol.38, No.13, City News Publishing Co., April, 1972, pp. 403-409.

"Revolution: Tomorrow is NOW." *Vital Speeches of the Day,* May, 1973, pp. 403-408.

"Address by Wilma Scott Heide, President of the National Organization for Women." ISCC EEO-Manpower (Sic) Conference, Illinois State Chamber of Commerce, May, 1973.

"From Institutional Sexism to Institutional Feminism." Keynote address, Hilles Conference, Yale University. *Proceeding of Conference,* 1973.

Welcome address to the First International Feminist Planning Conference convened by NOW at Lesley College and Harvard Divinity School, June 1-4, 1973. Proceedings prepared by NOW, pp. 1-4.

"A Feminist Perspective on Manipulation of Woman (Woman Includes Man)." The Genetic Manipulation of Man (Sic) Symposium of the University of Wisconsin in Stevens Point. Published by KNOW, Inc., P.O. Box 86031, Pittsburgh, PA 15221, Nov. 1973.

"Society's Responsibilities with Respect to War and Peace," presented at University of Idaho, Outlawry of War Symposium, Moscow, Idaho, 1973. Published by KNOW, Inc., P.O. Box 86031, Pittsburgh, PA 15221.

"Liberating Libraries and Librarians," address to American Library Association Convention, June 1973; *School Library Journal,* Jan. 1974.

"Sexism as Disease – Feminism as a Cure." MIT (Feb. 1975), reported in *Wellesley News,* Feb. 14, 1975.

"Feminist Imperatives for Education." Commencement address, Wheaton College, Norton, MA, June 1975.

"Human Rights are Indivisible." Ohio Education Association Winter Human Relations Conference, *Emphasis on Affirmative Action Programs,* Columbus, OH, Feb. 1976, pp.15-21.

"Feminism for Healthy Social Work." Commencement address, *Smith College School for Social Work Journal,* Winter, 1976, pp.1-4.

Name Index

Subject Index

Other titles available from Margaretdaughters:

Peace and Power: A Handbook of Feminist Process by Charlene Eldridge Wheeler and Peggy L. Chinn.

Feminism for the Health of It by Wilma Scott Heide.